Police Lea
in the
Twenty-First Century

PHILOSOPHY, DOCTRINE AND DEVELOPMENTS

The authors have in-depth experience of police leadership education and development through their work at the Police Staff College, Bramshill including within the National Police Leadership Faculty (NPLF) where they have been engaged for some years in higher police training in all its dynamics with police forces worldwide.

Robert Adlam joined the directing staff at Bramshill in 1976 and has worked extensively in developing the leadership of the police service through the Special Course, later the Accelerated Promotion Course and now the High Potential Development Scheme—which was reformed under his direction. He graduated in psychology (with zoology) at Aberdeen University and also holds an MA in management, a diploma in facilitation styles and humanistic psychology and a PhD in police ethics. He has published many articles on police psychology, leadership and reform. He is currently Reader in Ethics, Leadership and Human Rights at the NPLF.

Peter Villiers has lectured at Bramshill since 1986 and became Head of Human Rights there in 1998. He is the author of many publications on leadership, ethics and police studies. He graduated from Essex University with a BA in government in 1970 and also holds an MA in organizational psychology.

Police Leadership in the Twenty-First Century
PHILOSOPHY, DOCTRINE AND DEVELOPMENTS

Edited by Robert Adlam and Peter Villiers

Published 2003 by
WATERSIDE PRESS
Domum Road
Winchester SO23 9NN
United Kingdom ·

Telephone: 01962 855567
E-mail: enquiries@watersidepress.co.uk
Online catalogue and bookstore: www.watersidepress.co.uk

ISBN 1 872 870 24 4

Catalogue-In-Publication Data: A catalogue record for this book can be obtained from the British Library

Printing and binding: Antony Rowe Ltd, Eastbourne

Cover design: John Good Holbrook, Coventry/Waterside Press

Cover photographs of Bramshill House, Hampshire by Peter Abbott

Disclaimer *Police Leadership in the Twenty-first Century* is the work of the editors and individual contributors and represents their thoughts alone rather than the viewpoint of the Home Office or any other organization or body, official or otherwise.

Police Leadership
in the
Twenty-First Century

PHILOSOPHY, DOCTRINE AND DEVELOPMENTS

Edited by

Robert Adlam
Peter Villiers

With a Foreword by **John Grieve**

 WATERSIDE PRESS

Acknowledgements

We are indebted to the staff at Bramshill, police and non-police alike, who have contributed to the collective body of wisdom and understanding that has been established there. We salute them all, and in particular Richard Baker, John Hood, the Reverend James McKinney, Michael Plumridge and Colin Vick, who have influenced police thinking and development over the years.

The library staff at Bramshill have been, as ever, patient, courteous and helpful in helping us sort out some of the more obscure references for this volume, as well as charting the complexities of the ACPO administrative structure. Peter Abbott has provided invaluable help in Internet research and technical support. General Jonathan Bailey, currently Director of Development and Doctrine, was kind enough to offer his comments on the manuscript-in-being; as Colonel Defence Studies he launched the series of occasional pamphlets still published by the Strategic Combat and Studies Institute, which helped to shape our ideas on doctrine. Conor Gearty, Professor of Human Rights Law at the University of London, has been a constant source of inspiration on human rights and other matters. Ronnie Flanagan (now Sir Ronald) was a staunch colleague on the staff at Bramshill and went on to demonstrate great qualities of leadership as the last chief constable of the RUC.

It is a pleasure to acknowledge the debt that we owe to our publisher, Bryan Gibson, and editor, Jane Green, for their patience and encouragement. Finally, we are grateful to our families, who gave us the time when we needed it as what had seemed a very simple project became rather more.

Ultimately, this book is dedicated to all those police officers who aspire to lead with justice, integrity and humanity.

Robert Adlam and **Peter Villiers**
September 2002

Police Leadership
in the **Twenty-First Century**

CONTENTS

Contributors (in alphabetical order)

John Alderson CBE, QPM, barrister-at-law, held some of the highest and most influential positions in British policing including Commandant of the Police Staff College, Bramshill, Assistant Commissioner, New Scotland Yard and Chief Constable of Devon and Cornwall. His published works include *Policing Freedom* (1979), *Human Rights and the Police* (1984) and *Principled Policing: Protecting the Public With Integrity* (1998). He holds doctorates *Honoris Causa* from the Universities of Exeter and Bradford. John Alderson was a chief police officer who was ahead of his time. He pioneered community policing in Devon and Cornwall because he saw that it would be impossible to police the area without the active participation and support of the community—and where he led, others followed.

Ian Blair is Deputy Commissioner of the Metropolitan Police Service. He first joined the 'Met' in 1974 and has also served with Her Majesty's Inspectorate of Constabulary, Thames Valley Police and Surrey Police, where he was Chief Constable from 1998 to 2000. He is a visiting fellow at Nuffield College, Oxford and has also taught at New York University.

Jennifer Brown directs the masters course in Forensic Psychology at the University of Surrey. Professor Brown has researched gender issues in policing for nearly a decade, undertaking the first large-scale investigation of sexual harassment within the police service whilst she was the research manager of Hampshire Police. Since then she has looked at gender differences in conflict resolution, motivation for being an authorised firearms user, arrest rates and deployment patterns, as well as exploring the experiences of gay and ethnic minority police women. Her most recent collaboration was with Professor Frances Heidensohn with whom she co-wrote *Gender and Policing* in 2002.

Sir Robert Bunyard completed a long and distinguished police career, beginning as a constable in the Metropolitan Police and rising to become Chief Constable of Essex and then Her Majesty's Chief Inspector of Constabulary, as well as Commandant of Bramshill Police Staff College. He attended the Royal College of Defence Studies, wrote *Police Organization and Command* (1978) and was a member of the Royal Commission on Criminal Justice chaired by Lord Runciman which reported in 1993.

Garry Elliott joined the Metropolitan Police Service with a degree in physics in 1974, to which he later added an LLB and MBA. He is a police superintendent, having pursued his career as an operational police officer, force strategic planner and member of the directing staff at Bramshill (currently within the National Police Leadership Faculty of the Central Police Training and Development Authority) with equal interest and commitment.

John Grieve CBE, QPM joined the Metropolitan Police in 1966 at Clapham. He worked on the 'Flying Squad', Robbery Squad and Murder Squad in Europe, America, South East Asia and Australia. He introduced asset seizure investigation in the United Kingdom and was Head of Training at Hendon Police College. As the first Director of Intelligence for the Metropolitan Police, he commanded the Anti-Terrorist Squad as National Co-ordinator during the 1996-1998 bombing campaigns by the IRA. In 1998, he became the first director of the Racial and Violent Crime Task Force, until retiring in May 2002. He is now Senior Research Fellow at Portsmouth University, an honorary professor at Buckingham Chiltern University College and independent chair of the Greater London Authority's Alcohol and Drugs Alliance. He holds an honours degree in Philosophy and Psychology from Newcastle University and a master's degree in Drugs Policy Analysis from Cranfield University.

William C Heffernan is professor of law at John Jay College of Criminal Justice, City University of New York. He also serves as one of the editors of *Criminal Justice Ethics*, a publication of John Jay's Institute for Criminal Justice Ethics. His articles on search and seizure have appeared in numerous journals, among them the *Journal of Criminal Law and Criminology*, the *Georgetown Law Journal* and the *Wisconsin Law Review*.

Seumas Miller is professor of Social Philosophy and director, Centre for Applied Philosophy and Public Ethics, Charles Sturt University, Australia.

Terry Mitchell joined the Ministry of Defence Police as a graduate entrant where he served for 18 years. He spent part of his service as a syndicate director on the then accelerated promotion scheme at Bramshill Police College, helping to influence and develop the police leadership of the future. He holds a diploma in police management and is a member of the Institute of Management.

Milan Pagon ScD, PhD is Dean and associate professor of Police Administration and Management at the College of Police and Security Studies, University of Ljubljana, and associate professor of Organizational Behavior at the Faculty of Organizational Sciences, University of Maribor, Slovenia.

Mick Palmer is a police practitioner with 34 years' experience, including six years as Commissioner of the Australian Federal Police. He was Australia's first elected member of the Executive Committee of Interpol serving between 1997-2000.

Robert Panzarella PhD (Psychology) is professor of Police Studies at John Jay College of Criminal Justice, New York. He was exchange professor at Bramshill Police Staff College in 1986 and again in 1999. He has provided training and consultation for many police and fire departments and his research and publications have encompassed personnel, managerial and tactical studies of military, police and fire services.

Neil Richards BSc (Econ), M Phil, M Ed joined the directing staff at Bramshill Police Staff College in 1981 to become its *primum mobile* in ethics, working closely with the then Commandant, Sir Kenneth Newman (who went on to become Commissioner of the Metropolitan Police). As an expert to the Council of Europe, Neil Richards was influential in the council's publication of a new code of police ethics in 1999. Amongst other contributions, he set up the Human Rights Unit and the Chief Officers' Development Programme at Bramshill.

Roger Scruton is an internationally known writer with more than 20 books to his name, and is perhaps best known academically for his Kantian scholarship. Formerly a professional academic with professorships in aesthetics and philosophy in England and America, he is now a freelance writer and commentator who first visited Bramshill police Staff College to lecture on animal rights and wrongs as part of a conference on extremism.

Foreword

John Grieve

It is over 25 years since Robert Adlam first talked to me about police leadership. It was at his then puzzling instigation that I read the psychology part of my joint honours degree in philosophy and psychology; a choice greeted with hoots of derision by my immediate police supervisors at the time: 'As much good as flower arranging to the police service'. To contribute to this important volume and to be invited to write the foreword is both an honour and the payment of a debt.

Peter Villiers contributed to my thinking over the last dozen years, a period of both personal and organizational challenge. He and I, inspired by Neil Richards, another influence and contributor, developed some strategic workshops on ethics and latterly human rights and miscarriages of justice. In addition to my thinking derived from philosophy and psychology, I was able to revisit my father's library of military leadership and draw forth new links.

Those philosophical flowers, now tied into different bundles in this collection, are as old as Plato—Socrates' mother was a midwife, hence 'miscarriage'—and are at the forefront of the increasing challenges to senior police leaders as we enter the twenty-first century.

This is an important and timely book, not only because of the depth and breadth of the coverage of the issues but because it addresses the practical challenge of leadership at all levels. All police leadership is complex, and combines formal and informal elements—whether the leader in question be the highly experienced and respected late turn van driver as she races from call to call dragging her probationer constables in her slipstream, or the Chief Officer arguing with the Attorney General, Solicitor General and Director of Public Prosecutions about the merits of a prosecution. I have been involved in both situations and their outcomes, and earlier access to the ideas in this book would have been helpful to me then.

Police leadership is no longer a mechanical task, if it ever were. It is not enough, in order to be able to carry out a covert operation with official approval, for the senior detective simply to complete the latest proforma and hope for the best. When the challenges come, as come they will with increasing speed and subtle trajectory, an understanding of the underpinning principles and conflicting values of policing is vital for organizational survival. The need for a philosophy and doctrine of leadership and its application to everyday policing was never more important, both to the police and to society. For the challenges we face, both from the thoughtful and those of ill will, were never stronger, never more politically inspired nor more legally informed.

Many of those people who have contributed to this analysis of policing have played a role in the series of meetings and working relationships, operational and theoretical, that have characterised my working life over the last 37 years.

John Alderson has long been a hero and role model of mine. He has, like Roger Scruton, Terry Mitchell and Seumas Miller, delved into the philosophical basis for policing. Philosophy, like psychology, was not held in high regard by my peers when I chose to study the subject at Newcastle University on a Bramshill scholarship. Yet the need for the thinking police leader, who is prepared to examine a problem from first principles and reach a solution which will stand up to moral scrutiny as well as satisfy the practical dictates of the situation, has never been greater.

Sir Robert Bunyard trained me as a sergeant and later as a chief officer. The relationship of training and education to operational policing has long been debated, and his contribution will add fuel to that debate. It is essential that senior officers drill down to find out what is happening, not only on the streets but also within the stations under their command. Like Sir Robert, both Robert Panzarella and William Heffernan have argued that police leaders must find out what their subordinates are doing in reality, as well as in theory.

I was fortunate to work operationally very closely with both Ian Blair and Garry Elliott, in parallel teams in inner London. I then worked with each of them again when involved in cultural change, driven by the varying political agendas imposed on the police service. Ian changed my thinking about the investigation of sexual crimes. A decade later Jennifer Brown and I first worked together when introducing concepts of offender profiling in serious sexual cases and murders. She later influenced the way in which I responded to diversity.

John GD Grieve
September 2002

Introduction

For many years we have been responsible for the education and training of senior police officers. During those years we have been based at the Police Staff College, Bramshill, an institution constituted to support and develop effective police leadership within the context of a liberal democracy. Our own role has been particularly focused upon the design and delivery of training programmes that have taken as their overall goal 'the development of leaders with justice, integrity and humanity'. The current police leadership of the United Kingdom has experienced the ethos of these training programmes. We should add that this ethos has also pervaded the programmes of study offered to police officers from all four quarters of the globe. Most recently we have been engaged with the process of helping the police service in those countries wishing to join the European Community. The fundamentally important issues of police ethics and human rights have lain at the heart of those programmes.

This book has emerged as a result of our lengthy association with the past, present and future police leaders of the UK, the Continent and a very large number of police forces throughout the world. Through its pages we are primarily interested in making a contribution to the practice of morally principled and commendable policing, i.e. 'good' policing everywhere.

We should add that the book is also designed to further the effectiveness of police leaders and to 'strengthen leadership' in the public sector.

The reputation of the police

It is a necessary truism to begin by acknowledging that the British police service is the best known in the world, and still retains its reputation for innovation, experiment and excellence. Whatever Scotland Yard does is imitated elsewhere and its leaders—and those of other British police forces—are called in as experts, problem-solvers and reformers wherever there is a need.

> At the same time, policing is a controversial subject, and the British police are in the somewhat paradoxical position of being widely admired abroad, whilst on occasion heavily criticised at home. For example, the Metropolitan Police have been hauled over the coals on the matter of institutional racism in the aftermath of the inquiry into the death of Stephen Lawrence in 1993—an issue we explore in depth in this volume.

The attack goes wider, and is part of a structural criticism of public service leadership and management which is not confined to Great Britain, but which finds an acuteness of expression there. British police chiefs, it is believed in the higher echelons of Whitehall and its advisory discussion groups, are poor managers. They do not know what anything costs, and have no real idea of how to achieve efficiency. Their stock answer to any external scrutiny is that policing is unique and does not lend itself to measurement—which is very irritating in a performance management culture.

Police leaders, moreover, fail to think strategically and act positively. Whereas the Government is looking for inspirational or even 'transformational' leadership, the police service fails to rise to the challenge, but remains bland in its statements and fundamentally averse to achieving radical change in its actions— even though it may have mastered the jargon of reform. The leadership of the modern police service, by and large, continues to practice 'transactional' leadership—in other words, the leadership by bargaining that comes naturally to the *nomenklatura,* or indeed to any member of a pensionable bureaucracy.

A reasonable and relatively undemanding style of command, transactional leadership has served police leaders well in their careers, and indeed has much to be said for it in the uncertain and rocky terrain in which police operatives usually operate, whether within or outside the station. Moreover, it is at least arguable that transactional leadership is the norm for leadership within the public service as a whole; certainly bargaining, as well as idealism, is an indispensable part of political life.

The paradox of leadership

Police chiefs are expected to show exceptional levels of skill and commitment in both leadership and management, but without acknowledgement—or possibly, without even recognition—that these two requirements may clash with each other. The cautious, artful, consensus-seeking manager—who knows the cost of everything, who is determined to please everyone and upset no-one, and whose quota is always fulfilled—may be quite incapable of swift and dynamic leadership when the situation requires it. Indeed, the qualities of independent-mindedness and self-reliance that 'transformational' leadership requires may impel the leader in question to challenge either the objectives of the government, or the methods by which it chooses to address them—or both at the same time.

None of these courses of action is likely to prove very popular with the reforming administration, especially if it can claim a democratic mandate for its reforms: and the practice of 'transformational' leadership requires the addition of other qualities to back it up, as we shall later explore. (For an example of vigorous and independent-minded police leadership in practice, consider the current debate about the enforcement of the law concerning the use of illegal drugs, in which some police leaders have expressed views that dissent from governmental orthodoxy. However, police leadership as a body would appear to be disunited in its views on this issue—perhaps as a reflection of the lack of consensus within society as a whole.)

Police work can be a difficult and demanding occupation, and whilst it is not always a vocation it requires certain qualities of character in order for its practitioners to be successful. In one sense, every police officer is a leader; for all police officers exercise discretion, make decisions, and provide an element of leadership in the community. However, as Garry Elliott points out (*Chapter 15*), the police service itself requires organizational leadership. Its leaders must 'add value' to what goes on, not only in the narrow sense of contemporary reformist jargon, but in that they contribute something which the organization would not otherwise possess.

What is that something? Sir Robert Bunyard (*Chapter 5*) makes a historical analysis of the failure of the police service to eradicate institutional corruption, and points to the need for informed and effective supervision that is somehow able to reconcile trust and scrutiny. Seumas Miller (*Chapter 7*) quotes with approval David Bayley's notion of 'verifiable professionalism': in other words, professional judgement based upon demonstrable reasoning. John Alderson (*Chapter 2*) refers to principled policing and the need for the 'high police'—by which he means those with power to make and to implement policies affecting the police organization as a whole—to be able to strike the right balance between the maintenance of order and the protection of freedom, two principles which are in a permanent state of conflict.

> Societies in which policing is principled are less likely to suffer from policing injustices than where policing is driven by political opportunism, professional caprice, or bad law. If policing is to avoid the worse misuses and abuses of power there has to be a robust moral objectivity in the way in which it operates.

Roger Scruton (*Chapter 4*) explores the philosophical foundations of the need for police leaders to acknowledge and apply the categorical imperative. Milan Pagon (*Chapter 11*) argues that the present generation of police leaders needs to prove its suitability for the task. Jennifer Brown (*Chapter 13*) points to the need for the feminine as well as the masculine qualities of command to be recognised. Both Robert Panzarella (*Chapter 8*) and William Heffernan (*Chapter 9*) argue, from the American context, that the military or paramilitary model of leadership as applied in the police context is fundamentally flawed—as Pagon shows it also to be in eastern and central Europe, amongst the aspirant or re-established democracies.

We believe that all our contributors add value to the debate as to the proper ends and means of policing—its philosophy, in other words—and the doctrine of leadership that it needs to espouse. We may synthesise our theme as follows. Good policing rests upon informed consent, as the result of an authentic dialogue that is truly inclusive. Good police leaders provide a service to the community they police, which that community would not otherwise achieve for itself. That role is not restricted to 'fighting' crime, which in reality is a necessary but incomplete part of the duties of a public police service, and in which they may quite rightly be assisted by private policing (as our contributor Ian Blair (*Chapter 15*) has consistently argued elsewhere).

In a liberal democracy that is committed to the rule of law, the preservation of the peace, and the upholding of human rights, the police have a fundamental constitutional role and importance which cannot be reconciled with direct political control. Whilst it is important that the police exercise proper financial controls and are neither reckless nor profligate in their use of resources, efficiency is not the ultimate goal of policing, and cannot be the sole test of the success of any policing operation. (Indeed, when a police operation is successful, its cost is seldom queried.)

Despite the current emphasis upon public sector reforms, at a deeper level the constitutional importance of the doctrine of the separation of powers is still recognised, since the alternative is despotism—whether or not it be based upon the will of the majority. Whilst the so-called tripartite arrangement, whereby control over the police is shared between central and local government and the police themselves, is under some pressure, it remains of fundamental constitutional importance. The police continue to need to be led by men and women of appropriate judgement and calibre, who are capable of exercising a degree of independent far-sightedness in their interpretation of their role as guardians of the public interest.

The current emphasis upon public sector reform represents only a part of the body of established doctrine on the needs of the public service, which stretches back to the Northcote-Trevelyan reforms of the civil service in the mid-nineteenth century, and arguably before that. If we turn briefly to twentieth-century history we shall find that the British government itself laid down a very clear doctrine for the development of an independent-minded police leadership, based on the need to acquire and retain local respect. A national police college was set up in 1948, as a consequence of more than a century of conjecture and debate, in order that the police service should be able to foster and develop its leadership from within, rather than look elsewhere for its high command—such as to the military. (The contemporary example would be to look to business, or to those hybrid consultancies that specialise in public sector reform.)

It was intended that the officers who attended the Police College would be able to demonstrate: 'The growth of the broad outlook, the quality of leadership, and the independent habits of mind which are essential if a senior police officer is to command the respect of his men [*sic*] and the confidence of all classes of the community' (First Report of the Police Post War Committee, HMSO, 1946. Quoted in: *The First Fifty Years: The History of the Police Staff College*. Police Staff College, 1998). That doctrine is still valid, even if we would nowadays automatically extend the embrace of the leadership of the police service to those who have the appropriate ability, from any background.

This book serves to record the ideas on leadership developed at Bramshill and by police leaders, commentators and theorists who have been in some way connected with that police college in the years since 1948, and who continue to address its ideals. The resulting philosophy is incomplete and the doctrine of leadership is confined to broad principles. We have been able to record, however, that:

- leadership is less of a mystery than is often supposed, and there is a great deal of useful and applicable research on the principles of democratic leadership;
- much of mainstream leadership theory can be applied to police leadership; and
- although the 'natural' capacity to lead varies from individual to individual, the qualities required by police leaders can be developed by proper education and professional training.

Finally, we return to where we began. Police work can be a difficult and demanding occupation, and its leadership can make great demands upon the physical, mental and spiritual capacities of the person in charge. Police leadership requires more than a skill in performance management or an ability to read the political runes—useful, as these characteristics are to promotion within a self-serving bureaucracy. A healthy democracy depends upon an active and reflective police service, led by men and women with the capacity to serve the public good in a practical way. Those aspirant leaders who know or prove themselves to be unequal to that challenge had better look for work elsewhere.

Peter Villiers and **Robert Adlam**
September 2002

CHAPTER 1

Philosophy, Doctrine and Leadership: Some Core Beliefs

Peter Villiers

Many factors came together in influencing us to produce this book. They included:

- researching the origins and purpose of the Police Staff College for a fiftieth anniversary publication, and revisiting its key emphasis upon developing the present and future leadership of the police service;
- revising the Special Course and producing the Accelerated Promotion Scheme and Programme;
- rewriting the Overseas Command Course in order to produce a coherent and comprehensive body of thought on police leadership for international police commanders;
- scrutinising new developments in military thought and doctrine thorough liaison with the Colonel Defence Studies and Strategic Combat Studies Institute at Camberley and elsewhere;
- the creation of the National Police Leadership Faculty in 2001; and
- the influence of the Police Reform Agenda—a Whitehall initiative which began in the same year and led to the creation of the Police Leadership Development Board and a number of other ventures.

Whatever were the contributory factors that led us to wish to collate and edit this work, we expect to be judged, critically but not unfairly, by the outcome. Is it relevant? Is it valid? Is it useful? These are more interesting questions than what led to its creation. However, we cannot ignore the historical background to the project. For our starting point, like Descartes', was to assume a position of fundamental doubt. We asked ourselves three questions. Firstly, is there such a thing as police leadership? Secondly, if it exists, can it be formally articulated and shared? Thirdly, what is the relationship between police leadership and police philosophy? We believe that the answers to these questions will emerge as our text unfolds. However, we lay out our core beliefs now.

CORE BELIEFS

These are as follows:

- the police service needs to articulate an agreed philosophy of policing, and further agree an appropriate style of leadership, in order to achieve its full professional development;

- there is the basis for such a philosophy in the established tradition of policing by consent;
- there is as yet no established doctrine of leadership for the police service. However, there is a prototype for such a doctrine in the various sources which have been brought together in this volume, and which provide the principles upon which for the police to build its doctrine of leadership; and
- doctrine needs to be set in the political and ethical context of public service leadership.

The essential requirements of a doctrine of leadership

- a doctrine needs to provide for leadership requirements at different levels of the police service;
- a doctrine needs to be clear, comprehensive, memorable, and capable of being put into practice;
- a doctrine needs to be both aspirational and inspirational: the utmost that the service and those who lead it can achieve; and
- a police doctrine of leadership will fare better as an organic growth than a mechanical construction, and will continue to develop.

The meaning and uses of philosophy

We shall keep this brief, since we believe that semantic investigations of this kind are subject to the law of diminishing returns—but cannot be avoided altogether.

The *Shorter Oxford English Dictionary* defines 'philosophy', in its original and broadest sense, as' the love, study or pursuit of wisdom'.

Professional philosophers will naturally produce a rather more recondite analysis, both of what the word philosophy means and what it means to practice philosophy, which we need not pursue here, but to which we may have occasion to return.

In almost complete contrast, we have the everyday meaning of the word philosophy. Here it is harder to offer a clear and distinctive meaning. In everyday speech, we suppose a philosophy to mean a more-or-less coherent set of fundamental beliefs which imply some sort of commitment on the part of the person who is expressing them; but further than that we cannot go.

Current management jargon has debased the currency. Thus, a business may claim that it has a philosophy of putting the customer first, or respecting its suppliers, or playing its proper part in community life. Whilst we respect the way in which words are used in everyday life, we find this interpretation of the word philosophy too shallow to withstand scrutiny, let alone stand up to robust use.

The sociologists Burrell Gibson and Gareth Morgan (1979) made a bold attempt to chart both philosophy and philosophers. Their ambitious scheme identifies four 'paradigms' within which any philosopher operates:

- an ontology, or theory of existence;
- an epistemology, or theory of knowledge;
- a view of human nature; and
- a preferred method of research.

We find this scheme more applicable and less abstract than it might at first appear, at least for the drawing of broad contrasts. Thus the now utterly discredited but once enormously influential philosophy of Marxism–Leninism is both positivist in its epistemology and determinist in its view of human nature. In other words, we are all subject to the historical laws of nature, and we have no escape from them: whereas a voluntarist would think otherwise.

What is the relevance of this to policing? More, we would suggest, than might at first appear. Every practitioner makes philosophical assumptions, and many of them have profound practical consequences. Consider, for example, the notion of intelligence-led policing. We would suggest that its theoretical underpinnings tend towards positivism and determinism, rather than their opposites. This will influence the way in which the doctrine is applied, and the criteria that are chosen by which to judge both its relevance and success.

For our purposes here, we shall define the philosophy of an organization as its core beliefs as to its *raison d'être*, purpose and style. Under such a definition, philosophy and doctrine cannot be wholly separated, and policing by consent could be described as part-philosophy, part-basis for doctrine, and part-style. Before we go on to examine that phrase in more depth, however, we need to say something more about doctrine.

The meaning and uses of doctrine

The dictionary defines 'doctrine', *inter alia*, as 'a body of instruction or teaching'. Doctrine is a familiar part of theology, as exemplified by the 39 Articles of the Church of England; and indeed one of the religious philosopher Emanuel Swedenborg's works is entitled simply, *Doctrine of Life* (Swedenborg, 1954). However, our use of the word is taken from its current usage in the military context, where doctrine has been in fashion for some time. Both the usefulness of a shared doctrine *per se* and the operational doctrine which he developed have had an enormous impact since General Sir Nigel Bagnall (1927–2002) was Chief of the General Staff from 1985 to 1988; we shall begin our exposition in that area.

Military doctrine is defined by Colonel Mungo Melvin (1997) as:

> A formal expression of military knowledge and thought that the army accepts as being relevant at a given time, which covers the nature of current and future conflicts, the preparation of the army for such conflicts and the methods of engaging in them to achieve success.

Current military doctrine on operations asserts the need for the manoeuvrist approach:

> The manoeuvrist approach to operations is one in which shattering the enemy's overall cohesion and will to fight rather than his material is paramount ... It calls for an attitude of mind in which doing the unexpected and seeking originality is combined with a ruthless determination to succeed.

The style of command associated with manoeuvrist warfare emphasises the need for decentralisation. In the words of Field Marshal Slim, reflecting on the (manoeuvrist) campaign against the Japanese in Burma, 1942-1945:

Commanders at all levels had to act more on their own; they were given greater latitude to work out their own plans to achieve what they knew was the Army Commander's intention ... This acting without orders, in anticipation of orders, or without waiting for approval, yet always within the overall intention, must become second nature in any form of warfare ... and must go down to the smallest units. It requires in the higher command a corresponding flexibility of mind, confidence in subordinates, and the power to make its intentions clear through the force.

As we should expect from a disciplined and hierarchical organization with a highly trained general staff, the army has a hierarchy of doctrine, ranging from principles through procedures to practices. Doctrine has become part of the military mind-set, so that even the most practical soldiers preface their remarks with some acknowledgement of its importance, and specialist publications can become a positive orgy of doctrine. Colonel Charles Grant is very much at home with the notion of doctrine. He presents a useful overview of the nature of doctrine (Grant, 1997), which he divides into three parts:

- Doctrine in its purest form has a somewhat timeless, intellectual component. It draws principles from the experience of earlier successful armies and their commanders; principles that remain relevant to-day. We call them the Enduring Tenets and perhaps the simplest examples of such tenets are the Principles of War—Selection and maintenance of the aim, Concentration of force, Economy of effort, Maintenance of morale, and so on, all of which appear in remarkably similar form in the doctrine of most armies ...
- Doctrine also has a practical and dynamic component in that it interprets the Enduring Tenets in the light of current circumstances ...
- Finally, doctrine has a predictive component.

Current military doctrine
Colonel Grant agrees with Colonel Melvin that manoeuvre has replaced attrition as the central idea of the army in warfare at all levels. Seeking to shatter the enemy's cohesion is a fundamental element of this central idea. Doctrine identifies four factors that will achieve this: firepower, surprise, tempo and simultaneity. Grant goes on to define tempo as the rhythm or rate of activity on operations, relative to the enemy. Tempo has three elements: speed of decision, speed of execution, and the speed with which a force transitions from one activity to another. This is graphically illustrated by Liddell Hart, talking about the German invasion of France in 1940.

The pace of Panzer warfare paralysed the French staff. The orders they issued might have been effective but for being, repeatedly, 24 hours late for the situation they were intended to meet.

Colonel Grant goes on to comment:

Today the army uses another historical example to describe this and to explain the notion of getting inside the enemy's decision cycle. This is the Boyd Cycle or OODA loop based on Colonel Boyd's observation that the American pilots in Korea were more successful than their enemy, despite technically less capable aeroplanes. This was because they could observe, orientate, decide and act faster than their enemy.

Doctrine and core functions
Grant describes the core functions of the manoeuvrist doctrine as threefold: to find, fix and strike.

To find
- locate;
- identify; and
- assess.

To fix
- deny;
- distract; and
- deprive the enemy of the freedom to act.

To strike
- manoeuvre; and
- hit.

These three core functions are evident at the tactical, operational and military strategic levels.

Active doctrine
Grant quotes approvingly from the military intellectual, Major General J. F. C. Fuller, in order to illustrate the theme that doctrine needs to be active and revisited:

> The danger of a doctrine is that it is apt to ossify into a dogma, and be seized upon by mental emasculates who lack virility of judgement, and who are only too grateful to rest assured that their actions, however inept, find justification in a book, which, if they think at all, is in their opinion written in order to exonerate them from doing so. In the past many armies have been destroyed by internal discord, and some have been destroyed by the weapons of their antagonists, but the majority have perished through adhering to dogmas springing from their past successes—that is, suicide or self-destruction through inertia of mind. (Grant, 1997)

Commentary
This brief introduction to the nature and content of current military doctrine will have given the reader some notion of what is at issue. There is an intoxicating clarity and simplicity about military doctrine, at least in the operational context, and those who enjoy reading military history will already have noted contexts for themselves in which manoeuvrist doctrine was or was not applied. The words used in current military doctrine are deliberately chosen, we imagine, as being easy to memorise and apply. We may not all have read Clausewitz's reflections *On War* (1982), nor be able to summon them to mind and apply them in the appropriate way and at the appropriate time, but surely we can all grasp and recall that the essential mission of the armed services is to find, fix and strike the enemy.

Let us leave aside, at least for the moment, the interesting question as to how much doctrine influences army thought and behaviour in military action, whether before or after the event, and go on to consider its possible application in the context of policing. Can we apply such heady ideas in the police context? Here we must pause to draw breath.

We cannot simply transfer the content of current military doctrine from one context to the other, as if police work and soldiering were interchangeable activities carried out by interchangeable organizations, and the purpose of the police were simply to find, fix and strike the enemy—whatever the appeal of that notion to certain chief constables. A simple transfer of both notion and content is unworkable, for reasons that we are about to explore; but that does not mean that the two organizations cannot learn from each other.

POLICE AND ARMY RELATIONSHIPS

The underlying relationship between the police and the army, in Britain as elsewhere, is one of profound ambivalence. This is for both obvious and subtle reasons, which would form the subject of a fascinating monograph on organizational jealousy, but which need not detain us longer here. We shall simply remind our readers that:

- From 1829 onwards both the newly-created Metropolitan Police and the county and borough forces that were created in its wake needed to differentiate themselves as strongly as possible from the prevailing continental model of policing, which was based upon the idea of a *gendarmerie*—in other words, an armed body of men under military discipline, responsible to the state, and commanded by regular officers on secondment from the army.
- Having taken off in a new direction, the police still had to struggle for a century or more to emerge as an independent profession of its own, without the need to be commanded by retired military officers.
- The radicals in police ranks wish to complete the separation and to divest themselves of any resemblance, whether real or apparent, to anything either military or paramilitary. Conservatives, on the other hand, argue for order, hierarchy and discipline, and to retain at least some of the features of an organization of quasi-military origin. The dispute is a contemporary one, ranging from the drilling of police recruits to the question of whether the police are a force (military) or a service (non-military).

There is thus, we opine, a residual hostility or antagonism on the part of the police service towards adopting new ideas from the military, whatever their merits. Moreover, even if the will to adopt what might be seen as a military development were there, police difficulties of implementation would still be considerable.

Despite the survival of the regiment and the tribal loyalty that it engenders, the army is a national institution with a well-indoctrinated general staff, and is therefore capable of producing, promulgating and ensuring the acceptance and application of a general doctrine on command—or any other subject on which discipline and loyalty will ensure compliance.

The police of the United Kingdom, by contrast, still consist of some 60 or more autonomous forces, each commanded by an independent chief constable, and they have no central, authoritative, written doctrine of any kind. Despite the long existence of a Police Staff College at Bramshill, there is no General Staff, and if there were, there would be no Chief of the General Staff to command it. (See Villiers, 1998, for a history of the Police Staff College and a comparison with its military equivalent at Camberley.) Staff duties are not taught in the police service, and anyone who is selected as a staff officer will have to pick up the job as he or she goes along, without even the privilege of a hand-over from the previous occupant.

Moreover, whilst the service produces innumerable policies and other documents of every kind, there is no standard formula for their production or distribution, and their status is generally low. The police service might pretend to be a written culture, but it is in fact an oral one, so that those who argue that policing is still more craft than profession have a strong case. What is important is not necessarily written down, and what is written down is not necessarily important.

Under these circumstances, the oral traditions and tacit assumptions of policing have been of greater significance than any written doctrine; and some police strategists have undoubtedly argued very cogently (whether or not their ideas were committed to paper) that the flexibility of an unwritten constitution was greatly preferable to its alternatives.

We believe that the police service of the twenty-first century needs to recognise and declare its doctrine, in the sense of a recognised body of knowledge and an authoritative set of principles, in order to achieve its appropriate standing as a profession and fulfil its proper role in society.

We recognise that there will be opposition to this idea; that opposition emerges both from what we might term the natural critics of the police service, whatever its aspirations, and from within the service itself. Indeed, we would not have it otherwise: for there would be little challenge in writing a book simply to articulate ideas on which everyone had agreed in advance. Nevertheless, we are convinced that the service must move forward on this issue, and that the time to declare and uphold a doctrine of policing has arrived. The police service may not produce documents akin to Army Doctrine Publications; but it will produce their equivalent.

PROFESSIONS AND PROFESSIONALISM

Are the police a profession? We believe that they are moving towards a revised model of that ideal. The public services are changing in an era of increasing demand for accountability, and the idea of a profession must change with them. At the same time, the essence of what it means to provide a professional service cannot be allowed to wither away. For the true professional serves the community as a whole, not one faction or section within it.

The nineteenth-century model is obsolete
We need not mean by a 'profession' what is understood by that concept in the nineteenth-century: i.e. a group of learned gentleman who establish a monopoly

of professional knowledge and skills in a certain area, and are responsible for regulating both admission to their ranks and the practice of those once admitted. (See Greenhill, 1985, for a seminal contribution on the essential characteristics of a profession, which he identifies as having three essential characteristics: it has a unique body of knowledge, it performs work of social value, and it regulates itself. Against these three measuring sticks, we may only argue incontestably that the police service performs work of social value.)

Amateur or professional?
The police should be professional in their work, rather than amateurish. That is a trite point, although not always easy to achieve in practice: see some of the criticisms of police behaviour in the Lawrence Inquiry (Macpherson, 1999), and the subsequent debate as to whether the police are institutionally racist or institutionally inefficient. There is a conflict, however, when we come to consider whether or not all police work need be carried out by dedicated police officers.

The police service is officially dedicated to the recruitment and extensive use of special constables (i.e. voluntary and unpaid police officers, working when they choose to do so). It is therefore clear that policing is not an activity solely carried out by professional police officers, in the full sense of the word.

There is, nevertheless, a dynamic tension between the professional and the special or amateur police officer, which is recreated on a bigger scale in the tension between the public police service and the ever-increasing body of private security companies, special investigation agencies and the like, who have already taken some of the police service's business.

It is a tension which is likely to increase, and to which some of the best police minds have applied themselves. There is clearly a need to articulate, agree and apply a doctrine in this area—as our later contributor, the then chief constable of Surrey Police Blair, argued in a presentation, later taken forward by the Home Secretary, on two-level policing delivered at an ACPO conference in 1998.

Public service values
The police should be professional to the extent that they are reliant on their work as their major source of income, and should continue to be discouraged from the possibility of bringing the service into disrepute by part-time working or other activities that may represent a conflict of interests. In our view, the police service needs the security and predictability of long-term employment, which does not depend upon results and is not measured by crude and simplistic performance criteria, in order to preserve the professional ideals of integrity, dedication and disinterestedness that were once taken for granted as essential in the public service, but which are now under attack.

Here we refer only in passing to such onslaughts as the notorious Sheehy Report (1993), which sought to reduce police work to a semi-skilled occupation that anyone could take up or leave at any time, and to which any notion of a professional ethic was irrelevant. This was roundly attacked when it appeared and its impact was contained. But if Sheehy was a skirmish, the war goes on.

There has been a systematic and sustained guerrilla campaign against public service attitudes and values since the 1980s, and it has gained ground in the past few years under the twin dogmas of performance management and modernisation. Like many guerrilla campaigns, it has been supported by some of those who would have most to lose were it successful; and it has achieved its greatest success in undermining official morale.

An apparent digression on patrol work

Police chiefs, not unnaturally, will wish to be seen as modern, open-minded and progressive by those who are in positions of power. They must consider with at least apparent seriousness the current fashions, fads and fallacies of public service management: no matter what the evidence, or lack of it, on which they are based.

One of the prevailing assumptions in the newish and still rapidly expanding subject of police studies is that patrol work is ineffective. No one, we hasten to add, is arguing that this applies in the case of reassuring the public as to a visible police presence. Rather, it is argued that patrol work does not prevent crime; and we have social science research to support this contention, with the famous assertion that a police officer on patrol is statistically unlikely to encounter any crime in progress, let alone to prevent its completion.

As an all-purpose generalisation this is clearly fallacious, as any motorist is aware. It refers to foot patrol, and the bobby on the beat. But are that beat patrol officer's duties in reality so unlikely to affect crime? To his credit, at least one chief constable has taken on and challenged this item of conventional wisdom, on which so many organizational reforms have been based. David Westwood, the Chief Constable of Humberside, looked at the issue in a seminar on policing philosophies which he chaired at Bramshill on 26 July 2001. In his view, the research was fallacious since it was simply based on an arithmetical calculation. X number of constables randomly patrolling y miles of streets would indeed be unlikely to discover a crime in progress, such as a burglary, very often. (In fact, once in eight years is quoted as the statistical possibility for a random encounter.)

However, street patrols need not be random, but may be related to the patterns of crime in the area, the *modus operandi* of known local criminals, recent releases from local prisons, or other locally relevant information. On this basis, structured street patrolling can and should be both generally reassuring and effective in addressing crime, and the Humberside service was at that time being organized to do very much more of it.

In our view, this story illustrates two things:

- Police work may not be hard science, but nor is it a random activity. The professional police officer need not go out and wander the streets in the hope of coming across a crime, rather as if a doctor were to wander the streets, hoping to discover if anyone needed his or her services. In both cases, the true professional thinks about the most effective way to do good, but certainly does not set out to ignore the public's wishes.
- Police leadership may require the moral courage to go both against both conventional wisdom and political pressure. Interestingly, David Westwood has found that the greatest pressure against his policing policy has come from within the force: from the constables who do not know how to talk to the public any more, since they are so used to reacting at high

speed to critical demands for their services, and from the supervisors who do not know how to supervise them.

Professional management, or managing professionals?

Do professional people need to be managed? On the face of it, this sounds like a contradiction in terms. Professional people should not need to be managed, but should manage themselves: there is no place for time and motion studies (Brown, 1954) in the professions, (except, of course, to create another profession for the industrial psychologist—or perhaps nowadays the knowledge manager).

Traditionally, members of the professions have a degree of discretion about how they go about their work, since they are expected to exercise their professional judgement in the best interests of the client. We do not tell a surgeon how to perform an operation, even if it is our leg at stake; for we expect the surgeon to operate in our best interests. We do not tell the lawyer how to draw up a will, nor the clergyman how to preach a sermon. We may, at least in some of these cases, choose to go to another professional if we are dissatisfied with the service provided by our first choice; but we recognise the autonomy of the professional.

The situation changes, however, when it is the state that pays the bill. Policing is paid for almost entirely out of government funds. Home Office Circular 114 of 1983 began the drive towards the better use of that investment which remains with us, and which has resulted in a far greater central interest in and control over the use of resources. We have seen a sustained and increasing drive that the police provide value for money, and a shift in emphasis from controlling inputs (the cash provided) to a greater interest in how the money is used, and its longer-term effects (monitoring of outputs and outcomes). The drive for greater efficiency has assumed, if not ever more subtle and effective forms, at least ever more visible and bureaucratic ones; and measures adopted in other parts of the public services have been applied to policing.

The police are now, therefore, more accountable in practice than was the case in the past, since the performance management culture has weakened the protective constitutional barrier of operational independence which was the police version of professional autonomy. Indeed, the local identity and autonomy of each police force has been used against it, as it were; for in a culture of national performance indicators it is possible to compare one force's efficiency with another's.

We need a doctrine for the new public service professionals, which describes the extents of their powers and the ways in which they may be legitimately prescribed: for to define where power stops is to emphasise where it may be legitimately employed. We explore this further in this volume, under the idea of verifiable professionalism. But before we begin to explore the wider dimensions of doctrine, we need to spend some further time collating and considering the sources of police doctrine on leadership that already exist.

We have described police doctrine as an organic growth rather than a mechanistic construction, and our role will be therefore more that of a botanist describing what is to be found in the garden and how it might be cultivated further, than an engineer planning a new project. However, whether botanist or engineer, we must begin our task.

SOURCES OF POLICE DOCTRINE ON LEADERSHIP: GOVERNMENT POLICY

The police service is naturally, inevitably and rightly influenced by government policy and this must affect its doctrine of leadership. In some areas we see the elements of a doctrine already existing. For example, there is a clear set of criteria for selection to both the Accelerated Promotion Scheme and the Strategic Command Course. These criteria might be seen as the building blocks for a doctrine of leadership, for the graduates of those courses are the leaders of the service, and the qualities by which they are selected should therefore be the qualities needed by those leaders.

Here is an example of what we mean by organic development. There is a move afoot, in collaboration between the Association of Police Authorities (APA) and the Association of Chief Police Officers (ACPO), to attempt to establish a common set of criteria by which chief officers should be judged, both in selection for their posts and in their performance once in post. This is a potential further contribution to a common doctrine and therefore generally to be supported. We see no reason why ACPO should not contribute to its own development, as do the leaders of other professions to theirs.

The Police Leadership Development Board (PLDB), a central government inspiration, contains in its remit the need to revise selection procedure for fast track officers. It is right that a police doctrine of leadership should be influenced by such developments—although if it is to achieve the status of a modern profession it must ultimately decide such issues for itself, and reconcile government initiatives with what it knows to be needed. The doctrine that emerges will not reject government priorities, but absorb them into the enduring doctrine of police leadership that has already been articulated.

How? For an example of what could be done, let us consider the doctrine of equal opportunity. It is a long-established government policy that all public services should take active measures to promote a policy of equal opportunities in the selection, development and promotion of their staff. The need for this is stressed in every publication and on every occasion, to the extent that equality of opportunity has become something close to a creed.

In the police service, this means that women and members of minority groups must receive special attention, since they are under-represented both in the police as a whole and very much more so at the level of high command, where women are still a rarity and black faces most unusual. Since positive discrimination is both illegal and unfair, a police service cannot rectify this situation simply by promoting women or members of minority groups solely because of their womanhood or minority status, in an attempt to force an equality of outcome. However, it is assumed that were a genuine equality of opportunity to exist, there would be a greater variety at the top; and that it is both legitimate and desirable to attempt to promote that outcome by means of a policy of positive action. The mechanics of this need not concern us here, although we note in passing that it is part of the remit of the Police Leadership Development Board to work to achieve this outcome. There are, however, two points that we need to make:

- The promotion of equal opportunities is an essential part of government policy, and must therefore figure in police doctrine.
- Were its objectives to be achieved in full, there would still be a need for a police doctrine of leadership. In other words, even if police leadership adequately and fairly represented both women and minority groups, it would still need a collective identity and ethos. Hence the enduring need for this book.

In our view, a police officer is a police officer, whatever his or her race, sex, religious persuasion or other characteristics. Like MPs, they serve all their constituents, and must be both impartial and even-handed in so doing. They need not be colour-blind, a policy which was discussed at some length by the authors of the Lawrence Report (Macpherson, 1999); and we might learn from experience elsewhere in seeking how to achieve an impartial style of both policing and police leadership in a mixed society. What is certain, however, is that all police leaders, whatever their background, need to share a common ethos.

The need for professional confidence

There is a paradox in the police organization. On the one hand, police officers are usually, at least on the surface, entirely confident in their problem-solving abilities. It is a can-do culture, and any problem can be solved—even the production of a doctrine of leadership, to which the standard solution would be to set up an ACPO sub-committee to write it on a purely eclectic basis. On the other hand, we believe there to be a fundamental lack of inner confidence in many police leaders, which manifests itself in ways such as the following:

- *'Presenteeism'* There is an inability to let go, which the insightful police leader and commentator John Grieve will later in this volume characterise as 'presenteeism'. This shows itself in various ways, such as a disinclination to delegate, an unnecessary interest in tactical detail, and a failure to distinguish between urgency and importance. There is a pronounced tendency to confuse time spent on police premises with productive work, in which the presence of the leader adds value; and the mobile telephone and portable computer have worsened the situation.

- *Unwillingness to consider alternatives* There is, on the part of some chief officers, an unwillingness to test an idea, policy or solution to a problem which they have propounded, by comparing it with the best argument that can be raised against it, and thereby improving or discarding the original. Not carrying out real trials means that progress cannot be made, for the proper method is not being followed (Popper, 1977). To expose one's favourite ideas to the possibility that they may be wrong is to take a risk. It requires courage; and courage comes from confidence. The good police leader, as John Grieve points out in Chapter 14, needs to be able to handle risk, and to admit that an idea, policy or initiative may have been wrong, so that the organization can then find a better way forward.

- *Autocracy* Some chief officers confuse the ability to be decisive and to project vigour and confidence, with autocracy. The confidence achieved from autocratic leadership is a false one. It can lead to disastrous results both for the organization and the individual concerned, or more likely his or her hapless subordinates, who were unable to tell the chief in question that the initiative was not working. It is perhaps most simply described as an inability to listen; and listening too much is a very rare fault.

SOURCES OF POLICE DOCTRINE ON LEADERSHIP: THE POLICE STAFF COLLEGE

The national Police Staff College was created in 1948 in order to develop the police leaders of the present and the future, and it has addressed that purpose ever since. The development of leadership is a practical task, which need leave no record behind it; and indeed, much of the learning that has occurred at the College must remain unrecorded. Nevertheless, a collective body of practical wisdom has accumulated; and it is time to collate and comment upon what is in effect an informal doctrine of leadership.

Development may concentrate upon knowledge, skills or attitudes, or any combination of the three. Bramshill has addressed all three areas over the years, with different priorities as the needs of the service and the fashion of the time dictated. Rather than follow every twist and turn of the plot, let us sketch some of the main ideas that were developed on a leadership development course as it used to occur—the Junior Command Course (JCC) for all newly-appointed chief inspectors.

The assumption of any command course was that the officers who attended it already knew a good deal about leadership in practice. There was no formal and sustained attempt on the JCC to test or develop practical leadership skills. Instead, the JCC attempted to combine both professional and personal development, and to improve the knowledge and constructively challenge the attitudes of those attending it. Its primary method was the intensive use of the syndicate or discussion group—membership of which would have been, on at least some occasions, an experience not unlike living through a cultural revolution, but which was normally less intensive.

The learning was both collective and individual; but it was not recorded. There was no course historian to record what had occurred and no doctrinal specialist to shape it. This type of course produced not a single transferable doctrine of leadership, but a number of variations on a series of themes. Like the police service itself, each course was divided, and each syndicate developed an identity and approach of its own.

Provided that the JCC achieved results, only a purist would have looked for a collective doctrine. Even in its absence, however, it is possible to make some cautious generalisations about the views on leadership which were either reflected or developed. We shall present them as a series of propositions, and then draw some conclusions from them.

POLICE AXIOMS ON LEADERSHIP

Leadership exists
Leadership is a distinct phenomenon that can be distinguished from both management and supervision—but not by a neat and simple formula that everyone will recognise. The edges are blurred, and there is no clear, generally accepted and authoritative model as to where one begins and the others end.

Police officers are more used to management or supervision than leadership, whether as recipients or practitioners; and in fact police leadership is seen as relatively underdeveloped.

Every officer is a leader
Having said that, there is a school of thought that argues that by virtue of their original authority, need for the proper use of discretion, and powers of influence in the community, all patrol officers exercise leadership. Consequently, leadership is not a characteristic that only senior officers need possess or acquire, but is needed by all ranks who go on patrol or respond to emergencies. Most decisions on the streets are made by constables, who may be acting alone, or as 'tactical advisers' to more senior officers who may be officially in charge.

The 'military' style of leadership still exists
Whatever the reality of the demands of practical police decision-making on the streets, the police service has traditionally practised what it terms a 'military' style of leadership. By this is implied an autocratic style, supposedly suited to the harsh and immediate demands of war, although in reality it has a great deal more to do, we would suggest, with the practices of a mechanistic bureaucracy.

In fact, what the police refer to as the military style of leadership would probably be rejected by the contemporary armed services as something corresponding to the worst caricature of rule by non-commissioned officers under national service. However, the fact that a belief may be mistaken or distorted does not reduce the intensity with which it may be held.

Leadership by example has been neglected
The police understanding, or rather misunderstanding, of what is meant by military leadership makes no reference to the leadership by example that we should expect the better type of military leader to display.

That ideal may be ignored because it is considered that leadership by example is usually impossible in the police service. Police commanders very rarely *lead* the men and women under their command, in any very obvious sense; and few are the opportunities for heroic leadership in the police service. Even during a riot, the police officers in charge are more likely to require a sort of stoical endurance than any dynamic capacity for leadership; and on many occasions their fundamental role may be to restrain their officers from impetuous action.

Unheroic leadership
However, as William Heffernan argues in *Chapter 9*, there are in fact ample opportunities for the practice of leadership by example in such areas as not

making improper use of privileges and benefits, or simply by the leaders showing themselves to be honest and dedicated police officers, who are prepared to listen and learn from those around them. These are not heroic activities, but very necessary ones; and their impact need not be confined to the leader's immediate circle. Middle managers in the police service would like to see the demonstration of such qualities by their chiefs, on the whole, and are certainly quick to note their absence.

The need for a new style of command
There is a general agreement that the autocratic style of leadership is outdated and counter-productive, and the modern police service requires a much more democratic and less dictatorial style. But the old style is extremely difficult to eradicate, and has so far survived all attempts to achieve its extirpation.

The editors of this text have 40 years' combined experience of teaching at the Police Staff College, and have yet to hear any group of police leaders, at any level, argue for autocratic leadership, or against the need for a sea-change to a more consultative and democratic style of leadership.

Indeed, all those officers who attend any command course will support the need for change; and yet, we are forced to infer that despite this collective will, widespread cultural change does not occur. In reality, the bulk of senior police commanders remain autocrats—even those who advocated changing the culture when they occupied a position of middle management within it.

There is a need to change the culture of the police organization as a whole, before it can change its entrenched practices. Can the leaders be found within the police service who are prepared to take this on and see it through? Milan Pagon, as we shall see in *Chapter 11*, thinks otherwise. We have seen no sign as yet that contemporary police leadership is capable of putting into place the paradigmatic shift that both service and country require, but we believe it to be possible. We shall return to this theme in our conclusions.

The blame culture
Time after time, the police have been described as having a blame culture, or a fault-finding culture, rather than one based on a respect for professionalism and the proper use of trust. Senior officers tend to allow, if anything, rather too much discretion to the officers supposedly under their command, until something goes wrong. Then they investigate what has happened, as if they were old-style detectives investigating a crime; not in an objective search for the truth, but in order to find someone to blame. We have all seen this style of retrospective fault-finding caricatured in popular television series. Sadly, the caricature is based upon an element of truth.

A culture of generalised cynicism
The police are on the whole a cynical culture: about the public, about themselves, about their leaders, and about the limits of what can be achieved by their organization, whether in its reformed or unreformed state. Although they will produce mission statements and the like when pressed, any wholeheartedly aspirational statement of leadership is unlikely to meet more than a token approval, and more likely with a general scepticism. Police officers pride themselves on living and operating in the real world; and their real world does

not apparently contain very many transformational or even inspirational leaders. We quote here, of course, from the perspective of middle managers, who perhaps see the police chief as the valet sees the great man, i.e., unadorned by heroism. However, we believe that cynicism is a general characteristic of the service.

Police officers (of all ranks) tend to have an ambivalent attitude towards those who lead them, and unconditional declarations of admiration or even whole-hearted respect for chief police officers are conspicuous by their absence. Most police officers on a command course find it difficult to declare the names of more than one or two police chiefs whom they unreservedly admire for their leadership qualities. Those chiefs whom they do admire may be praised for qualities such as ruthless cunning or an unswerving determination to obtain results, rather than the sort of qualities which we should find recommended in the literature on the subject.

At the same time, however, we must add that when asked to list the qualities they would look for in a good police commander, most groups have tended to include such apparently unexceptionable virtues as honesty and integrity as being highly desirable. We must conclude that there remains a vein of idealism in even the most disillusioned cynic; but also that what is really meant by the apparently easily recogniseable concepts of honesty and integrity requires further investigation and debate.

Distrust of charisma

Paradoxically, although ruthless determination is admired, charisma is regarded with some suspicion, and a charismatic style of leadership is generally seen as neither necessary nor even desirable for police leaders. Putting it simply, very few senior police officers are regarded as being charismatic, even in the watered-down version of that much overused word; and those who do have such personalities are regarded with some suspicion. On intellectual grounds, the police quite rightly point out that their authority rests upon the constitutional grounds of legality and tradition, rather than force of personality or religious or ideological conviction. They further assert that the police officer who believes too strongly in what he or she is doing can be profoundly dangerous, as tending to be doctrinaire, unbalanced, or even extremist.

It is not the task of the police to solve society's ills, but to make reasonable progress under the law, and in some accordance with the elusive phenomenon of public opinion, in attempting to balance the competing and conflicting interests that emerge in any real dispute, from domestic violence to political demonstration. The police must not take sides, cut corners, or interpret the will of society before it has been able to do so for itself; and the charismatic leader may be tempted to try all three. Consequently, charismatic leadership is regarded with some suspicion, although firm leadership in emergency or crisis is very much welcomed, if not always supplied.

A masculine culture?

There is no reason why charisma should be exclusive to either sex. Military leaders have tended to be men, but that does not make the qualities of military-style leadership a male perquisite, as Queen Boudicca showed some time ago; and no presumption has been expressed at the Police Staff College, in the past 15 years at least, that men are either better than women at leadership or in some way better suited to it. Nor has the reverse point of view been expressed. Gender is not irrelevant to leadership, but nor is it an exclusionary factor.

Jennifer Brown will have more to say about male and female leadership patterns in *Chapter 13*. For the moment, let us briefly remind ourselves of the salient facts. Policing was traditionally an entirely male occupation, which women only entered during the acute labour shortages of the Great War, and then on special terms. Women were never easily accepted into the police, and the culture has remained an overwhelmingly masculine one. Under such circumstances, those women who joined the service, and the small minority who against the odds were able to obtain promotion to positions of leadership, have had, by and large, to conform to the prevailing culture, or at least not to rebel against it. (These remarks, of course, also apply to police officers of a non-majoritarian ethnic background—of either sex.)

Consequently, we do not know what a police service led by a proportionate representation of women police officers would be like, or what it could achieve. We may only for the moment comment on the absence of overt prejudice to women in the police service as shown on (mainly male) command courses at Bramshill.

A culture of anti-leadership?

If the police are suspicious of charisma, we must report our impression that they have mixed views about the whole notion of leadership, *in toto*. In some ways, there is almost a culture of anti-leadership in the police. Perhaps leadership is still associated with the army, with which organization the police have so ambivalent a relationship; and there is an unwillingness on the part of some police leaders, even when required by the situation to do so, to assume the mantle and trappings of leadership as traditionally conceived. Despite the symbols of authority which senior police officers display on their uniforms, and the often bizarrely confrontational nature of the relationship between the ranks—'Sergeant! In my office! Now!'—The police culture is still in some fundamental sense an egalitarian one, and it remains the creature of its origins.

The police do not believe in privilege and are uncomfortable with its rituals. Police officers, at least in popular detective fiction, do not enter at the main entrance of the local manor house, but go round to the back to talk to the cook. Moreover, the organization in which the police spend their lives has little time for pomp and ceremony. Its drill, when practised, is usually poor. It has difficulties with saluting, officers' messes, high tables and the other distinctions that the Police Federation takes such delight in lampooning—although it allows a collector's interest in memorabilia. In the detective branch, by tradition, uniforms are not worn at all; and although the terms 'Sir' or 'Madam' may occasionally be heard, they are much more likely to be replaced by the more down to earth 'Boss.'

Senior police officers recognize that they have to provide leadership, and will find a means to do so. But they are much less comfortable with the idea of officership, which they would appear to associate with the supposedly class-ridden and rigid distinctions of the armed forces; and which may not in any case be easily reconciled with the original authority of the constable which Seumas Miller reviews in depth in *Chapter 7*. Whilst some senior police officers will therefore exhort the students on a command course, that when they achieve senior rank they must look and feel the part, this message does not always reach open ears; for what does it feel like to look and feel like a leader?

Some police leaders set an excellent example. They manage to combine the ability to radiate warmth and a sense of unity with the person or group with whom they are interacting, *with* the need to pose some sort of challenge to its individual and collective capacities which is the essence of leadership. How did they learn how to do this? We do not know; but it is unlikely to have been either in a police training institution, or by the example of those who have led them in the past. Both factors are to be regretted; and both can be changed.

The pool of potential leaders

Although we have suggested that police leadership should be, in Napoleon's phrase, a career open to the talents, the service need not look outside its own ranks for the potential to lead. The potential for high quality leadership exists with the British police service and is acknowledged by its middle management— although not all are averse to looking outside for new talent and a fresh look. Cynical as some of these officers are, they do not doubt the potential for leadership that exists within the service; and nor do we. The service recruits more than enough intelligent, well-educated, dedicated and resourceful candidates, both through its accelerated promotion scheme and through the normal patterns of recruitment, to provide an ample pool of high quality future leaders. The mystery is what happens to their vision and idealism as a result of 20 years' experience of policing, rather than why it was never there in the first place.

Recognition of the need for doctrine

The British police are often described as pragmatic, which can be seen as a polite word for having no interest in theory. Some analysts go further, and brand them as positively anti-intellectual; our contributor Sir Robert Bunyard will reflect on this theme from an historical perspective in *Chapter 6*. We have not found an absence of interest in the theory of leadership amongst the officers who have attended command courses at the Police Staff College. Indeed, the reverse is true. There is an interest in what works; and some theories do. Police commanders are keen to further professionalise their occupation, and we sense a frustration with the absence of progress in this area.

In exploring leadership theory, the contribution of Professor John Adair and his action-centred theory of leadership (1979) has been recognised as being both illuminative and helpful. The role of the leader is to achieve the task, build the team and develop its individual members, in conjunction; and it is a fundamental but easily followed error, to concentrate on one or even two tasks, at the expense of the three as a whole.

The notion of situational leadership holds a similar intellectual appeal. It is recognised that the good police leader should be able to change his or her style of leadership according to the current motivation, experience and ability of the group, and that no one style could fit all occasions. It is also generally agreed that the same leader may not be equally comfortable as delegator, facilitator, coach or director, and there is likely to be an individual developmental need here.

More recent theories of leadership—and here we are referring to the developments of the 1990s and the emphasis, for example, upon transformational rather than transactional leadership—have generally proved of interest, despite our earlier comment about a general absence of recognition of transformational leadership at work in top police leadership. In case any of our readers are unfamiliar with what is at issue here, we quote from command course material:

Transformational leadership:

Values and visions
More important than charisma, bearing, or interpersonal skills is the secret ingredient of leadership; the ability to convey a sense of vision and mission in a way that transforms and enhances the follower's sense of the possible.
Leaders motivate their followers to:

- Transcend self-interest for the sake of organizational goals and values
- Raise their need level up from security and safety to self-esteem or autonomy
- Share with the leader a common vision of the importance of the leader's goals or values to the future of the organization

In the process, leaders motivate followers to achieve more than they thought possible, strengthen their commitment to the organization, and induce feelings of trust, admiration, loyalty and mutual respect.

Given the cynicism that we have already described as a prevailing characteristic of the police, it is a positive factor that the achievement of some aspects of transformational leadership is seen as a possibility for the service: a theme to which we shall return.

REFERENCES for *Chapter 1*

Adair, J (1979), *Action-Centred Leadership*, Aldershot: Gower.

Bailey, Col. JBA, OBE (1994), 'The First World War', *SCSI Occasional Bulletin* No. 7, Camberley: British Army Review Publications.

Blair, I (1998), 'Off-beat Solution', *Guardian*, 17 July 1998.

Brown, JAC (1954), *The Social Psychology of Industry*, London: Penguin. This contains a lucid account of the pioneering work of the industrial psychologist and management consultant F W Taylor, and his global impact upon the organization of work.

Clausewitz, C von (1982), *On War*, London: Penguin Books.

Descartes, R (1968), *Discourse on Method*, Harmondsworth: Penguin Books.

Grant, Col. C, OBE (1997), Contemporary Doctrine, *SCSI Occasional Bulletin* No. 30, Camberley: British Army Review Publications.

Greenhill, N (1986), 'Professionalism in the Police Service' in *Modern Policing*, Pope, D and Weiner, N (eds.), London: Croom Helm.

Macpherson, Sir William of Cluny (1999), *The Stephen Lawrence Inquiry*, Cm. 4262, London: Stationery Office.

Melvin, Col. R (1997), 'Camberley Doctrine on Command and Leadership', from a lecture given at Bramshill on 19 June 1997.

Morgan, G and Gibson, B (1979), *Sociological Paradigms and Organizational Analysis*, London: Heinemann.

Popper, K (1977), *The Logic of Scientific Discovery*, London: Routledge.

Sheehy, Sir P (1993), *Inquiry into Police Responsibilities and Rewards*, London: Stationery Office, Cmnd 2280.

Swedenborg, E (1954), *Doctrine of Life*, London: Swedenborg Society.

Villiers, P J (1998), *The First 50 Years: A History of the Police Staff College*, Bramshill, Hampshire: Police Staff College Publication.

CHAPTER 2

Nice People, Big Questions, Heritage Concepts

Robert Adlam

This article urges leaders to make sure that they have done sufficient groundwork upon which to base their claim to lead. It cautions against the beguiling blandishments of 'best practice', the promise of 'solutions to problems' and the managerial rhetoric of improved efficiency and effectiveness, and recommends police leaders to rekindle and display their passion, their commitment to a cause, and their clarification of the worthwhile ends to which the police aim.

If we wish to remain human, then there is only one way, the way into the open society. We must go into the unknown, the uncertain and the insecure, using what reason we may have to plan as well as we can for both security and freedom. (Popper, 1943: 200)

INTRODUCTION

The practice of senior police leadership impresses as a difficult task for at least two reasons. First, the role of the police in liberal democratic society remains ambiguous and contested. Moreover, it is not entirely clear how police effectiveness is to be measured. Even if police leaders do manage to establish definite aims and objectives for policing it is by no means easy to reform and re-structure the police organization as a design to achieve these goals. Yet, in spite of these problems, police leaders remain public figures appraised and evaluated in terms of police 'efficiency, economy and effectiveness'—as well as fairness and integrity. Their competence is judged against an extensive range of criteria and in relation to a general but somewhat opaque model of 'professionalism'. Second, they are embedded within an occupational culture that is characterised by more or less shared—yet sometimes contradictory—notions concerning the definition of the 'appropriate' conduct that is expected from them. As Schein's (1988) analysis of the cultural rules of interaction demonstrates, they have to 'pay their dues' if they are to earn widespread legitimation of their status and if they are to secure the goodwill of their subordinates.

They must, for example, spend time attending to the wants, needs and interests of those subordinates if their social performances are to be satisfactory. They must also manage the strategic dramaturgical arts of self-presentation and interpersonal style if they are to meet other demands attaching to their superordinate role. By way of example, Schein observes that the 'superior' must display him or herself as 'being in control of the situation' and must 'communicate clearly so that orders can be followed'. Schein also emphasises additional demands that weigh heavily upon the most senior figures in the organization including those associated with 'bearing' and 'deportment' as well as those connected with their ambassadorial function. He remarks that: 'High ranking leaders have to manage their public image very carefully, lest they "disappoint" their subordinates and leave them feeling cheated' (Schein 1988: 80).

How well does police leadership meet these challenges? To the extent that criticisms of and concerns about its adequacy continue to be raised from both within the service (e.g. Woodcock, 1992, Bunyard, 1993, ACPO, Quality of Service Committee, 1993, the Police Federation, 1995, HMIC Inspection, 'Police Integrity', 1999) and from a number of external stakeholders—including successive home secretaries, Home Office departments and the Police Authorities Association (Vick, 2000)—it seems that significant numbers of police leaders do 'disappoint' and fail to meet the taxing demands of full 'professionalism'.

One of the constant ambitions of police leadership and management development programmes (Plumridge, 1985, 1988; Villiers, 1998) has been to help police officers acquire the perspectives, knowledge, understanding and skills that, in principle, might enable them to be excellent practitioners. These programmes have represented one facet of a more general attempt to produce effective police leaders from within the ranks of the police service itself. Even if it is unreasonable to expect any obvious and straightforward connection between the provision of these programmes and subsequent 'improvements' in police leadership it is still reasonable to subject the nature and content of the curriculum to critical scrutiny. Just how 'sophisticated' is that curriculum? Does it, for example, provide sufficient 'coverage' of the difficult and demanding issues surrounding the shift to a 'single status' society (Feinberg, 1973) that is entailed through adopting concepts of human rights? Does it help police officers appreciate the constitutional foundations of the police? Does it explore the notion of 'authority' and probe the bases of police leaders-as-authorities? In short, does it provide police leaders with anything like the conceptual adequacy commensurate with their role?

A number of years ago Richards (1985) noticed that most of the content of 'command' courses at Bramshill (the centre for higher police training in England and Wales) was given over to an admixture of police-related social science and 'management' studies—along with a focus upon police operational matters. However, 'ethics' and the exploration of other serious spheres of philosophy relevant to policing were 'set aside'. Since Richards made those observations some attempts have been made to secure 'ethics', as a named subject of study, on the police leadership development curriculum (Villiers, 1998; Adlam, 1999). However, this has proved to be remarkably difficult. In part, this is because the selection of subjects for inclusion on programmes of study at Bramshill has tended to depend on 'student' feedback. Ethics has often failed to please its 'customer'. In addition, the curriculum at Bramshill has proved to be unstable because of its vulnerability to the changing regimes installed by the incoming senior staff. As a result, subjects such as 'ethics' may simply disappear.

Nonetheless, curriculum planners and managers (as well as faculty staff in universities) always have some room for manoeuvre and are free to ask: 'What sorts of knowledge should the present and future leaders of the police service draw from in order to guide their professional practice?' This paper attempts to provide part of an answer to that question. It sets out to bridge the gap between theory and practice—through the application of ideas and concepts. Written against the backdrop of concerns with the effectiveness of police leadership it assumes a tone of advocacy: it reflects the belief that police leadership would be improved if it were systematically informed by the results yielded from certain fields of philosophical inquiry. It also commends a revision of the police leadership development curriculum. It suggests that the content of that curriculum should do more to rest policing and police leadership practice upon proper foundations—foundations that can be provided through an engagement with applied philosophy.

The paper draws from a lengthy period of association, at Bramshill, with the design and delivery of a number of police leadership development programmes—including the Police Management Programme and the Accelerated Promotion Course. This experiential data is supplemented by material emerging from a long-term study of the 'character of police leadership' involving questionnaires, interviews and observation of the professional performances of police leaders. The empirical claims made in the paper are largely based on this source of data.

The main idea to be developed in the course of the paper concerns the general proposition that discussions in certain fields of philosophy have produced insights that can enhance the quality of police leadership and management practices. There is something of an irony here. This is because philosophy itself—via the particular contributions of Nietzsche and Wittgenstein—has hastened the arrival of the postmodern condition (Harvey, 1990, Connor, 1989, Best and Kellner, 1991) along with its erosion of confidence in authority and a general affirmation of 'relativism'. In the world of no certainties bequeathed by Nietzsche and Wittgenstein it is paradoxical to expect philosophy to do anything more than destabilise, subvert and undermine 'authority' (and, therefore, police leaders). Nonetheless, advances have been made in the philosophy of existence, as well as in social, political, legal and moral philosophy, that could be used to promote better police leadership.

PHILOSOPHY AND THE PRESENT

Relatively recent engagements by philosophers with the different and difficult practical issues attending 'cosmopolitanism' (Derrida, 2001), 'immigration and refugees' (Dummett, 2001), the development of the Internet (Dreyfus, 2001), the 'impossible people' of religion (Caputo, 2001), free speech (Arthur, 1997), 'environmental ethics' as well as 'animal rights' (Sterba, 1995), alternatives to the 'emptiness of self-interest' (Singer, 1994) and 'political liberalism' (Rawls, 1996) reflect an exciting trend in philosophy: a concern to put the discipline to work in the public domain. Philosophy has responded to the charge that its esoteric character has rendered it remote, exclusive, arcane and irrelevant, by confronting, directly, some of the most demanding social and political issues of contemporary times.

Bauman's (1993) 'postmodern ethics' extends this philosophical concern into the more general arena of 'postmodern society' and its 'postmodern types' of people. He finds, for example, the increasing genesis of 'persons-as-tourists' viewing society as an endless series of opportunities for garnering aesthetic pleasure. A consequence is the hastening of a tendency to exploit others—in what he, Bauman, perceives as a 'your value for my money situation'. His précis of the 'postmodern perspective' and its constituent wisdom finds it redolent with a new and pervasive mood of 'scepticism':

> What the postmodern mind is aware of is that there are problems in human and social life with no good solutions ... The postmodern mind is aware that each local, specialised and focused treatment ... spoils as much as it repairs. The postmodern mind is reconciled to idea that the messiness of the human predicament is here to stay. This is, in the broadest of outlines, what can be called postmodern wisdom. (Bauman 1993: 245)

Bauman's analysis is important for practical leadership: it underlines the fragility of its foundations. It urges leaders to make sure that they have done sufficient groundwork upon which to base their claim to lead. It cautions against the beguiling blandishments of 'best practice', the promise of 'solutions to problems' and the managerial rhetorics of improved efficiency and effectiveness.

The fact that philosophy has been 'taken to its public' (Critchley and Kearney, 2001a) is, however, no guarantee that it has found itself influencing the practice of policing. Indeed, not one essay in LaFollette's (1998) recent anthology devoted to 'ethics in practice' included the word 'police' in its title. Nor, in his comprehensive 'companion to ethics' was Singer (1993) able to make any reference to the moral problems encountered in policing. This is curious because police are constituted (at least in part) to achieve moral 'products'. Moreover, as the enduring facts of history show, the police are always liable to serve malevolence and evil. In this respect, Alderson (1998) is even moved to ask whether the police are essentially amoral. A part of the explanation for the lack of this reference to 'police' in contemporary philosophy lies in the rather underdeveloped nature of philosophical thinking about police. What, though, has been achieved?

A DEVELOPING PHILOSOPHY OF POLICE

Whilst Ker Muir (1977) in his bibliographical essay, identifies some of the solid ground upon which to rest policing (e.g. Packer, 1968, Skolnick, 1966)—as does Klockars (1985) in his 'idea' of police—it seems that a full philosophy of police has yet to be articulated. Richards (1985, 1993) recommended that applied ethics be given more attention within the police service. In line with the earlier findings of Sherman (1978, 1982) he observed the tendency, in police training, quickly to pass over questions of how officers *should* act—particularly in problematic or conflicting circumstances. Richards believed that a genuine engagement with 'ethics' might render moral problems more tractable. In addition he pointed out that the study of ethics would raise questions about the values that policing seeks to attain—as well as focusing upon *how* those valued ends might legitimately be achieved. Laugharne and Newman's (1985) 'principles of policing' achieve an intermediate stance between a genuine philosophy of police and a set of concrete prescriptions providing broad practical guidelines for police conduct. In consequence it might be more accurate to characterise their work as a doctrine of policing. They draw heavily from discussions within the realms of political and legal philosophy as they underline the paramountcy of upholding the 'Rule of

Law'. Central to this remains the unswerving commitment to protecting human rights and preserving fundamental freedoms.

Lustgarten's (1986) discussion of police 'governance' constitutes an important contribution to philosophical thinking about 'police' through his emphasis on 'democratic constitutionalism'. In the course of redressing the analytic imbalance that had befallen the study of policing (as a result of the sheer numerical dominance of social scientific inquiries) Lustgarten reminds his readership of the widespread tendency of humans *qua* humans to abuse power. Drawing from a Rawlsian conception of justice (Rawls, 1971) he insists that police—in virtue of their power and their 'virtual monopoly of legitimate violence in the name of the political order'—be subject to a regime of control which ensures that everyone be treated equally. Plainly Lustgarten covers that aspect of a philosophy of police concerned with legitimacy, accountability, the proper exercise of police power and the relationship between police and government. Thus, his work overlaps with Alderson's (1979, 1998) continuing search for a set of philosophical principles upon which to base the practice of policing in a liberal democracy.

Kleinig (1996) offers a relatively comprehensive ethics of policing that is perhaps the closest approximation to a comprehensive philosophy of police. Even this work falls short of addressing the full range of conceptual (analytic) and normative (justificatory) questions with which a genuine philosophy of police would deal. Kleinig includes important references to social, political and legal philosophy in the course of his search for the 'moral foundations of policing'. An exhaustive philosophy of police would need to draw extensively from these spheres of philosophical inquiry.

Golding's (1975), 'philosophy of law' sets out a framework that might be readily appropriated in order to define the topics, issues and problems with which a philosophy of police might deal. These would include investigations into the 'essence' of police, analysis of the 'limits' of police and policing, as well as a clarification of key concepts such as 'authority', 'human rights', 'coercion' 'legitimacy' and 'community'. Golding's framework can be supplemented by drawing from a range of philosophical discussions that have yielded plausible solutions to organizational problems. Hodgkinson (1983) adumbrates a philosophy of leadership whilst Thomas (1989) provides a philosophy of administration—reminding public servants (including police) of the principles and doctrines upon which public service (in the United Kingdom) is based. So, notwithstanding the absence of a 'full' philosophy of police plainly it is possible to re-invigorate practical policing and police leadership with studies of police that are philosophical in nature.

There is also a specific branch of philosophical thinking that has much to offer the practices of police leadership and management. A philosophy of persons—stemming from Nietzsche's emphasis on creativity and artifice, Kierkegaard's exploration of 'existence' and Heidegger's notion of 'being'—has rekindled faith in the creative nature of human powers and in the exercise of choice. These conceptions of the person underpin the emergence of the post-positivist inquiry frameworks as well as the related emphases upon the social construction of persons. A philosophy of persons (Shaffer, 1978) explores what humans may become—and the types of social arrangement and social ethos that might encourage an increased realisation of human potential. Presumably part of the current fashion for 'transformational leadership' (Van Maurik, 2001) reflects the need for 'lived experience' to have passion, meaning and purpose.

THE INADEQUACIES OF POLICE EDUCATION: A VIEW FROM THE 'INSIDE'

It is far from certain that the police professional development curriculum has been touched, in any significant way, either by some of these *recent* developments in philosophy or by the developments in philosophical thinking about police. There are probably two reasons for this. The first centres on the fact that philosophical reflection and analysis is difficult. In the 'your value for my money' situation, that Bauman identifies, the consumer of police development programmes wants a set of pleasing experiences and useful management 'tools'. Philosophy rarely promises anything so straightforward. The second reason lies in the simple fact that an actual 'philosophy of police' is still in the process of being constructed. In consequence, if philosophical questions and issues are included on the curriculum they are more likely to be associated with an existing discipline (such as criminology and sociology) rather than the police *per se* or the practices of policing and police leadership.

Does this mean it is fair to claim that the police leadership development curriculum fails to provide police generally—and police leaders and managers specifically—with an adequate basis for the practice of policing? The study of the 'character of police leadership' provides direct support for this idea. Of 18 superintendents and chief superintendents who were interviewed in 2001 not one was familiar with the nature of a 'philosophy of police'. Rather respondents tended to confuse a philosophy of police with some orthodoxies of police doctrine—such as 'We police by consent' or 'We provide a service to the customer'. Two made the following observations:

> I don't think we, as an organization, know what a philosophy of police actually is. (Superintendent, Strategic Command Course)

> Sometimes people come out with their 'philosophy of police'—but it is pretentious—they haven't really got a true philosophy—they haven't even studied philosophy enough to have a real philosophy of police. I certainly haven't—though I realise there is a need to do so. (Superintendent, Strategic Command Course)

Other features of the police leadership development curriculum that point to the relative 'silence' in relation to the philosophical foundations of police include:

- *A failure to appreciate and deploy the concept of 'authority'* It is difficult, for example, to find any contemporary exploration of police and police leadership that understands 'command' (the issuing of directives and orders, the making of pronouncements and the granting of permissions) as an expression of authority. In consequence there remains a complete failure in police thinking to appreciate the overlapping yet distinct characters of 'command', 'leadership', 'power' and 'influence'. Moreover, following Peters (1985), to be in authority is to be an author—of states of affairs and states of being. Authority (and its authorial character) rests upon personal credentials. Taken seriously, persons in authority will come to ask: 'Just what personal credentials do I have to legitimate my "authority"?'

- *An antipathy towards 'government' and the wider 'administration'* The peculiar and 'sacred' doctrine of constabulary independence (Savage, Charman and Cope, 2000) seems to help sustain a generalised negative attitude towards the institutions and processes of government. So, for example, Accelerated Promotion Course students admitted that they viewed central government either as an impediment, or a largely intrusive constraint, or, an inconvenience 'around which they had to navigate'. Only a handful of these students had any appreciation of the way political ideas and ideals underpinned the concrete manifestation 'the police'.

- *An impoverished and inadequate conceptualisation of the nature of police leadership* 'Leadership' is coming, increasingly, to be viewed as if is an entirely context-free practical skill or 'competence'. No systematic analysis is offered concerning the ways in which police leadership is a) like all other manifestations of leadership b) like some other types of leadership (e.g. public service) and c) like no other form of leadership (in virtue of its specific tasks and functions). Paramount amongst the latter is the 'leadership of constraint' (Richards, 1999 personal communication). The assumption that police leadership is 'just like any other kind of leadership' ignores critical and distinctive features in the 'life-world' of police officers. As Ker Muir puts it:

> The policeman's [sic] authority consists of a legal licence to coerce others to refrain from using legitimate coercion. Society licenses him to kill, hurt, confine and otherwise victimise non-policemen who would illegally kill, hurt, confine or victimise others whom the policeman is charged to protect. But the reality and the subtle irony, of being a policeman is that while he may appear to be the supreme practitioner of coercion, in fact he is first and foremost its most frequent victim. The policeman is society's 'fall guy', the object of coercion more frequently than its practitioner ... Contrary to the more unflattering stereotypes of the policeman, it is the citizen who virtually always initiates the coercive encounter. (1977: 44, 45)

Ker Muir moves on to show how the police officers' authority coupled with their sense of civility and reasonableness impose 'terrible limits' on their freedom to react successfully to the coercive practices of others. His subsequent analysis of the development of police officers serves to underline how police leadership and management *has* to be deeply sensitive to the unusual dynamics that powerfully influence the evolution of their character and personality. Ker Muir's analysis also helps to provide an appreciation of some of the distinct features of police culture: 'If you get grief from the public then you don't want to get grief from the "guvnor" '. As a result, techniques of 'feedback', 'constructive criticism' 'assertiveness' and other 'management skills' are perceived as rather 'inappropriate' in the police cultural milieu.

- *A failure to distinguish 'ethics' from moralising* Whilst Richards (1983) and Kleinig (1990) argue that some grasp of the rudiments of moral philosophy—and an analysis of the difficult issues surrounding e.g. 'loyalty' and 'impartiality'—should feature as components of a police ethics education, the actual 'ethics' that police leaders and managers encounter on programmes of study, at Bramshill, consists of a disguised form of moralising. Whilst police officers are exhorted to be 'more ethical' and appeals are made to the immense importance of 'integrity' there is virtually no critical examination of concepts such as 'rights', 'duties', 'role responsibilities' or the striking challenges involved in living a life ethically.

It would be possible to cite a number of other examples indicating the inadequacies of the police leadership development curriculum if it is taken as a design to enhance connoisseurship and artistry in relation to role-filling. Amongst these would have to be included the superficial discussions that are proffered in the name of 'managing and valuing diversity'. Enough, though, has been said. If a plausible case has been made suggesting that the sophistication of the curriculum is inadequate it is now necessary to indicate how improvements might be made through 'putting philosophy to work'.

PHILOSOPHY FOR POLICE LEADERSHIP IN PRACTICE

The contribution to police leadership practice that an emerging philosophy of police can make may be organized into three partially differentiated areas. First, it can elaborate and clarify the ends to which police should aim, guide and shape styles of interpersonal encounter and suggest forms of organization and organizational ethos likely to generate sympathetic professionals. It can, therefore, affect leadership conduct in a relatively direct way. Second, it can provide a deep appreciation of the logic upon which the institution 'police' rests. In consequence it offers police leaders 'sapience'—and therefore a justifiable form of power/knowledge (Foucault, 1991). Third, through its understanding of central concepts in the western intellectual tradition it can illuminate the nature of the tensions and contradictions that 'structure' current practical dilemmas in policing; in consequence, it offers subtle forms of illumination. It can protect decision-makers from hoping for too much. Always, too, it offers an 'alternative'—a sense that there are never complete answers but temporary points of view. In this respect a philosophy for police acts to subvert the absolutism of the dogmatist.

MacCallum's (1989) political philosophy, *inter alia*, asks: 'At what should governments aim?' Similarly a philosophy of police must ask: 'At what should police leadership aim?'

Weber (1967) provides part of the answer in his famous discussion concerning a basic ethical question facing the leadership of organizations. Since such leaders, by virtue of their power and influence, 'hold a nerve fibre of historically important events' in their hands Weber wanted to know 'through what qualities could they hope to do justice to this power?' Weber believed three 'pre-eminent qualities' were 'decisive': passion (a devotion to a 'cause'), a feeling of responsibility, and a cool sense of proportion. Weber's notion of 'passion' resonates with Kierkegaard's (1962) idea concerning the importance of 'vocation' (a calling)—the experience of being 'gripped' by an ineluctable psychological force. Together, Weber and Kierkegaard invite police leaders to contact and display their passion—their commitment to a cause—their clarification of the worthwhile ends to which police aim.

However, in the face of the 'wide menu of police responsibilities' (ACPO, Quality of Service Committee, 1993), the restless shifts in emphasis concerning the role, function and basic conceptualisation of the police, and the postmodern cultural mood of uncertainty and relativism (Moult, 1990) it has become increasingly difficult for police leaders to provide, consistently, any such clear sense of direction. Meanwhile, the research literature on leadership and management effectiveness emphasises the importance of vision, mission and purpose. Police leaders need, if they can, to resolve the question of the police purpose. One answer to this question is capable of providing an enduring, robust and stable idea about the aims of policing. It derives from considering an essential feature of what we, unavoidably, are as humans. The sheer variety of ways that we can lead an individual life, the rich diversity in the cultural forms of social groupings, and the plasticity of the human condition indicate how we are, in 'nature', creatures of social learning. Kleinig observes that:

> What is most characteristically and distinctively human is the result of a long process of learning. And this process of learning is essentially social. It requires the ongoing engagement of human beings, and if it is to be successful, this social environment must be characterisable in certain relatively determinate ways. (Kleinig 1996: 14)

The work of child and clinical psychologists, as well as personality theorists has identified the kind of environing social and experiential conditions that will facilitate learning, adjustment and the full development of the human personality. The fully developed personality is, according to Kleinig, one distinguished by 'care, stability, moral sensitivity, diversity of experience, interaction with others, attention to individuality' and so on. For Heron (1977a) it features the ability to meet three *sui generis* personal needs: the need to be loved (and to love), the need to be understood (and to understand), and the need for choice (and the need to be chosen). Since the police institution is concerned with establishing security, with promoting order and stability, and with enabling the emergence of an environment in which sufficient safety exists for individuals to pursue their own and shared designs for living then the basic function of the police is to help support the conditions, noted by Kleinig and Heron, in which 'good' learning and development can take place.

Security and sympathy

Police leadership has another more 'inner directed' aspect. It centres on the question: 'What sort of person should the individual police officer be like?' To this question, the pragmatic postmodernist, Rorty (1993), has a surprisingly simple answer: 'nice people'. Rorty's idea of 'nice people' refers to individuals who, brought up in the shadow of the Holocaust, believe that 'prejudice against racial or religious groups is a terrible thing' and who are 'eager to define their identity in non-exclusionary terms'. He identifies the importance of two socio-psychological conditions that are necessary to produce such 'nice people': 'security' and 'sympathy'. He defines these as follows:

> By 'security' I mean conditions of life sufficiently risk-free as to make one's difference to others inessential to one's self-respect and sense of worth. These conditions have been enjoyed by Americans and by Europeans—the people, who dreamed up the human rights culture—much more than anyone else. By 'sympathy' I mean the sort of reaction that the Athenians had more of after seeing Aeschylus' *The Persians* than before ... the sort that we have more of after watching television programmes about the genocide in Bosnia. (Rorty, in Ishay, 1997: 266)

Rorty explains the intimate relationship between security and sympathy by noting that:

> Security and sympathy go together, for the same reasons that peace and economic security go together: the tougher things are, the more you have to be afraid of, the more dangerous your situation, the less you can afford the time or effort to think about what things might be like for people with whom you do not immediately identify. Sentimental education only works on people who can relax enough to listen. (Rorty in Ishay, 1997: 266)

If Rorty is right then his is a critical observation for police leaders. Thus, in order to generate 'nice people' they need to be able to provide conditions of physical and psychological security in which a 'sentimental education' can take place. Unfortunately, it appears that something is at work in the police organizational milieu that compromises the feeling of 'security'. It takes the form of an ever-present possibility: it is the diffuse pervasive threat of 'wrong-doing'—or, in police vernacular, 'the bollocking'. A recurring theme emerging from the research study examining the character of police leadership concerns the fact that most respondents perceived the 'modal' style of leadership as 'right of centre', inclined to be crude, threatening and mildly intimidatory. If the ethos of the police organization remains permeated by currents of fear and anxiety then police leaders have failed to provide those conditions that help to generate 'nice', empathic people.

A thorough reading of Heron (1977a, 1977b, 1988, 1989) also suggests that a huge amount of 'personal' (or self-developmental) work needs to be done before police leaders and managers are equipped to provide an environment in which the full positive blossoming of their subordinates can be effected. Heron's cataloguing of 'degenerate interventions' (i.e. dysfunctional interpersonal actions) includes those that are 'unsolicited, manipulative, compulsive and unskilled'. His more detailed analysis of specific types of degenerate intervention describes many standard patterns of police interactions. For example, in the context of 'prescriptive degenerations' he documents the 'interfering take over'—consisting of 'giving advice' to a person 'who doesn't need it and doesn't want it, and whose self-direction needs honouring', the 'insulting take over'—'the content of which implies that the person is an idiot', and 'moralistic oppression'—which imposes on the person 'authoritarian 'shoulds' and 'oughts' and 'musts' such that the person comes to feel alienated from a sense of his or her true needs and interests'.

Clearly, a great deal needs to be done. Yet it is hardly likely to be achieved if the police leadership development curriculum simply focuses upon leadership and management techniques (through the medium of 'training') and abstract academic study. To the extent that it appears to have jettisoned the 'whole-person—applied knowledge' curriculum model—which tried to inculcate enhanced sensitivity and greater self-awareness there is little reason to be optimistic.

A philosophy of persons can provide concrete ideas concerning the ideals that might guide and illumine practice. Without them, we merely 'fumble around in the dark' (Heron, 1989). These ideals have been painstakingly articulated by Heron—who argued that in the field of interpersonal encounter 'interventions' should be designed to effect 'self-direction and co-operation', 'informed judgement and open communication' and 'emotional competence and sensitivity'. The beauty of Heron's philosophy lies in its capacity to remind us all of what we may be. The possibility of enjoying something resembling the fully-functioning person (Rogers, 1961) lies within everyone's grasp.

POLICE LEADERS AND THE INSTITUTION 'POLICE': BIG QUESTIONS IN FOUR BRANCHES OF PHILOSOPHICAL THINKING

Police leaders occupy roles within a complex organizational architecture. This architecture reflects the fundamental design that is the police institution. The police institution as a 'design' or artifice can be understood as an answer to a series of questions or a solution to a perceived set of problems. In its 'modern' form (i.e. from 1829 onwards) it represents a complex logic derived from an amalgam of fact, concept and value. To the extent that the police are a design to help a legal system 'work' they are constituted as a jural agency. Thus, certain of the philosophical foundations for 'police' are likely to be discovered in the philosophy of law. To the extent that police can be viewed as a design aiming to guarantee the possibility of certain types of social relations and forms of social experience—such as the expression of 'freedom'—then other philosophical foundations of the police institution might be found in social philosophy. Freedom of expression is not, of course, unfettered. It is often limited by coercive power. Whilst social philosophy explores the grounds upon which coercion might be defended, this important topic is taken up in particular ways within the field of political philosophy. At the heart of political philosophy lie questions concerning the nature of government, types of political system and expressions of power. Typically, governments demand conformity to their regulations and directives—and police supply some of the coercive force necessary to secure that conformity. Political philosophy, therefore, constitutes, the third major field of philosophical inquiry that will have much to say to police leaders.

When the subject 'government' is explored it is impossible to overlook phenomena of authority and authorisation. Who, though, are the authorities? How fit are they to issue orders and commands? In short, 'Who *should* govern?'

Thus, there is an overlap between political philosophy and ethics. Perhaps, the most profound feature of the police institution lies in its potential capacity to help achieve morally worthwhile ends. Inseparable from the idea of 'police' is the belief (however imperfectly developed and however ideologically peculiar) that the police institution can make a contribution to the common good. There is good reason why police should understand themselves as a design to promote human flourishing and to curb human limitations (Warnock, 1971) Thus, in addition to legal, social and political philosophy the police institution finds itself embodying ideas taken from the long history of moral philosophy. *Prima facie*, reflections, in legal, social, political and moral philosophy promise to provide important knowledge for the practice of police leadership. What relatively tangible contribution has each of these branches of philosophy to offer? This is illustrated in the following four short sections. In each case, one example is taken from the vast and extensive literature that has grown up in relation to each of these fields of enquiry.

Philosophy of law and a perspective on 'police'

The philosophy of law provides police leaders with the opportunity to clarify their conceptions of the nature of 'police'—and raises a central question concerning the police identity. Golding's (1975) study of legal philosophy includes a device to begin this process. In the context of searching for a definition of law Golding invites his readership to ask the question: 'What does it mean to say that a legal system exists in a society S? Analogously, in searching for the definition of 'police', or the 'essence' of police, the same starting point can be employed: 'What does it mean to say that a police system exists in society X?

Golding (in the context of identifying the nature of a legal system) asks us to suppose that we are members of a party of anthropologists studying the communal life of an island people ('islanders') in a known location that remains uninvestigated. As a group of anthropologists we plan to write a book about the society—describing, for example, its economy, its religious beliefs, the structure of its family etc. We shall also include a chapter on 'the law' of this community (if there is any). Golding notes:

> In order to carry out a systematic investigation, we must have at least a rough idea of the data that would be relevant to it. That is, we must know, broadly, what to look for, although we cannot be sure that we will find it. Our first step, then, is to formulate, in this light, specific subjects for inquiry. A number immediately suggest themselves [e.g. dispute settlement] ... we would be interested in how disputes are settled. Is there an agency, a social mechanism or institution for settling disputes between individuals? And if so what kinds of dispute will it undertake to settle? (Golding 1975: 9)

Golding's 'islander' example provides him with clues for the elucidation of what it means to say that 'a legal system exists in a society'. As he uncovers the various elements that constitute a 'legal system' (e.g. an agency for changing and making the laws, an agency for determining infractions of the laws) he points out that we might also ask: 'How are the laws of the community enforced?' He adds:

The enforcement of the laws is another jural activity of interest to us. Is there an agency that has this task, or does the society rely on diffuse social pressure to secure compliance? What methods are available to this end (e.g. capital punishment, ostracism, imprisonment, fines, expressions of disapproval)? ... If there is an agency for enforcing the laws, how is it constituted and how is its membership recruited? Is there anything like a police force, permanently on guard to prevent violation of the laws? (Golding 1975: 10)

Golding thus identifies 'an agency for enforcing the laws' within the wider framework of a legal system. This illustrates how the concept of 'police' may come to be entirely subsumed within a wider philosophy of law. It tends to place, at the centre of policing, the 'law enforcement' function. The essence of police is taken to lie in 'law enforcement'.

But rather than arrive at the institution 'police' through an examination of 'legal systems', what might happen if we begin with an analysis of police systems in their own right? Imagine that we were to set off as anthropologists intent on writing a chapter on the 'police system' within our island people. What, broadly, would we be looking for? From this starting point, we would be looking to see what social arrangement, device or institution existed that was concerned with achieving 'compliance'. The interest in compliance would not be entirely restricted to compliance with 'law'. It would also be with a) the issuances of 'authority' (i.e. the commands, directives, rules and regulations issued by 'people in authority') and b) with the network of rules concerned with 'order' (i.e. tranquillity, decorum) that criss-cross and constitute the fabric of society-as-a-whole. In other words, far from subsuming the agency 'police' within a wider justice system, the police institution is essentially concerned with sustaining order and discipline. Instead of seeing police as officers of the law Golding's device suggests that police are officers of order. Moreover, to the extent that a police system is concerned with adherence to 'rules' and with calibrated responses to rule-breakers then it is a system concerned with managing deviance. The police system, on this analysis, is a rule-compliance system constituted in order to achieve, sustain and enhance security, predictability, tranquillity, order, and social peace, necessarily through the actual or potential exercise of coercive force.

This conceptualisation of the police system provides it with a hard edge; in the words of a moral and political philosopher (Richards, 1999: personal communication) 'policing is inescapably about hitting people over the head'. This idea may have an advantage over other attempts to identify the functional heart or essence of policing—such as Kleinig's (1996) portrayal of police as 'social peacekeepers' or Laugharne and Newman's (1985) emphasis on police as 'upholders of the Rule of Law'—because it is neither overly benign nor does it base itself on an extended and sophisticated legal conceptualisation. Instead, it has a Foucauldian tone: police systems conjoin reason and violence. In short, police systems exist because we still need to be made frightened into adopting forms of conduct that will provide those preconditions (e.g. order) which enable us to develop types of society in which specialisations may be co-ordinated sufficiently well enough for us to flourish.

Social philosophy and the importance of 'freedom'

The western liberal democratic tradition understands that a primary precondition facilitative of human flourishing is 'liberty'. Feinberg (1973) begins his exploration of social philosophy with an analysis of what someone is doing when they assert that they are 'free' before examining grounds for coercion. He sets out the 'presumptive case for liberty' observing that whatever else we believe about freedom, most of us believe it is something to be praised, or 'so luminously a thing of value that it is beyond praise'. He asserts that:

> Whatever the harmful consequences of freedom in a given case, there is always a direct effect on the person of its possessor which must be counted a positive good. Coercion may prevent great evils, and be wholly justified on that account, but it always has its price. Coercion may be on balance a great gain, but its direct effects always, or nearly always, constitute a definite loss. (Feinberg 1973: 21)

In the light of this Feinberg recognises that there is always a 'presumption in favour of freedom' even if, on occasion, it is over-ridden by more powerful reasons on the other side. Why, though, a 'presumption in favour of freedom'? Feinberg draws from a number of writers (e.g. Mill, 1974) who have concluded in favour of the primacy of liberty noting that:

> The presumption in favour of freedom is usually said to rest on freedom's essential role in the development of traits of intellect and character which constitute the good of individuals and are centrally important means to the progress of societies.
> (Feinberg 1973: 21)

He goes on to add that the highest good for persons is neither enjoyment nor passive contentment but rather, a dynamic process of growth and self-realisation. Feinberg proceeds to elaborate this notion of the 'good'; it is reflected in the greatest possible amount of individual self-realisation and through this, as a result of the inclinations of different human natures, the resultant diversity and fullness of life. In addition:

> Self-realisation consists in the actualisation of certain uniquely human potentialities, the bringing to full development of certain powers and abilities. This is turn requires constant practice in making difficult choices among alternative hypotheses, policies and actions—and the more difficult the better. (Feinberg 1973: 21)

Feinberg's reminder as to *why* freedom is so prized is fundamentally important to the practice of police leadership. It is rare to hear senior police officers support, defend and champion freedom—yet if they were to do so it is clearly one way to inspire subordinate officers. Through articulating the defence of freedom police leaders can transform the perception of police work; in principle they can transmute the process of 'breaking stones' into 'building cathedrals'.

Political philosophy and the exercise of coercive power

Feinberg juxtaposes the presumption in favour of liberty with an analysis of the grounds for coercion. Governments, especially through their invocation of the need to prevent harm, find reasons to justify coercion. MacCallum's (1989) political philosophy includes a fairly detailed analysis of the nature of government—an analysis which underlines the intimate association between police and government. Thus he writes:

> Governments are organizations of officials charged with responsibility for directing and administering the political affairs of political communities ... Governments fulfil their responsibility typically, through not exclusively, through the use of co-ercion backed rules, regulations, orders and commands. (MacCallum 1989: 66)

Police, in part, have to make sure that 'orders' are 'executed'. Although Locke's (1991) celebrated thesis concerning the need for a separation of powers in relation to three aspects of civil government (i.e. the legislature, the judiciary and the executive) is approvingly cited by police leaders and managers in order to preserve their 'immunity' from 'governmental interference' it seems absurd to imagine that police are somehow hermetically sealed from the wider (and serious) functions of government. Further, as MacCallum's discussion of 'government' shows, its characteristic mode of operation is to employ, whenever necessary, co-ercion (and the ever-present threat of coercion). This also shows the absurdity of overlooking or denying the fact that coercive power is a necessary and constituent thread woven into the very fabric of policing.

It seems sensible to reiterate Ker Muir's (1977) analysis of the psychological development of police officers, an analysis that pays close attention to the ways in which this aspect of police work creates remarkable problems for individual adjustment. He contends that unless police officers sustain a 'tragic' as opposed to a 'cynic' understanding of the human condition and simultaneously find ways of constructing a moral system integrating the exercise of power as 'means' in the pursuit of morally worthwhile ends then police officers will remain liable to moral collapse. Unsurprisingly, Ker Muir recognises the significance of the 'chief's choices' and the potential impact of police education as way of helping police officers 'keep faith' with the positive ideals of policing and with standards of integrity.

Sadly, there are no guarantees that the official provisions for police leadership development are able to provide analyses of the complex relationships between police, government, power and authority. Yet, as MacCallum pushes his analysis of government and the problems of ruler-ship further he arrives at the question of 'who should rule?' He writes:

> Concentrating now especially on the reliability and fruitfulness of the orders and commands, supposing that they will come from some persons or other ... we would want them to be well-informed, skilful in the use of the information they posses and well-intentioned. We might, depending on the situation, desire them to possess other characteristics as well. (MacCallum 1989: 76)

MacCallum immediately proceeds to mention Plato's answer—an answer particularly developed in *The Republic*—to the question 'Who should rule?' Plato thought that the rulers should be the most intelligent, knowledgeable and best-intentioned people who could be found and developed. (He also wanted them to be physically healthy, vigorous, strong, steadfast, and well balanced.) In this way, MacCallum reminds us that there has, since classical antiquity, been a very long interest in the types of person who are selected to be rulers or, in more contemporary terms 'leaders of organizations'. He thus touches on the way ethics and political philosophy come to overlap: answers to the question, 'Who is to lead?' include reference to the type of character who *authors* or originates the commands and orders.

Ethics and police leadership

Frankena (1973) begins his short introduction to 'ethics' by choosing to examine the questions raised by Socrates in Plato's dialogue, *The Crito*. He uses the dialogue between Socrates and Crito to serve as an example of moral reasoning. Significantly, however, before examining the specific content of Socrates' argument, Frankena includes a reference to the correct method (after Socrates) for carrying our any such inquiry. Thus:

> Socrates first lays down some points about the approach to be taken. To begin with we must not let our decision be determined by our emotions but must examine the question and follow the best reasoning. We must try to get our facts straight and keep our minds clear. Secondly, we cannot answer such questions by appealing to what people generally think. They may be wrong. We must try to find an answer we ourselves can regard as correct. We must think for ourselves. Finally, we ought never to do what is morally wrong. The only question we need to answer is whether what is proposed is right or wrong, not what will happen to us, what people will think of us, or how we feel about what has happened. (Frankena 1973: 2)

In many ways this short piece of text begins to raise profound doubts about the adequacies of police leadership practice. Thus, for example, it is difficult to find any consistent indications that such practice is based on fact and evidence. Moreover, in the field of policing it seems that the 'best reasoning' is often subordinated to the emotions generated by *esprit de corps* or by a person's 'reputation' or the cultural climate that cautions against 'making waves'. In addition, whilst it is clear that most police leaders have opinions on many matters it is not so clear that these opinions reflect genuine independence of mind. In short, it is not certain that they genuinely 'think for themselves'. Finally, and more precisely, the relatively recent concerns about police ethical standards (Woodcock, 1992), the flurry of activity surrounding questions of police integrity (HMIC, 1999), the debate over the degree of police corruption (Newburn, 1999) and the proliferation of textual material dealing with 'police ethics' (e.g. Villiers, 1997, Crawshaw, Devlin and Williamson, 1998, Neyroud, Beckley, Collier and Clayton, 2001) lend support to the idea that 'police took a holiday from ethics' (Richards, 1999: personal communication).

Any review of philosophical activity constituting the field of ethics will quickly reveal a rich vein of material with a direct bearing on police leadership. At the outset, and fundamentally, for example, it is plausible to argue that the police institution has been created as part of the answer to the question: 'How should one live?'

However, the discussion here will confine itself to making just two observations. First, Frankena, after reviewing a number of major ethical theories, suggests that a satisfactory answer can be given to the question, 'How should one act?' (in any given situation): thus, he finds that we should, in the first instance, adopt the principle of beneficence and the principle of justice. He thinks that we have a prima facie obligation to maximise the balance of good over evil only if we have a prior prima facie obligation to do good and prevent harm. It is this prior principle that he calls the principle of beneficence. Frankena believes that many rules of right, wrong or obligation can be derived from the principle of beneficence—including for example, the injunction 'we ought to promote knowledge'. He points out, however, that not all of our prima facie obligations can be derived from the principle of beneficence because it does not tell us how to distribute the goods (and evils). It is here that we need a principle of distributive justice. This does not mean that we should treat people identically but, rather, that we should treat them equally—in the sense that we should tailor their treatment in ways that are designed to provide them with an equal chance of living and experiencing a good life.

This analysis allows Frankena to find a supremely logical answer to the questions 'What sort of person ought one to be?' or 'What sort of moral values ought we to possess and cultivate? Thus, if it is the case that our actions should be guided by the principles of beneficence and justice then we should develop aspects of character (those moral virtues) which will most incline us towards expressions of beneficence and justice. In other words we should be 'benevolent' and 'just'. Frankena claims that these two virtues are cardinal. It follows that character traits like honesty should be acquired and fostered.

He then fills out his sketch of the virtuous (or ideal) person by identifying a set of 'second order' virtues. These include: 'conscientiousness'; 'moral courage' (or 'courage when moral issues are at stake'); 'integrity'; 'good-will' (understanding 'good-will' in the Kantian sense of respect for the moral law); 'a disposition to think clearly'; 'moral autonomy'—the ability to make moral decisions and to revise one's principles if necessary; and, 'the ability to realise, vividly, in imagination and 'feeling', the inner lives of others'. Frankena concludes his analysis of moral virtues by focusing on the importance of this latter ability:

> If our morality is to be more than a conformity to internalised rules and principles, if it is to include and rest on an understanding of the point of these rules and principles … then we must somehow attain and develop an ability to be aware of others as persons, as important to themselves as we are to ourselves, and to have a lively and sympathetic representation in imagination of their interests and of the effects of our actions on their lives. (Frankena 1973: 69)

Thus, Rorty (1993) reprises Frankena as he underlines the importance of empathy—of a 'sentimental education'.

Again, what this example of philosophical thinking demonstrates is that philosophers have produced answers to difficult and fundamental questions. These answers emerge after long and thorough processes of analysis and reasoning. Thus, they avoid the character of cliché-ridden dogmatic assertion that sometimes befalls police leadership discourse.

An attempt has now been made to show how the quality of police leadership might be enhanced if it were to draw from discussion and analysis in each of four branches of philosophy. Questions in legal philosophy can serve to clarify the very identity of the police itself. Familiarity with social philosophy sharpens an appreciation of liberty and fosters commitments to human rights. To engage with political philosophy is, eventually, to come to ask the question; 'How well is a society likely to do without the accoutrement police?' And, as Ker Muir (1977) maintains, police have to deal with the 'big insistent problems of existence'. They cannot take a holiday from ethics.

Heritage concepts: more on 'ethics' and police leadership

Critchley and Kearney (2001) describe the method Derrida uses to analyse contested and emotive issues as a prelude to influencing political action. They note that much of Derrida's recent work might be described as the historical analysis of concepts—or 'a form of conceptual genealogy' where, characteristically, a concept is selected from '*l'heritage*' (or, 'the dominant western tradition') and then proceeds 'via an analysis that is at once historical, contextual and thematic' to reveal 'the logic of that concept'. The logic that Derrida so identifies takes the form of a contradiction or a double imperative. In the example of the 'heritage concept', cosmopolitanism, he, Derrida, finds that:

> on the one hand, there is an unconditional hospitality which should offer the right of refuge to all immigrants and newcomers. But on the other hand, hospitality has to be conditional: there has to be some limitation on rights of residence.
>
> (Critchley and Kearney 2001b: x)

All the political difficulty of immigration 'consists in negotiating between these two imperatives'. Significantly, the two 'injunctions' of the unconditional and the conditional are in a relation of contradiction 'where they remain both irreducible to one another and indissociable'. Responsible political action and decision-making entails negotiating between the two irreconcilable yet indissociable demands. This is an exciting development. Derrida demonstrates how leadership remains wedded to the permanent instabilities generated by the content of heritage concepts.

It is not difficult to unearth a range of such 'heritage concepts' involved in the practice of policing and the discourses of police leadership. Amongst those that present themselves are 'care', 'Utopia' and 'the other'. Each of these heritage concepts functions in complex ways in relation to 'performance', 'security', 'progress and reform' and 'diversity'. In this final section of the paper a concise Derridaean analysis will be presented to illustrate a third way in which philosophical thinking can be brought to bear on the police situation.

The consuming demands caused by commitments to provide 'best value', the procedures of the new managerialism, and, the aspiration to install a 'performance culture' generates a profound ethical dilemma for police leaders. The ethical dilemma becomes apparent through analysing the heritage concept of 'security'. Before focusing directly upon this concept some preliminary discussion is necessary concerning the outcomes connected with the new managerialism. All these developments promise *more* police service. This means more surveillance, more crime prevention, more targeting of prolific offenders, more crime reduction 'partnerships', more specialisation and so on. The ideal is to make the very best use of police resources. This also means improved time management, improved 'human resource management systems' as well as reductions in the numbers of police involved in ancillary rather than core activities. It means less absenteeism. A form of super-efficient performance is the goal.

More police service is promised because police are supposed to guarantee public safety; they are supposed to protect all the citizens of the nation state; they ought to help everyone enjoy the right to the security of their person. Thus, Article 3 of the UN declaration of human rights states that: 'Everyone has the right to life, liberty and security of person' whilst Article 5 of the European Convention On Human Rights states that 'everyone has the right to liberty and security of person'. Moreover, the police explicitly acknowledge that they are morally obligated to protect the public. Laugharne and Newman's (1985) clarification of the principles of policing underlined the fact that police had a duty a) to respect individuals' rights and b) to protect and assist citizens. Subsequent statements of ethical principles and 'shared values' (Whitehouse, 1995) included commitments to 'upholding fundamental human rights'.

The commitment to supply protection is linked to the very *raison d'être* of the police organization. Police officers 'bind themselves over' to something other than their own selves—something to which they have sworn an oath. Giving oneself up to policing and its ideals is akin to the way religion 'kicks in' (Caputo, 2001). As Caputo puts it:

> Something grander and larger than us comes along and bowls us over and dispossesses us. Something overpowers our powers, potencies and possibilities ..... Something makes a demand upon us and shakes us loose from the circle of self-love, drawing us out of ourselves and into the service of others. (Caputo 2001: 31)

At some point however, the unconditional promise (or commitment) to supply protection and guarantee security begins to run up against a cluster of opposing injunctions.

The quest for improved efficiency threatens to turn police officers into a form of exploited stock. Heidegger in the 1950s and 1960s perceived the 'limitless domination' of modern technology. In a Western world wedded beguiled by the promises of high modernism, Heidegger found that a measuring, calibrating, calculating logic had come to be applied to everything. Nature, including its human subjects, was to be commanded, manipulated and controlled. There was emerging a complete 'technisising' of the world and of people. Technology operated to make 'things' (people, materials etc.) completely available for use; in so doing, everything was becoming turned into forms of 'stock' to be acted upon, or, as Heidegger put it 'set upon'. In the course of his criticism of this tendency, he revisited the original meaning of the term *'techne'*—the ancestor of the word technology. *Techne* not only meant the activities and the skills of the craft worker but also the 'arts of the mind' and the creative arts. *Techne* therefore included the idea of *'poiesis'*—a 'bringing forth' or a 'bringing into presence'. Heidegger concluded that the modern technological tendency had denied *poiesis*. For Heidegger this was disastrous: it led humanity further and further away from its being.

A first resistance to the emergence of a 'set upon stock' stems from the oppositional energies evoked by another 'human right'. Some philosophers, including Feinberg (1973), suggest that the right not to be exploited (and not to be made into a docile object to be used for the purposes of others) is one of the few rights that has a claim to being absolute and exceptionless. In other words, there are *no* circumstances that justify turning human beings into types of domesticated animal. Thus, the techniques of the new managerialism and the desire for 'more' police service to achieve utopian security runs up against the counter injunction asserting the right not to be exploited.

In addition to this first vector of resistance a second stems from the suffocating 'life denying' logic of 'protection'. Ultimately, it seeks to exclude any form of unpredictability, any form of deviation. It leads, as Foucault (1991) demonstrates, to the 'carceral' society—a society dominated by the science of discipline. Against this state of ubiquitous measuring, monitoring, grading and judging is pitted a very long history that prizes 'freedom'. It may be simply the freedom from present frustration or it may be something more: thus, as Feinberg (1973: 6) puts it: 'The love of freedom can be a love of breathing space, of room to manoeuvre, of a chance to change one's mind.'

It is also possible to find another vector in opposition to the purifying tendencies of complete protection. Without risk and experimentation, without 'difference' there remains little more to life than safe repetitive movements. Human society becomes roboticised. There is no permission left for the 'leap into the unknown' that is one of the hallmarks of the 'open society'.

Police leadership entails a constant adjustment to this ethical dilemma. It is not a dilemma with any simple, single resolution. Heidegger believed that it was possible to rescue *'poiesis'*. Its emergence, he thought, could be 'enticed'—through, for example, reflective thinking. Ironically, it was, in part, to encourage this form of thinking that an institution like Bramshill was established. Is it possible that the new designs for police leadership development will help to make this happen?

CONCLUSION

A clearly perceptible and readily apparent phenomenon displayed by most of the police leaders and managers who have contributed to the study of the character of police leadership has been their readiness to express themselves in crude, blunt and abrasive terms. Coupled with this has been their admission that, in broad, terms, they have not developed a sophisticated understanding of the 'difficult' issues attending the leadership and management of police in a liberal democracy. In addition they have acknowledged the relatively superficial nature of their preparation for police leadership. This paper has advocated a remedy; it can be found in the construction of and engagement with a philosophy of police.

REFERENCES for *Chapter 2*

ACPO, Quality of Service Committee (1993), *Getting Things Right*. Available from: The National Police Library, NPT, Bramshill House, Bramshill, Hook, Hampshire, RG27 0JW, UK.

Adlam, R (1999), 'We Need a Night Shift: Notes on the Failure of an Educational Design for Police Leaders and Managers', *Educational Action Research*, Vol. 7, No. 1, 1999, pp. 34-51.

Alderson, J (1979), *Policing Freedom: A Commentary on the Dilemmas of Policing Liberal Democracies*, Plymouth: McDonald and Evans.

Alderson, J (1998), *Principled Policing: Protecting the Public with Integrity*, Winchester: Waterside Press.

Arthur, J (1997), 'Sticks and Stones' in, LaFollette, H (ed.) (1998), *Ethics in Practice: An Anthology*, Oxford: Blackwell Publishers.

Bauman, Z (1993), *Postmodern Ethics*, Oxford: Blackwell Publishers.

Best, S and Kellner, D (1991), *Postmodern Theory: Critical Interrogations*, New York: Guilford Press.

Bunyard, R (1993), 'The Future of Policing', The Frank Newsam Memorial Lecture, 1993. Available from: The National Police Library, NPT, Bramshill House, Bramshill, Hook, Hampshire, RG27 0JW, UK.

Caputo, J (2001), *On Religion*, London: Routledge.

Connor, S (1989), *Postmodernist Culture*, Oxford: Blackwell Publishers.

Crawshaw, R, Devlin, B and Williamson, T (1998), *Human Rights and Policing: Standards for Good Behaviour and a Strategy for Change*, The Hague: Kluwer Law International.

Critchley, S and Kearney, R (eds.) (2001a), *General Introductory Remarks to the Series 'Thinking in Action'*, London: Routledge.

Critchley, S and Kearney, R (2001b), 'Introduction' to Derrida, J (2001), *On Cosmopolitanism and Forgiveness*, London: Routledge.

Derrida, J (2001), *On Cosmopolitanism and Forgiveness* (trans. Dooley, M and Hughes, M), London: Routledge.

Dreyfus, H (2001), *On the Internet*, London: Routledge.

Dummett, M (2001), *On Immigration and Refugees*, London: Routledge.

Feinberg, J (1973), *Social Philosophy*, Englewood Cliffs, NJ: Prentice Hall Inc.

Frankena, W (1973), *Ethics*, Englewood Cliffs, NJ: Prentice Hall Inc.

Foucault, M (1991), *Discipline and Punish: The Birth of the Prison*, Harmondsworth: Penguin Books.

Golding, M (1975), *The Philosophy of Law*, Englewood Cliffs, New Jersey: Prentice Hall Inc.

Harvey, D (1990), *The Condition of Postmodernity*, Oxford: Blackwell Publishers.

Heidegger, M (1953), 'The Question Concerning Technology' in Krell, D (ed.) (1993), *Martin Heidegger: Basic Writings*, London: Routledge.

Her Majesty's Inspectorate of Constabulary (HMIC) (1999), *Police Integrity*. Available from: The National Police Library, NPT, Bramshill House, Bramshill, Hook, Hampshire, RG27 0JW, UK.

Heron, J (1977a), *Catharsis in Human Development*, School of Educational Studies, University of Surrey, Guildford, Surrey, UK.

Heron, J (1977b), *Behaviour Analysis in Education and Training*, School of Educational Studies, University of Surrey, Guildford, Surrey, UK.

Heron, J (1988), *Cosmic Psychology*, London: Endymion Press.

Heron, J (1989), *Six Category Intervention Analysis*, School of Educational Studies, University of Surrey, Guildford, Surrey, UK.

Hodgkinson, C (1983), *The Philosophy of Leadership*, Oxford: Basil Blackwell.

Ker Muir, W (1977), *Police: Street Corner Politicians*, Chicago: University of Chicago Press.

Kierkegaard, S (1962), *The Present Age* (Trans. Alexander Dru), New York: Harper and Row.

Kleinig, J (1990), 'Teaching and Learning Police Ethics: Competing and Complementary Approaches', *Journal of Criminal Justice*, Vol. 18, pp. 1-18.

Kleinig, J (1996), *The Ethics of Policing*, Cambridge: Cambridge University Press.

Klockars, C (ed.) (1985), *The Idea of Police*, Beverly Hills, California: Sage Publications.

LaFollette, H (ed.) (1998), *Ethics in Practice: An Anthology*, Oxford: Blackwell Publishers.

Laugharne, A and Newman, K (1985), *The Principles of Policing and the Guidance of Professional Behaviour*, Metropolitan Police Public Information Department, New Scotland Yard, London, UK.

Locke, J (1991), *Two Treatises on Government*, Cambridge: Cambridge University Press.

Lustgarten, L (1986), *The Governance of Police*, London: Sweet and Maxwell.

MacCallum, G (1989), *Political Philosophy*, Englewood Cliffs, NJ: Prentice Hall Inc.

Mill, J (1974), *On Liberty*, London: Pelican Books.

Moult, G (1990), 'Under New Management', *Management Education and Development*, Vol. 21, Part III, 1990, pp. 171-182.

Newburn, T (1999), *Understanding and Preventing Police Corruption: Lessons from the Literature*, London, Home Office Police Research Series, Paper 110.

Neyroud, P, Beckley, A, Collier, P and Clayton, J (2001), *Policing, Ethics and Human Rights*, Cullompton, Devon: Willan Publishing.

Packer, H (1968), *The Limits of the Criminal Sanction*, Stanford, California: Stanford University Press.

Plumridge, M (1985), 'Dilemmas of Police Management and Organization' in Thackrah, R (ed.) (1985), *Contemporary Policing: A Study of Society in the 1980s*, London: Sphere Reference.

Plumridge, M (1988), 'Management and Organization Development in the Police Service: The Role of Bramshill' in Southgate, P (ed.) (1988), *New Directions in Police Training*, Home Office Research and Planning Unit, London, HMSO.

Police Federation (1995), 'You and Your Views', *Police*, Vol. 27, No. 10, June 1995, pp. 16-18.

Popper, K (1943) *'The Open Society and Its Enemies* (Vols. 1 and 2), London: Routledge and Kegan Paul.

Ràwls, J (1971), *A Theory of Justice*, Cambridge, Mass.: Harvard University Press.

Rawls, J (1996), *Political Liberalism*, New York: Columbia University Press.

Richards, N (1982), 'Towards a Police Professional Ethics', unpublished paper, included as a teaching aid for students attending the Junior Command Course, The Police Staff College, Bramshill, Bramshill House, Hook, Hampshire, RG27 0JW, UK.

Richards, N (1985), 'A Plea for Applied Ethics', in, Thackrah, R (ed.) (1985), *Contemporary Policing: A Study of Society in the 1980s*, London: Sphere Reference.

Richards, N (1993), 'A Plea for Applied Ethics' (including an appendix) in Thomas, R (ed.) (1993), *Government Ethics*, Vol. 1, Cambridge: Centre for the Study of Business and Public Sector Ethics.

Richards, N. (1999), personal communication.

Rogers, C (1961), *On Becoming a Person*, London: Constable.

Rorty, R (1997), 'Human Rights, Rationality and Sentimentality' in Ishay, M (ed.) (1997), *The Human Rights Reader*, London: Routledge.

Savage, P, Charman, S and Cope, S (2000), 'The Policy Making Context: Who Shapes Policing Policy?' in Leishman, F, Loveday, B and Savage, S (eds.) (2000), *Core Issues in Policing* (second edition), Essex, England: Pearson Education.

Schein, E (1988), *Process Consultation* (Vols. 1 and 2), New York: Addison-Wesley.

Shaffer, J (1978), *Humanistic Psychology*, Englewood Cliffs, NJ: Prentice Hall Inc.

Sherman, L (1978), *The Quality of Police Education*, San Francisco: Jossey-Bass.

Sherman, L (1982), 'Ethics in Criminal Justice Education', *The Teaching of Ethics*, Vol. X, Hastings-on-Hudson, New York, Institute of Society, Ethics and the Life Sciences, The Hastings Centre.

Singer, P (ed.) (1993), *A Companion to Ethics*, Oxford: Blackwell Publishers.

Singer, P (1994), *How Are We to Live? Ethics in the Age of Self-interest*, London: Mandarin.

Skolnick, J (1966), *Justice Without Trial*, New York, Wiley.

Sterba, J (1997), 'Reconciling Anthropocentric and Nonanthropocentric Environmental Ethics' in LaFollette, H (ed.) (1998), *Ethics in Practice: An Anthology*, Oxford: Blackwell Publishers.

Thomas, R (1989), *The British Philosophy of Administration*, Cambridge: Centre for Business and Public Sector Ethics.

Vick, C (2000), 'Aspects of Police Leadership', *Police Research and Management*, Summer 2000, pp. 3-14.

Villiers, P (1997), *Better Police Ethics*, London: Kogan Page.

Villiers, P (1998), *The History of the Police Staff College: the First 50 Years*, Bramshill: Police Staff College Publications.

Warnock, G (1971), *The Object of Morality*, London: Methuen.

Whitehouse, P (1995), Untitled paper published in *Police Ethics in a Democratic Society*, Strasbourg: Council of Europe Publishing.

Woodcock, J (1992), 'Trust in the Police: The Search for Truth', International Police Exhibition and Conference, Seminar Reprints, London, Major Exhibitions and Conferences Ltd.

CHAPTER 3

Police Leadership: A Search for Principles

John Alderson

John Alderson has held some of the highest and most influential positions in British policing, including Commandant of the Police Staff College Bramshill, Assistant Commissioner New Scotland Yard, and Chief Constable of Devon and Cornwall. He was a chief police officer ahead of his time, including in pioneering community policing when he saw that it would be impossible to police the counties for which he was responsible without the active participation and support of the local community. Where he led, others followed. Practice and theory have always in John Alderson's case been intertwined, and he continues to apply himself wholeheartedly to the study of the fundamental principles upon which policing—and especially police leadership—should be based. This chapter contains the essence of his conclusions.

INTRODUCTION

Around 8.30 p.m. on 22 April 1993, a young black student, Stephen Lawrence, was stabbed to death in a vicious, gratuitous attack by a gang of white youths whilst he was waiting at a south-east London bus stop. His death was to become a *cause célèbre*, not only for the racist nature of the attack itself but also for the subsequent failings of the police action and their racist attitudes towards the investigation of the crime in which they failed to bring about a prosecution. Allegations of police racism were persistently made by Stephen Lawrence's parents, who pressed for an independent inquiry into the whole affair.

On 31 July 1997 the Home Secretary, the Rt. Hon. Jack Straw MP appointed Sir William Macpherson, a judge of the High Court, assisted by a team of advisers, to inquire into 'the matters arising from the death of Stephen Lawrence in order particularly to identify the lessons to be learned for the investigation and prosecution of racially motivated crimes'. What became known as the Stephen Lawrence Inquiry submitted its report[1] on 15 February 1999 after a nationwide inquiry into police practices and attitudes concerning racial minorities.

The inquiry report pays tribute to Neville and Doreen Lawrence, parents of the murdered youth, for their courage and persistence in the face of their tragedy and their bitter disillusionment with the police. The inquiry said that 'their dignity and courage have been an example to all throughout'. It further stated:

> The conclusions to be drawn from all the evidence in connection with the investigations of Stephen Lawrence's racist murder are clear. There is no doubt but that there were fundamental errors. The investigation was marred by a combination of professional incompetence, institutional racism and a failure of leadership by senior officers. A flawed MPS (Metropolitan Police Service) review failed to expose these inadequacies.

Any consideration of this affair and the outcome of the inquiry is likely to come to the conclusion that the principles under which the police should operate in a modern society, with its multi-racial make-up, have not been as clearly defined as is desirable. It is not possible to demand accountability for excellence in police affairs if the road to accountability is not clearly defined.

It is not only the police who have the responsibility for defining their excellence, but it is a matter also for the community itself to express the standards which it desires. What follows is a commentary on what I have called 'principled policing' as a contribution to the fulfilment of the recommendations of the report of the Stephen Lawrence inquiry.

POLICE, GOVERNMENT AND SOCIETY

Principled policing should be of such a nature that it applies to all people in all societies, since it concerns reconciliation of the maintenance of order with the protection of freedom: two principles which are in a permanent state of conflict. Too much of one means less of the other. Striking the balance between them is the true goal of the best policing. Societies in which policing is principled are less likely to suffer from policing injustices than where policing is driven by political opportunism, professional caprice, or bad law. If policing is to avoid the worse misuses and abuses of power there has to be a robust moral objectivity in the way in which it operates.

To seek rationalisation of the police mission, and to give it coherence and form in both theory and practice, has always presented a personal challenge to the present author. When leading and managing a major police organization by what is commonly called 'the seat of the pants', a good deal of luck or overweening power is required to avoid the worst results of such professional sin. Consistency demands that the command of policing and formation of policies should be based on some coherent framework. My own tried and tested formula was to link philosophy, ideas, policies and performance.

PHILOSOPHY AND POLICING: THE SEARCH FOR PRINCIPLES

The police need to know what it is that is fundamentally valued by society, what they are supposed to be protecting or defending. That set of values will be influenced by the ideology of the state and its effect on social attitudes: what is respected in one society may be otherwise regarded in another. Consider, for example, the protection of property. In a bourgeois democracy one of the main functions of the police is to protect private property, whether that property is owned by private individuals or corporations. The need to protect private property more effectively was one of the major reasons for the creation of the Metropolitan Police in 1829—as it is the main reason for the growth of the private security industry today.

However, it is a noted experience in liberal democracies that the theft of government property, whatever the law may say about it, is not so serious as is theft of private property.

In a socialist state such as the former USSR, by contrast, the (1936) Constitution stated that: 'it shall be the duty of every citizen of the USSR to safeguard and fortify public, socialist property, as the sacred and inviolable foundation of the Soviet system.' And we may assume that someone who stole state property would face severe penalties for his crimes against the people.

Here we have two very different sets of attitudes to property, with profound implications for the role of the police. We must conclude that respect for property *per se* does not give us a universal principle on which to found proper policing.

Utilitarianism, or the greatest happiness of the greatest number

On the face of it, the principle that policing should contribute to the greatest happiness of the greatest number is very attractive. However, there are difficulties with utilitarianism as a general principle, as many philosophers have indicated.

The police should be aware that in enforcing laws and restricting freedoms it is not always immediately obvious that police activity is likely to increase anybody's happiness, though their protective role may reduce fear.

The police need to have regard for the common good and, therefore, may at times be required to make the greater number unhappy in order to serve or protect a smaller number, e.g. ethnic minorities or religious or political groups. Northern Ireland is a case in point.

The founder of the school of the political philosophy of utilitarianism, Jeremy Bentham (1748-1832), paid little heed to the work of Kant (1724-1804), and in particular Kant's reputation as 'the philosophical defender *par excellence* of the rights of man and of his equality'.

Russell[2] tells us that 'Bentham's ideal, like that of Epicurus, was security and not liberty'. Liberty is diminished when people feel afraid to exercise it, but to stress security to unnecessary extremes plays into the hands of would-be high police despots. Such despots are quick to exploit fear in order to secure unlimited power.

The exploitation of fear seems to have characterised much of the rise of Hitler and his National Socialist Party in Germany in the 1930s. Nazi propaganda spoke of the Communist Party of the Weimar Republic as the 'Red Terror'. When the Reichstag building 'mysteriously' went up in flames on the night of 27 February 1933 public fear was intensified. This provided the pretext for government by decree. 'The day after the fire, on 28 February, Hitler promulgated the degree signed by the President 'for the protection of the people and the state'. The decree was described as 'a defensive measure against Communist acts of violence'.[3] It suspended the guarantees of individual liberty under the Weimar constitution, and provided very heavy penalties of life imprisonment and execution for political crimes.

This cameo of calculated political tyranny plays on fear and then takes away liberty. This is not to suggest that utilitarianism intends such behaviour but that the central place of human rights in modern politics may not be compatible with the doctrine.

The theory of protectionism

In his critique of *Plato's Politics*, Karl Popper unearths a theory which he calls 'Protectionism'.[4] According to Popper, Aristotle tells us that Lycophron (c. 400 BC) considered the law of the state as a 'covenant by which men assure one another of justice'. He relates that Lycophron looked upon the state as an instrument for the protection of its citizens against acts of injustice (and for permitting them peaceful intercourse, especially exchange), demanding that the state be a 'cooperative association for the prevention of crime'. This appears to adumbrate a theory of the state that was later to be described as a contract. The theory called 'protectionism' seems to offer much for the high police leader.

The high police official faces the question as to whether a particular police institution is well adapted to producing a well ordered society. A humanitarian (and we hope that our high police officials are humanitarians) would answer: 'What I demand from the state is protection, not only for myself but for others too. I demand protection for my own freedom and for the freedom of others.' I am happy to say that when I was a senior police official I held a view founded on principles along these lines, which would be a humanitarian philosopher's theory of protection.* In practice, however, it is not easy to convince police practitioners that they are to protect an abstraction such as 'freedom' or 'liberty'.

We should note that, when speaking of freedom, Popper wants us to know that he is ready to have his own freedom curtailed by the state, provided that the freedom which remains is protected by the state. Thus, 'the fundamental purpose of the state' should be 'the protection of that freedom which does not harm other citizens'. Furthermore, any limitations put on the freedom of citizens should be applied as equally as possible. I agree with this entirely and as a senior police officer sought to ensure that this principle was well understood by those for whom I was responsible.

It is of great help to police leaders when fashioning their policies to have a theory permitting a rational approach to political challenge.

We noted earlier that the theory of protectionism foreshadowed the subsequent development of the social contract theory, so it seems appropriate to ask in what sense, if any, might policing be described in social contractual terms?

Social contract theory and the police

An examination of the social contract theory and its pertinence for policing does not rely on the idea that in natural law there existed in the mists of time, beyond which the memory of man runneth not, an original agreement between ruler and ruled. In a politically developed and plural society, however, political ideas, nuances, and a vocabulary are necessary to progress. The concept is thus of an implied contract, rather than the existence of an original contract arising from historic binding agreement.[5]

The 'contract' does not explain either the origin of civil society or the state; rather it is a principle of political government that deals with ideals of legislation and legal justice as well as administration.

What has now to be addressed is the notion that a contractual relationship of one form or another exists in most, if not all, societies between persons *inter se* and between persons and those who exercise government over them.

In the 1994 United States Congressional Elections, the Republican Party published its manifesto called the 'Republican Contract with America', in which it promised to do many things if elected. At around the same time, the various parties involved in the Algerian political crisis were meeting in Rome in order to seek a way out of the bloody *impasse* that agonised Algerian society. The Algerian delegates of the parties involved published the results of their findings for a pathway to peace and order in the country, which they call 'a platform for a Peaceful Political Solution of Algeria's Crisis; or a National Contract.'[6]

Though some philosophers dispute the theoretical basis for the social contract, nevertheless the idea as being some form of 'legal fiction' is of political utility when discussing and carrying on government. It would seem from the United States and Algerian examples quoted above, that the vocabulary of politics finds ready use for the language and meaning of the social contract theory.

Henry Maine observed in his famous work *Ancient Law*[7] that the theory is 'an ingenious hypothesis, or convenient verbal formula'. Maine believed that 'the positive duty resulting from one man's reliance on the word of another, is amongst the slowest conquests of advancing civilisation', and, 'that the movement of progressive societies has hitherto been a movement from status to contract'. [8]

As police come to understand the doctrine of the dignity of the person, they would find it advantageous to accede to the notion that the people upon whom they exercise their power, or those for whom they are exercising it, stand in the kind of implied contractual relationship which calls for moral standards of behaviour with which to characterise the exercise of their legal power.

Protectionism is not a selfish theory, since it is not a matter of self-protection but applies to each and every person. To protect the weak from being bullied by the strong is a moral obligation with contractual implications, and we can say that principled policing has a moral obligation to the protectionist theory and is obliged by social contractual terms to carry it out.

JUSTICE

The idea of 'justice' has to be considered very carefully and seriously by officials responsible for enlightening members of their organization concerning criminal justice. So, it is prudent to enquire what connection there may be between distributive justice and criminal justice. Would a society, or part of it, being denied distributive justice present more problems for policing? There is plenty of historical evidence that it would.

The roots of terrorism within a state can often be traced to distributive injustices. Minority rights denied through discrimination on racial, ethnic, or religious grounds are the most common causes of terrorism: to combat which the high police have to develop policies and strategies which rely on force, and sometimes on Draconian legal measures. These measures have included detention without trial, criminal courts without juries, forcible restriction of movement and geographical confinement, and internal exile.

The policeman or woman is not only concerned with what is called criminal justice but also with what amounts to criminal injustices. But what is justice?

There are numerous answers (and much sophistry) to this question, which has occupied philosophers from Plato to the present time, with differing results. A good starting point is provided by the work of John Rawls, whose modern treatment of it is comprehensive and respected. He describes justice as fairness and the first virtue of social institutions. Much of his philosophy is sympathetic to the social contract theory of justice.

Justice as fairness

Rawls insists that justice in the widest sense of the meaning of the term is the first claim on governmental institutions, and this concept conflicts at the outset with the utilitarian idea that all that matters is the greatest happiness of the greatest number. People live in society in a contractual relationship which insists on the moral criteria of rights and duties. Rawls puts forward two principles of justice; these are very relevant to the policing of a society since, when social strategies and public order are under consideration, these principles of justice and fairness might be brought into use.[9]

The First Principle is that each person shall have an equal right to the most extensive total system of equal basic liberties compatible with a system of liberty for all. An understanding of the social implications of this First Principle is required by high police, since it is not only morally correct under the equalitarian principle, but those societies which are in blatant disregard of it face problems of social unrest and potential, or actual disorder.

The Second Principle concerns social and economic inequalities. Here Rawls attempts to justify those that are inevitable, and considers how to deal with those which are not. It is his 'Priority Rules' which have the greatest relevance for police.[10]

Rawls' First Priority

His First Priority Rule requires that the principles of justice are to be ranked in lexical order, and therefore liberty can be restricted only for the sake of liberty. There are two cases where it is therefore legitimate to restrict liberty:

- the judicial imprisonment of the dangerous; and
- voluntary restrictions accepted in the private lives of those belonging to organizations such as police, military, and religious orders.

Rawls' Second Priority

Rawls' Second Priority Rule (the Priority of Justice over Efficiency and Welfare) is primarily concerned with the distribution of economic and other goods. As a principle, it can have relevance to the policing of a society in that justice cannot be sacrificed in the cause of efficient criminal investigation and prosecution.

Rawls' General Conception

Finally it is worthy of note that what Rawls calls 'the General Conception' means that 'all social primary goods—liberty and opportunity, income and wealth, and the bases of self-respect—are to be distributed equally, unless an unequal distribution of any or all of these goods is to the advantage of the least favoured'. All this seems to differ from the social morality of utilitarianism.

Rawls' formula calls for policing policies that reflect the paramouncy of liberty rather than the priority of power. Power should only be applied to enhance liberty, and the liberty of a few may have to be restricted for the freedom of the many—provided that such arrangements comply with the equalisation principle.

A controversial restriction of liberty in the United States would be to diminish the liberty to possess firearms (a right which is claimed under the Constitution), since privately held firearms damage the liberties of many innocent victims, thereby denying their freedom.

Injustice, discretion and deseutude
The ideal situation for police is one in which they are able to operate in a just manner in a just society. If operating in what is generally a just society it is possible, to some extent, to ameliorate a degree of injustice by using discretion (in those police systems which permit such discretion, for some do not) and not enforcing laws generally regarded as unjust e.g. through desuetude. Care has to be taken however not to be in neglect of duty through failing to fulfil the will of the legislature. This is a difficult line for police to tread, and it should be trodden with great care.

High police officials will realise that the repeal or amendment of archaic and unjust laws is a matter for the political process. The situation presents a moral dilemma. In a liberal democracy police may not take an active role in party politics. Police can only justify involvement in law reform through constitutional channels, and particularly where unjust laws are considered to be in conflict with the constitution.

Police are sometimes presented with opportunities to exert pressure on the system of laws by putting them to the test; this is particularly the case where the law may be uncertain. Such an opportunity presented itself to me in a case which has been fully covered in law reports and legal textbooks.[11]

The Central Electricity Generating Board, a nationalised industry, sought to test a site within my jurisdiction for a nuclear power station. Peaceful protests ensued, and farmers owning the land, who had objected to this exploration, were neutralised by being served with High Court injunctions, as were many local residents.

Other protestors arrived from elsewhere and obstructed the vehicles and machinery of the Board on what was private land, the owners of which did not declare them to be trespassers. The Board tried to persuade me and my constables to arrest the protestors, deeming them to be in breach of the criminal law. I refused to do this on the grounds that I was exercising my discretion not to arrest as the law was not clear. Subsequent appeals by the Board to the High Court and later to the Court of Appeal for Order of Mandamus failed. In effect, the Board were told to exercise their own powers at common law, which they declined to do. Although the entire operation lasted for six months, no persons were arrested, injured or assaulted. Had the police used a more heavy hand in this situation, injustice and anger may have been aroused.

It seems that this is a situation fitting Rawls' principle of liberty: that justice comes before efficiency. I think it important for high police to address the question of the two justices, namely distributive and retributive justice, and their relationship.

Rawls stresses that the basic structure for society and the way in which major social institutions provide for fundamental rights and duties is the key to distributive justice and to the maintenance of the Queen's Peace. After all, in 'justice as fairness' society is interpreted as a cooperative venture for mutual advantage, just as Lycophron demanded that the state be a 'cooperative association for the prevention of crime'; and any markedly unjust distribution of fundamental social assets would tend to vitiate the social contract involved.

Once freed from the moral obligation of mutual cooperation, behaviour which is inimical to a well ordered society is, from experience, predictable, and police contingency planners would be well advised to understand this, and to warn governments accordingly. The high police leader will need to consider any relationship there may be between distributive and retributive justice, since distributive injustice, if marked and obvious, may lead to public disorder, crime, insurrection, and even to terrorism.

One only has to read daily newspapers, or listen to news reports, to find confirmation of this. Rawls says:

> It is true that in a reasonably well-ordered society those who are punished for violating just laws have normally done something wrong. Of course such a society, like any society, has to have a system of punishment for wrong-doing in order to uphold basic moral duties.

> The distribution of social and economic goods, however, is another matter.

> The arrangements are not the converse, so to speak, of the criminal law, so that just as the one punishes certain offences the other rewards moral worth.[12]

Criminal justice is not fully realisable since it admits of acquittal of the guilty, and from time to time conviction of the innocent, since the system can only arrive at decisions through the evidence and rules constructed for its purpose; it must always remain flawed and imperfect. This is what Rawls describes as a partial compliance theory. There is no such fundamental flaw in the theory of distributive justice which 'belongs to strict compliance theory and so to consideration of the ideal'.

KANT, JUSTICE, AND THE POLICE

Kant[13] is very helpful to the police where he addresses the questions of the use of coercion and of justice. After all, although coercion is not the only purpose of the police arm of the state or of government, it is a central one.

> Everything that is unjust is a hindrance to freedom, according to universal laws. Coercion, however, is a hindrance or opposition to freedom. Consequently, if a certain use of freedom is itself a hindrance to freedom according to universal laws (that is, is unjust) then the use of coercion to counteract it, in as much as it is the prevention of hindrance to freedom, is consistent with freedom according to universal laws; in other words, this use of coercion is just. It follows by the law of contradiction

that justice [a right] is united with the authorisation to use coercion against anyone who violates justice [or a right].

This equates with Popper's view as previously developed, that the fundamental purpose of the state (and therefore the police) should be the protection of that freedom which does not harm other citizens. When we set this test against police excesses that deny freedom around the world, we are able to talk of the police as handmaidens of either justice or of injustice. The high police have to face that they are either just or unjust, and therefore morally condemned.

THE RULE OF LAW

In considering whether coercive police action is moral even when it accords with the so-called 'rule of law ', we need further clarification of is meant by the rule of law, and what might be a rule of law which is morally just.

In English constitutional law, according to Dicey[14], the rule of law:

means in the first place the absolute supremacy or predominance of the regular law as opposed to the influence of arbitrary power, and excludes the existence of arbitrariness, of prerogative, or even of wide discretionary authority on the part of government.

This principle should motivate police to defend freedom through laws, since to do otherwise is to act unjustly and unconstitutionally.

Dicey's second point is that the rule of law 'means, again, equality before the law, or the equal subjection of all classes to the ordinary law of the land administered by the ordinary law courts'. This ensures that police and other public officials are not exempt from the duty of obedience to the same laws as are other citizens.

Dicey's last point is a formula for expressing that in Great Britain the laws of the constitution (which in some countries are part of a constitutional code) are not the source but the consequence of the rights of individuals as defined and enforced by the courts and thus the constitution is the law. But this is not enough. Dicey leaves us short of the idea of the justice and morality of laws. After all, there may be a duty of civil disobedience as a moral reflex to unjust laws, and this places great strain on the morality of the police function.

According to Fuller[15] there is what he would described as the 'inner morality of law'. He goes on to argue for the 'rule of law' to be prospective in its effect. (There should be no retrospective legislation making past action into new crimes.) Laws should be extant, comprising general rules, but not vague. (People have to know what the laws are saying if they are to comply). Laws should embody constancy and not caprice. Laws should be possible of compliance so as not to punish people for failing to do the impossible. Lastly, police and other government officials stand in the same position as to laws as do the general public.

The high police official in the Federal Republic of Germany would know that Article 1 of the Constitution of that republic concerns the protection of human dignity, *viz.* 'the dignity of man shall be inviolable. To respect and protect it shall be the duty of all state authority'. Now the police leader would have a duty to translate the idea of the rule of law, and the dignity of the individual into policies for the direction and conduct of police.

It is, however, no longer sufficient to regard the rule of law as restricted to the domestic state. International law requires that police officials comply with certain international treaties and conventions. The European Convention on Human Rights and Fundamental Freedoms requires that the states which are parties to the Convention shall acknowledge jurisdiction of the court of the Council of Europe, and this body of law is designed to produce certain standards of behaviour affecting police as well as other government officials.

In the past the lengthy procedure and the cost of seeking justice under the Convention in Strasbourg deterred many complainants from seeking redress of grievance. Now that the issues can be dealt with through the state's legal system it is likely that more complaints will be registered. Clearly this is a matter for governmental guidance and effective collaboration between the police and the prosecution services.

The response to the impact of incorporation of the European Convention On Human Rights and Fundamental Freedoms into the law of the state should generate a fresh police ethos towards achieving its ideals. Through leadership and training the police services might be expected to respond to the shifting political and civic morality towards a culture of rights. This places a heavy demand on the leaders of the police service, for with the shifting morality of politics from utility to rights it might be said that policing is entering a new and progressive phase.

As peoples become more aware of the concept of the dignity of the individual and of human rights, they are likely to criticise and complain about police behaviour which in another age would not have been regarded as wrong. This phenomenon may lead to the false impression that police have deteriorated in behaviour, but closer consideration may reveal that it is the higher demands being made upon them, and reflected in various Codes of Conduct for law enforcement officials.

CONCLUSION

Supreme police power, given the opportunity, can produce the most debased and debasing of human institutions. It is a power that needs not to be fettered into impotence but to be bound by the highest of principles.

Utilitarianism failed to recommend itself as the guiding theory of police, due largely to ethical uncertainties.

Through Popper we have acquired the theory of *Protectionism* based on his assessment of Lycophron's ideas; the law is a 'a covenant by which men assure one another of justice'; and the state is a 'cooperative association for the prevention of crime'.

In considering the theory of the *social contract*, we accepted that it has some measure of truth as a legal fiction to justify government. The police function might best be understood and articulated through the philosophical theory of the social contract, even conceding that neither it, nor other theories of government, are likely to offer the perfect answer. At the end of the day, as Clausewitz[16] reminds us, in the practical arts, it is 'experience which is their proper soil'.

Finally we are able to synthesise three elements we have considered which appear to support the theory of principled policing. These are the *social contract theory* as advanced by Rawls's conception of 'Justice as Fairness'; the second is the *theory of protectionism* through Popper, and the third is the *theory of policing the common good* as discussed in this chapter.

The evolution of the social contract

Although the social contract as an abstract idea might remain unchangeable, its terms or contents cannot do so, for they must change as societies change.

Thus the terms of the social contract in the former USSR were markedly different from those which now exist in the liberal democracies which have emerged from the Soviet bloc. Amongst the most important of these changes would be the principles of policing, particularly in relation to freedom, and the remit and the powers of the secret police. Further strengthening of the contractarian society is likely to emerge from the growing characteristics of civil society.

Even in liberal democracies, in recent times, many adjustments to the terms of the social contract have had to be made to ensure that justice keeps pace with plural and multi-racial characteristics. For example, policing principles have been required to adjust to protect minorities from discrimination, and to protect the legitimate expectations of justice for women. With more changes ahead, the important, indeed key, consideration is that there must always be a claim on cooperation and morality of people and government. Constant attention to the ideals of the theoretical contract is also a test for the efficacy of developing policing from principles.

Not only do the terms of the contract change, but the frontiers do too. There is a constant process of expansion to bring within its moral compass the alienated, and the 'barbarians'. There is now a contract to deal with the whole human family within the terms of the Universal Declaration of Human Rights, and, for example, to prosecute war criminals through an international dimension of the social contract theory.

The role of the police in its widest moral sense can be conceived of as advancing and facilitating contractarian purposes, not in the purely theoretic way of philosophers, or in the remote prescriptive way of legislators, but in the practical way within the actual life of society day by day. Police have to expect not simply to be called upon to exercise force, but to acquire an understanding of how to deal with people constructively in their role as trustees of the social contract, establishing cooperation and morality based on justice as fairness.

Protection of contractarian freedoms would rest on the theory of protectionism as described by Popper, the principles of which are equalitarianism, individualism, and protection from injustice, which must be central to the morality of principled policing.

The police function should be based on the notion and principles of trusteeship. Trusteeship carries with it moral obligations, such as those of honourable and ethical conduct in the application of power and authority. As trustees under the social contract, police are required to use their position 'constructively'.

High police

The use of the term 'high police' in this chapter is not to be confused with the old French usage which described those elements of the police which kept a close watch on plotters, and political machinations amongst high society. In the aftermath of the French Revolution, as is the tendency following all resolutions, counter-revolutionaries posed a threat—offering scope for a powerful minister of police like Fouche, Duc d'Otranto (1759-1820) who it is said saw his role as 'policing internal politics'.[17]

Believing that the monarchy failed in 1789, 'through the nullity of high police', he said, 'the minister himself had to get in contact with the outstanding and influential men of all opinions, all doctrines, all superior classes of society. This system always succeeded with me, and I knew the secret France better from oral and confidential communications and from untrammelled talk than from the hotch-potch of writings that passed under my eyes. Thus nothing essential to the security of the state ever escaped me'.

High police today, in the Fouche sense, is to be found in the secret and political police, sometimes described as security services. *In our case, the expression 'high police' is used to denote those with power to make and to implement policies affecting a police organization as a whole.*

REFERENCES for *Chapter 3*

1. Macpherson, Sir Williamof Cluny (1999), *The Stephen Lawrence Inquiry and Report,* Cmnd 4262, London: Stationery Office.
2. Russell, B (1961), *History of Western Philosophy,* London: Unwin, p. 742.
3. Bullock, A (1963), *Hitler: A Study in Tyranny,* London: Penguin pp. 262-8.
4. Popper, K (1989), *The Open Society and Its Enemies,* London: Routledge, pp. 114-117.
5. Locke, J (1967), *Two Treatises on Government,* Cambridge University Press, second edition.
6. Royal Institute of International Affairs, *International Affairs,* Vol. 72, No. 2, April 1995, p. 259.
7. Maine, Sir H (1917), *Ancient Law,* London: Dent.
8. *Ibid,* p.100.
9. Rawls, J (1973), *A Theory of Justice,* Oxford: Oxford University Press, p. 573.
10. *Ibid,* pp. 109-110.
11. 3 WLR 961.
12. Rawls, J (1973), *A Theory of Justice,* Oxford: Oxford University Press, p. 119.
13. Kant, I (1965), *The Metaphysical Elements of Justice,* New York: Bobbs-Merrell, p. ix.
14. Dicey, A V (1985), *An Introduction to the Study of the Law of the Constitution,* London: Macmillan Education.
15. Fuller, L L (1964), *The Morality of Law,* Yale: Yale University Press.
16. Clausewitz, C von (1982), *On War,* London: Penguin Books.
17. Stead, P J, (1977), *Pioneers in Policing,* Maidenhead: McGraw-Hill, p.72.

CHAPTER 4

Strategic Depth: The Core Values of Policing

Neil Richards

Neil Richards joined the directing staff of the Police Staff College, Bramshill, in 1981 to become its *primum mobile* in ethics. He was later appointed as expert to the Council of Europe and was instrumental in drawing up its European Police Code of Ethics in 2001. That document lays down the fundamental principles on which the policing of any democratic state should be based, and is of primary doctrinal significance for any serious practitioner of police leadership. Its tenets are reflected throughout this work. In 1993, Neil Richards made an appraisal of the background, purpose and value of the Statement of Common Purpose and Values which was produced by the Association of Chief Police Officers, and that appraisal is here revised and updated. The Statement, which is both short and profound, is the closest thing to a doctrine of which the British police service is in possession.

> The purpose of the police service is to uphold the law fairly and firmly, to prevent crime; to pursue and bring to justice those who break the law; to keep the Queen's peace; to protect, help and reassure the community; and to be seen to do all this with integrity, common sense and sound judgement.
>
> We must be compassionate, courteous and patient, acting without fear or favour or prejudice to the rights of others. We need to be professional, calm and restrained in the face of violence and apply only that force which is necessary to accomplish our lawful duty.
>
> We must strive to reduce the fears of the public and, so far as we can, to reflect their priorities in the action we take. We must respond to well founded criticism with a willingness to change. (ACPO, 1992).

INTRODUCTION

One of the major tasks facing the strategic leadership of any contemporary organization concerns the need to frame, clarify, refine and communicate the organization's purpose. In addition to identifying the *raison d'être* of an organization, the leadership is responsible for determining the valued means through which the organization's purpose can be realised. Here, my concern is to place in the foreground and explore the relatively succinct statement that outlines the ends to which policing aims and the means through which those ends are to be achieved.

The police service of the United Kingdom began the process of redefining its mission, vision and role when it set out to adopt a 'quality of service' philosophy in the early 1990s (ACPO, 1992). The *Statement of Common Purpose and Values* (ACPO, 1992) was published in the same year. Sir George Woodcock, then Her Majesty's Chief Inspector of Constabulary, stated in a supporting paper (1992):

Every effort of the police service must be thrown into making the ACPO statement of common purpose and values come alive for each and every officer and member of the civil staff.

Woodcock's recommendations were taken seriously at Bramshill and, at least in the years immediately following its publication, programmes of study at the Police Staff College used a range of imaginative designs to secure support and affection for the statement, its ethics and values.

As the debate about the purpose and nature of the police unfolded throughout the 1990s the statement of common purpose and values was able to withstand the critical scrutiny of academics and police alike. Thus, for example, the Independent Committee of Inquiry into the Role and Responsibilities of the Police (Cassels, 1996) began the summary of its findings and recommendations by supporting the 'definition' of the police mission that is expressed in the statement: 'In our view, the definition contained in the police service's statement of common purpose remains a helpful one ... We endorse this definition' (Cassels 1996: 53).

Despite all the reforms and revisions of policing that have been introduced through New Labour's 'modernisation' programme, the statement of common purpose and values continues to influence and structure the core identity of the police. Most recently, for example, Baker (2001)—writing from the perspective of a police strategist—contends that: 'The statement of common purpose still represents our role as we see it'.

Plainly, the statement of common purpose and values provides a framework of priorities to which police leaders can make appeal in the justification and legitimisation of their policy and decision-making. However, in the light of the enduring concerns about police integrity (HMIC, 1999), professionalism and fairness (Macpherson, 1999) and effectiveness (Home Office, 2001) I think it sensible to re-visit the statement of common purpose and values in order to 'bring-out' its ethics and its implications for policing.

THE STATEMENT OF COMMON PURPOSE AND VALUES: UNDERLYING CONCERNS

When the British police service embarked upon formulating its 'Statement of Common Purpose and Values', it was concerned to provide guidance to police officers in their practice of policing, and help them to achieve some certainty of purpose in their difficult and demanding roles.

Its concern was to provide a general framework of answers to questions about the values and ethics of policing that police officers were likely to ask themselves, and, it is worth noting that the Statement was conceived and written by police officers. However, the questions, to which the Statement could be taken as a response, are nowhere made explicit. If they had been articulated, I believe they would have been as follows: What professional, legislative and public needs must we fulfil to meet the demands of our roles? What are the values that we should defend during our daily practice? What sort of moral world should we strive to uphold? Are the values and ethics that we represent similar or different from those of the public we serve? How do we harmonise police values and needs with public values and needs? What part should a police code of ethics play in helping to solve the problem challenges raised by these questions? How can I be prepared through experience, professional development, training and education to meet the ethical demands of my policing role? These questions will be linked to the substance of this chapter.

THE MORAL QUALITY OF EFFECTIVE POLICING

The police are able to secure the consent of the public in a democracy to the extent that they police towards morally worthwhile ends in a morally acceptable manner. The moral quality of both the ends and means of policing are critical for effective policing. Moreover, criticism of the police is usually framed in terms of moral shortcomings. To take an example of this principle in practice, if the police do not have the co-operation of the public, criminal intelligence will be lacking and a wide range of police activity made extremely difficult, if not impossible. This is the reality of the situation in countries where authoritarian police regimes are in place, or where the police have not won the trust and confidence of the people they should be serving.

Under such conditions, policing becomes particularly difficult and the police a 'people apart' with the result that the police themselves become disillusioned and cynical. Surely, it is when the police are 'citizens in uniform', and share the values of the people they serve that they are at their most effective.

THE QUALITY OF SERVICE PROGRAMME IN THE UNITED KINGDOM

Historically, the British police service has always recognised that the public has a right to expect to be treated with fairness, courtesy and sensitivity, but the style of policing required by the public has not always been clear. The public disorders and riots of 1981 in Brixton, London, highlighted the challenge of policing a more fragmented society. Also, a significant number of well-publicised cases revealed that professional standards were not being met by a minority of police officers. These developments were made worse by a shortage of resources and severe budgetary constraints. The essence of the problem was that the police had got into the habit of setting their own priorities and standards without finding out whether the service they were prepared to provide met with the expectations of the public they were supposed to serve. And they had not looked carefully enough at which choices they needed to prioritise in situations where they could not realise all their legitimate objectives. For example, whether the prosecution of minor crime in racially sensitive areas did not involve too high a price in terms of the breakdown of public order and the hostility of the community that they were there to serve.

In October 1990 the Association of Chief Police Officers (ACPO) published a strategic policy document *Setting the Standards for Policing: Meeting Community Expectations*, which found that the police service was not providing a consistently acceptable standard of fairness, courtesy and sensitivity in its delivery of services to the public. It recommended enhancing the standard of service to meet, as far as possible, public expectations. Hence the *Police Service Statement of Common Purpose and Values.* This was a landmark document. For the first time in 160 years of its history, the entire police service of the United Kingdom had a single statement of its values and core ethical principles. The Statement aimed to identify the values and ethics specifically needed for the police environment, and to make them explicit and understandable for police officers and citizens alike. A major part of the implementation programme was focused on training, with the Statement playing a key role.

THE POLICE SERVICE STATEMENT OF COMMON PURPOSE AND VALUES: AN ANALYSIS

This Statement can be analysed into what are claimed implicitly by it to be morally worthwhile ends, or purposes, and the morally acceptable manner in which they should be achieved. Taken together they provide the core criteria or necessary conditions to be fulfilled by someone in the role of a police officer. They are necessary but not sufficient conditions. They also identify the values of policing in the sense that they specify what is valued for policing. But only in a few cases do they identify values in the sense that they set standards as such. How well does the *Police Service Statement of Common Purpose and Values* measure up to the everyday requirements of morality?

Following Warnock (1967) our core moral commitment is, or ought to be, to non-malevolence, benevolence, non-deception and fairness. Morality supports those activities that are generally agreed by human beings within particular societies and cultures to promote human flourishing and well being, and protects those social arrangements that secure desirable outcomes on the basis of freedom of choice.

The phrases in the Statement on upholding the law, bringing to justice law breakers, preventing crime, keeping the Queen's or public peace, helping the community, and reducing the fears of the public all presuppose the value of helping citizens to be free from the predatory designs of those who would harm their persons, lives or property, practice deception on them, treat them unfairly and illegally, and disrupt their legitimate pastimes and activities. Given this presupposition, the phrases can be seen to enjoin police to provide just the sort of moral antidotes to human limitations that I have characterised as moral activity. And it is a moral activity that is common to police and citizens alike: the good citizen is concerned with it as much as the good police officer.

Of course, the phrases also assume the context of an open, representative democracy and a positive, criminal law that is reasonably fair in substantive and procedural terms. If this assumption is allowed, then morality also seeks to support the law as a constructed institution that confers considerable benefits upon society. As a matter of empirical fact, United Kingdom criminal law does build on common sense morality to counter malevolence and deception, promote fairness as justice, and help establish the conditions for the exercise of benevolence. This is true, too, of the institution of the Queen's, or public, peace which also is seen as conferring benefits on all citizens, including those who would flout it locally in pursuit of their own, narrow self interests.

To turn to what morality demands in terms of the manner of policing, clearly, the injunctions to uphold the law fairly, to behave with integrity and with compassion involve the direct evocation of moral requirements. It is worth noting that the prescription to uphold the law fairly does not go quite far enough to make explicit a key requirement of the rule of law: that those who apply the law should be subject to the same law. To achieve this the reflexive nature of fairness would have to be made explicit. For example, the phrase might read, 'to be bound by and uphold the law fairly'. Nonetheless, the number of bookings of chief officers for exceeding the speed limit by police in their own police forces would seem to provide a fair indication that the cardinal principle of the rule of law is being honoured in practice.

Courtesy and patience are part of the small morality or etiquette of good manners, and are ways of being benevolent. They are also part of the repertoire of ways of ensuring procedural fairness. Time and again in the everyday police activity of intervening to arbitrate between contesting and conflicted citizens, police officers try to ensure that each party to a dispute or conflict has the opportunity, in the small court of the street, to have their point of view heard before a police decision is pronounced. Acting without fear, favour or prejudice are all species of the requirement to act fairly. If police officers are fearful of those in power, be it social, political, or economic then they are likely to apply morality or the law unfairly.

In a society, which is racially, culturally and religiously pluralistic, the exhortation to act without prejudice has a particular importance. Prejudice impedes fairness. To discriminate between people on grounds of prejudice is both irrational and immoral: irrational, because prejudice identifies human characteristics that are not, and cannot be, relevant to treating equals equally and unequals unequally—the formal requirement of fairness, and hence morality.

The Statement expresses the need for police officers to be professional, which means in this context the need to be equipped with the necessary practical peace keeping and peace restoring techniques, to be calm and retrained in the face of violence, and apply only that force which is necessary to accomplish their lawful duty. This accords with the moral requirement to have the capacity to be able to act in a moral manner—to be professional—and to refrain from acting malevolently. This requirement places a particularly difficult and delicate moral demand upon the police, and one for which they have to be trained. When confronted by and offered violence, human beings generally take to fighting back or fleeing. A retaliatory response is likely to be at least proportionate to the violence offered, if not excessive. That is, passions and temper trigger malevolence.

Without training and professionalism, this can happen to police officers too with the result that, on occasion, they are in danger of doing more public damage through their interventions than would have resulted without such interventions, which is contrary to the police mission. Seriously injuring a petty thief who resists arrest, responding to public disorder in a way that leads to a police riot and, in a related fashion, driving in hot pursuit so zealously and carelessly that innocent bystanders are needlessly injured or killed are all instances of the problem and the challenge.

The focus on common sense and sound judgement links with discretion. Lord Scarman, in the report about the Brixton riots that bears his name, instances the wise exercise of discretion as the key to good policing. To quote from his report:

> Discretion lies at the heart of the policing function ... The good reputation of the police as a force depends upon the skill and judgement which policemen display in the particular circumstances of the case and incidents which they are required to handle. Discretion is the art of suiting action to particular circumstances. It is the policeman's daily task. (Scarman, 1981)

From the vantage point of the police's moral mission, this focus is about morality securing its own moral capacity. The mission would be impossible without sound judgement and common sense.

The phrases in the Statement which urge the police to reflect public priorities and respond to well founded criticism could also be seen, in the light of the police's moral mission, as morality safeguarding its own capacity. If police officers become too insular, and professionally arrogant, they begin to distance themselves from their public, lose the huge benefits of public co-operation—in crime intelligence alone they would pay a high price—and undermine their capacity to discharge their moral mission. As I indicated earlier, this problem is being taken very seriously by the British police service.

I should add that, in my experience, police officers are generally reluctant to recognise the moral nature of their mission, and for good reasons. Such a mission carries with it a very considerable responsibility for personal probity and integrity on the part of individual officers: those who uphold morality and law with, and on behalf of, their fellow citizens must themselves be worthy to do so. But the police are human, and the exercise of morality is by its very nature fraught with dilemmas that are invariably resolved by decisions that are uncertain and contentious, so they more readily talk in terms of best practice and the requirements of the law. Nonetheless, it is this deep moral character that helps explain many of the arrangements and features of policing that are not fully intelligible otherwise.

The other main reason for avoiding such a characterisation is that police officers, I think wisely, wish to be classed with the citizenry as merely human, as imperfect, as capable of virtuous or vicious conduct, not as an army of saints on a moral mission aimed at human perfectibility. It is one of the hallmarks of police in authoritarian regimes that they embark upon moral missions in a quest for ideologically inspired goals of human perfectibility. The moral character of the police mission also helps to explain why it is that police interventions to resolve all manner of disputes between citizens are often brought to a successful conclusion by police officers having recourse not to the law but to the application of common-sense morality.

THEORY AND PRACTICE

Policing is above all a practical activity, which, like other practical activities is made more intelligible when it is theorised about and explained in appropriate terms. Inspired by Michael Oakeshott (1991), for many years I have employed the metaphor of cooking in my own thinking about the difficult relationship between theory and practice. The metaphor suggests that practice precedes theory, and that in the practical business of cooking, theory is to likened to a recipe for a dish. Theory, like a recipe, is an abstraction out of the practical business of the kitchen, which leaves much of the reality of the cooking experience, and particularly the know-how of the chefs, behind. However, the best chefs know how to write recipes to capture, in outline, their culinary creations, and they also swap recipes with other chefs in the confidence that they have the practical knowledge to apply them in their own kitchens.

When applying unfamiliar recipes they are able to add in the vital ingredient of their own experience and judgement. To apply this model to morality, the vital tensions between what 'is' the case and what morally 'ought' to be the case, and the actuality of what 'can' be done and what, morally 'ought' to be done, are analogous to that between practice and theory. And the best way of encouraging a thorough exploration of the practical and moral kitchen that is policing is as age-old as the symposia of Plato. It is that of promoting a lively, open learning climate in which police practitioners can engage in the logic of question and answer, with critical attention to the moral pros and cons of police practice.

THE EUROPEAN CODE OF POLICE ETHICS (2001)

The recent appearance of the European code of ethics for police—along with its associated textual material—reprises many of the issues surfaced by the statement of common purpose and values. Clearly, it can and should be used to supplement and extend the professional development of police officers. I hope that through reflecting upon the moral sophistication and finesse that suffuses the statement of common purpose and values as expanded upon in the European Code of Police Ethics (Council of Europe Publications, 2001), police leaders will consolidate the moral foundations of policing, promote an open learning climate and strengthen the quality of police professionalism and integrity.

REFERENCES for *Chapter 4*

Association of Chief Police Officers (1992), *Setting the Standards for Policing: Meeting Community Expectations*. This includes the Statement of Common Purpose and Values. London: ACPO.
Baker, R, Chief Superintendent (2001), *A Review of the Purpose and Design of the Strategic Command Course at Bramshill*, National Police Training, Bramshill (unpublished).
Cassels, Sir John (1996), *Role and Responsibilities of the Police: The Report of an Independent Inquiry*, London: Police Foundation/Policy Studies Institute.
Council of Europe (2001), *European Code of Police Ethics*, Strasbourg: Council of Europe Publications. (This code replaced the 1979 publication by the Council of Europe: *A Code of Ethics for the Police*).
Her Majesty's Inspectorate of Constabulary (1999), *Police Integrity: England, Wales and Northern Ireland: Securing and Maintaining Public Confidence*, London: HM Inspectorate of Constabulary.

Home Office (2001), *Policing a New Century: A Blueprint for Reform*, London: Stationery Office, Cmnd. 5326.

Macpherson, Sir William of Cluny (1999), *The Stephen Lawrence Inquiry* (Cm. 4262-1), London: Stationery Office.

Oakeshott, Sir M (1991), *On Human Conduct*, Oxford: Clarendon Press.

Scarman, Lord (1981), *The Brixton Disorders, 10-12 April 1981*, London: Stationery Office, Cmnd. 8427.

Warnock, M (1967), *Existentialist Ethics*, London: Macmillan.

Woodcock, Sir G (1992), 'Trust in the Police: The Search for Truth', (Presentation given on 13 October 1992 at the International Police Exhibition and Conference, 1992).

CHAPTER 5

A Kantian Approach to Policing

Roger Scruton

Roger Scruton is a moral philosopher, Kantian scholar and author who was formerly professor of Aesthetics at Birkbeck College of the University of London. In this chapter he reviews human rights as a basis for police doctrine, and decides in favour of reason. Where reason and duty clash, police leaders must attend to Kant's Categorical Imperative: they have a duty to apply the law, but also a duty to speak out against it. This chapter links to others exploring the seminal influence of Immanuel Kant as a moral philosopher, and the applicability of his ideas to policing.

Laws are constantly added to the statute book, and rarely deleted from it. Innumerable regulations emerge from Brussels each month, to pass into law without a moment's discussion by our Parliament. It is therefore almost certainly true that the ordinary constable could turn his attention at any moment to a large number of crimes in his vicinity. Given the shortage of officers and the constant expansion in the number of laws, good officers need some criterion of relevance. The authority of the police force therefore depends upon distinguishing true from invented offences, in a manner that commands the endorsement of the public.

The training manual might here speak of the need for officers to use their discretion. But there is more to it than that. We live at a time when law is expanding and the respect for it declining. Police officers can uphold the law only if they can renew the public's trust in law, as the reasonable and equitable solution to social conflict. This means that they must show, through their conduct and demeanour, that they recognise the distinction between laws that uphold the social order, and laws that erode it, and that they are prepared to overlook misdemeanours if this is necessary to uphold the law. If a mugger is captured by a law-abiding bystander with a rugby tackle, it should be a matter of course that you do not arrest the bystander for assault and let the mugger go free. Hence you must be able to distinguish fundamental from ancillary laws, which in turn requires a framework of values—a framework shared between police and public—in terms of which the fundamental laws of society can be justified and recognised.

This is particularly necessary now, when society is threatened with internal conflicts of loyalty. Hitherto, confronted by questions of right, wrong and ultimate value, both police and public could refer to religious authority, to Biblical precedent, or to a shared sense of God's purpose. In the wake of the Islamic terrorism of 11 September 2001 in the United States of America, few people are disposed to believe that a reference to God's will can produce an immediate consensus, or a solution to social conflict. Hence the need, in a multi-cultural society, for a legislative framework whose authority transcends that of any particular religious creed.

RIGHTS

From what material can such a framework be built? The fashionable answer is: rights. In the concept of a right modern people find what seems to be a clear, rational and objective criterion to distinguish genuine law from bossy regulation. Society exists to protect my rights; the law is legitimate so long as it does not infringe my rights; important laws protect rights, trivial laws are merely policy. Finally, police officers have authority because they are the guardians of my rights; they too must respect my rights, therefore, and if they do not do so they lose their social standing and their right to enforce the law.

Those ideas have a cogency and appeal that is all the greater in that they seem to make no reference to any religious faith or supernatural authority, being addressed to everyone everywhere. We all have rights, and the fundamental rights—'human rights'—are those that stem from our humanity alone, and not from the legal jurisdiction under which we happen to live. If there are such rights, then they must apply universally, regardless of ethnic, religious or sectarian background.

The idea of universal human rights has a long and respectable history, going back to Greek philosophy and to Roman Law. 'Natural law' is a branch of Roman Law devoted to laws which owe their authority to no human institution and which allegedly lie in the nature of things. All rational people, the Roman jurists supposed, would spontaneously assent to natural law, regardless of the particular jurisdiction under which they live. This theory was re-formulated by Saint Thomas Aquinas (1225-1274) and other medieval philosophers, and given a secure place in Western political thinking by Jean Bodin (1530-96), Thomas Hobbes (1588-1679) and John Locke (1632-1704), though with little agreement as to what the natural law actually says, or whence it derives its authority. (For references to these and other authors cited in the text, please see the bibliography at the end of the chapter.)

At some time in the late seventeenth century the emphasis shifted from natural law to natural rights. Natural law points towards God as its author; natural rights point towards human beings, since it is we who possess them. Hence the shift from natural law to natural rights can be seen as part of the general shift—which began in the Renaissance and was completed at the Enlightenment—from a God-centred to a man-centred view of the human condition. Theories of natural rights therefore go hand in hand with modern secular ideas of society, in which the freedom of the individual is seen as the true purpose of government.

In the writings of Jean Jacques Rousseau (1712-1728) and Immanuel Kant (1724-1804), the idea of natural rights became the cornerstone of a moral and political outlook which we now know as 'Enlightenment Universalism'—by which is meant the attempt to define a system of law which could command the assent of all people everywhere. Such a system would be based on purely rational premises and make no reference to place, time or history. In a famous drama—*Nathan the Wise*—the German poet and critic Gotthold Ephraim Lessing took the Enlightenment vision to its natural conclusion, by making religion no more than a private avenue to a universal order based in tolerance. In this play a Jewish merchant (Nathan), a Christian soldier and a Muslim Prince (Saladin) are reconciled through a drama in which love, the highest and most universal of human values, discards all distinctions of faith, to establish a moral order in which dogma and doctrine retreat into the private sphere where they can do no damage.

The Founding Fathers of the American Constitution were more influenced by Locke than by the German Enlightenment. But the Constitution that they drew up, and the Bill of Rights appended to it in the form of the first ten Amendments, perfectly express the Enlightenment vision. Their concern was to create a legal system which would have purely rational authority, since all citizens would see the reason for adopting and obeying it, without the benefit of any supernatural revelation. The Enlightenment vision has persisted into our day. Despite the tragedy of the French Revolution, allegedly founded on a universal 'Declaration of Rights', and despite all the ups and downs of American politics, the hope has remained of distinguishing legitimate from illegitimate law in terms of universal and objectively binding human rights.

This hope was enshrined first in the League of Nations (the idea for which had been put forward by Kant in 1795), and then in the United Nations Charter of Human Rights, and finally in the European Convention On Human Rights, all of which have tried to specify an objective test for the validity and legitimacy of laws, transcending the demands of place, faith and history and enabling us to reach agreement about the things that really matter.

The right to due process

Rights cannot be qualified or cancelled by the state without due process of law, in which the citizen is heard before an impartial judge. Otherwise they are not rights at all, but meaningless pieces of paper. The French Revolutionaries issued a *Declaration of the Rights of Man and of the Citizen*; but no sooner were they in power than due process disappeared, so making the entire document utterly meaningless, since no citizen had the power to summon it in his defence. In the Revolutionary Tribunals the accused were forbidden to retain a defence counsel, lest legal niceties (i.e. rights) should get in the way of justice (i.e the guillotine). The same is true of the rights of the Soviet citizen as specified in Stalin's Constitution of 1936—hailed by gullible Westerners as the most liberal constitution in the history of mankind, but never once upheld in court, there being no courts empowered to apply it.

More recent attempts to specify universal rights, such as the UN Charter and the European Convention, have been clear on this point. If there are any rights at all, then there is a right to due process, since without due process no rights are effective.

Rights and duties

Whatever rights the state sets out to guarantee—and we could argue that the process is necessarily an inflationary one, since new rights are always added and old ones never subtracted—the concept of rights fails to provide a complete framework for proper law enforcement. The exclusive concentration on rights turns attention away from the more basic concept of duties—more basic since, while there can be duties without rights, there are no rights without duties.

Roughly speaking, your right is my duty, and in conferring rights on one person the law lays a burden of duty on the rest of us.

A right therefore involves a claim against others, and it seems legitimate to ask how that claim is earned. The obvious suggestion is that you earn your rights by performing your duties, since that is what you are asking others to do on your behalf. It is only in a society of mutual duties that the demand for rights is sustainable. To specify rights and say nothing about duties is to hold society hostage to individual demands. Hence, if you go on defining, claiming and upholding rights, without defining and imposing duties, the whole arrangement will collapse. Which, of course, is what we are seeing.

This, to me, is why Kant is so important. For, while he defended universal rights as the foundation of legal order, he believed that rights in turn need a foundation, and that this foundation is duty. Duties form the objective basis for both morality and law. I believe that it is possible to state Kant's moral and political position in a way that makes it plausible and defensible even in an age of religious scepticism and rooted selfishness, and that this is our best hope for developing a consensus about the nature and the scope of law, and about the authority of those who enforce it.

THE CATEGORICAL IMPERATIVE

Crucial to all questions of morality and law is the concept of obligation, enshrined in the word 'ought'. Anybody who claims a right must establish not merely that he or she wants or needs a certain benefit, but that someone ought to provide it. If there is no person or no institution that is under the obligation to grant the benefit, then it cannot be a right. A world governed by rights, is in fact a world governed by 'oughts'. What does this word mean? Kant's answer to this question is not accepted by every philosopher, but it is the best answer ever given, and as near the truth, I believe, as we are likely to get. Here, in outline, is what he said.

There are two kinds of 'ought': the hypothetical ('If you want x, you ought to do y') and the categorical ('You ought to do y, no "if" about it'). The second kind of 'ought' is what we have in mind when we claim a right, or announce a duty. To justify a hypothetical imperative (as Kant called them) is easy: you just show that y is the best means to x. But how do we justify categorical imperatives? What can be said in favour of the call of duty, other than that it is the call of duty? Kant's view was that we can never arrive at a final justification by appeal to any external authority. To say that you ought to keep your promises because that is what God commands simply raises the question: why ought I to do what God commands? This question too demands a reasoned answer. If God commands me to commit a crime, then He does not deserve my obedience. Only if we know that God commands us to do what we ought, should we obey Him. Which means that we stand in need of some independent test, which will tell us what our duty really is.

Surely what disturbs us in the pronouncements of Islamist fanatics is the constant invocation of God as the source of commands which are given no further justification, even if they fly in the face of common morality, and even if they contradict the equally intransigent commands issued in God's name by rival fanatics or by the same fanatics on some other day. Without an independent test, this reference to God's will as the source of morality is, Kant believed, not merely irrational: it is a kind of blasphemy against God Himself, since it sets Him entirely outside the sphere of moral judgement.

This independent test is reason: for nothing else can provide a final justification for anything. Hence Kant's search for a law of 'pure practical reason'. All rational beings would consent to this law, he believed, regardless of their circumstances or desires. Moreover, there is such a law—the Categorical Imperative, which tells me to adopt a principle only if I can consistently will that every other rational being should also adopt it. This is the golden rule of Christian morality, more normally stated in the form: do as you would be done by. All rational beings accept this principle, since it is assumed in practical reasoning, just as the laws of logic are assumed in ordinary argument. It is at the back of all our minds, when we use the word 'ought'.

Kant's Categorical Imperative is universal since it makes no reference to the circumstances, the history, the ethnic identity or religious belief of the individual who adopts it. That, in Kant's view, is what we have in mind when we use the word 'ought' categorically. We are trying to rise above the impediments of our human circumstances, of our aims, ambitions and desires, even of our religious faith, so as to look on ourselves as just one instance of the human multitude, who, like our fellows, have only reason as our unquestionable guide. And if we think it through, Kant argued, we must accept that lying, promise-breaking and other forms of dishonesty are wrong—these are things that we ought not to do, since the motive behind them cannot be consistently willed as a universal law.

Kant drew other conclusions from the root idea of an 'imperative of reason'. One in particular deserves mention. The Categorical Imperative, in Kant's exposition, is equivalent to the view that we must base our motives on reason. Hence we must respect reason, both in ourselves and in others. This means that we must treat others as though reason were the guide to their actions, and seek to persuade them by argument rather than to constrain them by force. We can argue with others, however, only if we listen to their arguments, and that means being open to persuasion.

The Categorical Imperative therefore requires that we come to terms with our fellows through rational argument and mutual respect, not treating our own desires and aims as sovereign but being open in all things to rational persuasion. This is what Kant meant by his famous re-formulation of the Categorical Imperative: Act so as to treat humanity, whether in yourself or in another, never as a means only but always also as an end in itself.

More simply: treat people as ends, not means. This is our fundamental duty towards the human world—not to exploit, manipulate, enslave, defraud, constrain, still less to kill or maim or torture, but to be always ready to set aside our aims, if the reasonable interest of another requires us to do so. It is from this principle that the doctrine of universal rights can be seen to spring. If we all have a duty to treat each other as ends, then we all have the right to be treated with respect, as rational moral agents, capable of making up our minds for ourselves. Human rights are simply the rights which must be granted, if we are to be treated as ends in ourselves.

Kant had much to say about the motive of duty. He set before us a model of the human being that is austere in outline, but persuasive in substance. He saw the rational human being as set apart from the rest of nature, compelled to live by the moral law, and finding freedom and happiness in so living. On Kant's view, the motive of morality is quite different from that of interest or desire. It rules us absolutely and necessarily, we feel its power even when we are most defying it. It is not one consideration to be balanced against others, but rather a compelling dictate which can be ignored but never refuted.

This accords, he thinks, with common intuition. If someone is told that they can satisfy the greatest of their lusts, only on condition that they will afterwards be hanged, then they are sure to refuse the offer. But if they are told that they must betray a friend, bear false witness, kill an innocent, or else be hanged, then their interest in their own life counts for nothing in determining what they ought to do. They may bow to the threat; but only with a consciousness of doing wrong; and the moral law itself, unlike any motive of desire, propels the individual onward to destruction.

DUTY, PUBLIC SERVICE AND LEADERSHIP

Kant's noble vision of the moral motive corresponds to something within all of us, even if we find it hard to live up to, and even if, for most ordinary mortals, duty requires the backing of religion if it is to be fully obeyed. The important point, however, is that it is only by living in the way Kant suggests, putting duty before pleasure and treating others as though they too did the same, that people earn the respect of their fellows. There is no other path to authority, than the path of duty. People whose sole motive is self-interest and who learn how to imitate dutiful conduct in order to advance their aims, but who set duty aside as soon as their aims are achieved—such people always lose our respect, and therefore the motive to do as they say.

We know this from the current disaffection with politicians, whose principles always seem to be set aside when a conflict arises with self-interest. And it is one reason for the great respect in which the police force has been held in this country, that it has been seen to be animated by a sense of public duty, and not by self-interested calculation.

But this raises the question how we transfer the Kantian vision of duty into the public sphere. Kant was concerned to show that the ordinary morality that requires us to put 'ought' before 'want' is rationally justified, that it frees us from all external pressures, and puts us on an equal footing one with another. But this ordinary morality is equally binding on all of us, and says nothing about the special duties of the public servant, or about the social and political conditions that enable people to fulfil a public office as they should. Can we extract from Kant any further message, concerning the special circumstances of the police force in the modern world? I believe that we can.

First, we must confront some unpleasant facts. Although Kant is right in believing that his morality of duty is justified by reason, and stands higher in our thoughts than the demands of self- or group-interest, increasingly many people no longer act as though this were true. Without religion or disciplined schooling young people are disposed to reject every attempt to deny their pleasures.

Discipline imposed by others is regarded as meddling presumption, and a violation of their 'rights'. Discipline imposed by oneself is simply foreign to their experience. The connection between rights and duties is no longer clearly taught to the young, who are in any case given a hundred motives to ignore it. I do not believe that they are any the happier for this: why else the recourse to drink, drugs and mind-numbing hooliganism? But when people are really unhappy, they are seldom able to see that they are, and in any case ill-disposed to emerge by their own efforts from their predicament.

The police in this country have to bear the brunt of this moral decay, in the form of vandalism, assault and all the petty and not-so-petty crimes that are the inevitable by-product of the drug culture. So how should they behave?

Rights can be respected only in a society that puts duty first: such is the message taught by Kant. When the ethic of duty is in decline, the only recourse for the police officer is in some way to set an example: to make it apparent that there are other forms of human behaviour than those that appeal to the hooligan, and to show this to the hooligans themselves. The officer must display in his or her person and conduct that the *claim* for rights is meaningless without the *respect* for rights, and that both stem from the sense of duty. The art of making this apparent to others through one's own behaviour is what we mean, or ought to mean, by leadership.

The leader is the one who sets an example, not as a pop star does, through making his behaviour seem glamorous, but as a person of principle does, by making self-sacrifice and self-denial seem right. The leader is one who is undaunted by taunts and mockery, who is prepared to take risk on behalf of his duty, and who shows himself to be strong in the face of temptation.

I believe that young people are disposed by nature to esteem those qualities, and that in doing so they will discard their self-centred ways and gradually come to align themselves with the vision set before us by Kant—the vision of a society in which disputes are settled by reason, in which people treat one another with respect, and in which the fundamental duties of the moral life take precedence over the imagined rights of those who reject the call of duty.

TWO KINDS OF LEADERSHIP

For many people, however, the idea of leadership is a tainted one. After all, if you think of the people who have recently assumed the title of leader— Mussolini (the *Duce*), Hitler (the *Führer*), Mullah Omar (Leader of the Faithful), and Osama bin Laden—the record does not look very good. A leader of this kind has charismatic power, with which to stir up sympathy in his following. To follow such a leader means renouncing independent judgement, ceasing to be a rational decision-maker, and losing oneself in an all-comprehending and all-excusing purpose. The comfort of this lies in the fact that everyone else is doing likewise. Charismatic leaders appeal to the herd instinct. They offer refuge from doubt and hesitation, certainty without knowledge, and courage without remorse. The experience of leadership of this emotional kind has led many people to believe that we are all better off without leaders, simply pursuing our own interests and trying as best we can to respect the interests of others.

The problem is that, without leadership of some kind, most human beings don't learn to respect the interests of anyone except themselves. What is needed is not the abolition of leadership, but leadership of another kind—based not in emotion but in reason. This is the Kantian idea of leadership. You become a leader, in the Kantian sense, by taking command in difficult situations, thinking things through and doing what is reasonable, even if your emotions tend the other way. You seek to persuade people, by showing that what you are doing is right, not just in your eyes, but in their eyes too. The confidence that such leadership imparts is not that which comes from immersion in the herd, but that which comes from trusting another's judgement, and making that judgement your own.

RESPECT FOR THE LAW

Those thoughts bring me back to the question from which I began. To what framework of values can we appeal, which will bring public endorsement to the police officer's role? I think that a Kantian should have no difficulty at all in saying which laws must be given priority, in a time when there are too many laws. Murder, rape, theft and fraud are all directly contrary to reason, as embodied in the Categorical Imperative, and such offences are crimes in the very nature of things. Kant's outlook lays down a clear 'natural law' as the root of social order. This natural law is the law which we must all uphold if we are to live under a regime of mutual respect. Many of the regulations that now encumber our lives form no part of that natural law: the Categorical Imperative says nothing in their favour and may even lead us to reject them, should they prove oppressive.

When the officer has to decide, between enforcing an oppressive regulation, and enforcing a law that has the full backing of the Kantian imperative, it is clear what his or her choice should be. Respect for the police is eroded by the belief that they enforce whatever regulations are easiest. It is also enhanced by the knowledge that, in a real crisis, the fundamental laws on which society depends take precedence, in the thinking of the average police officer, over the regime of bureaucratic control.

At the same time, the police force must adhere to its professional duties. The police officer, like the soldier, is not just a moral being with a conscience. He or she is also acting under orders, and is duty-bound to obey the commands of their superiors. At the head of the chain of command stands the Queen in Parliament, and if laws are handed down by Parliament, the police officer must apply them. What is essential, however, is that the officer should apply these laws impartially and, when they are foolish, unnecessary or unjust, not be afraid to say so. By speaking out against bad legislation, the police force wins the friendship and trust of the people, and is therefore better able to secure popular support in enforcing the laws that really matter. If the police force has been reluctant to speak out in this way in recent years, it is partly because it has been unsure of the basis of criticism. If the only criterion for the validity of a law is that it issues from the mouth of Parliament, then how can we distinguish, among the laws passed by Parliament, between the good and the bad?

If, however, there is a point of view outside Parliament from which its laws can be judged, then criticism makes sense. Such a point of view is what people have sought in the European Convention On Human Rights. Its purpose was to establish an objective, philosophical test of the validity of legislation, and one that could be used to strike down oppressive laws as illegitimate. In practice, however, the Convention has proved vague and contradictory, and also insensitive to the very different social expectations and historical conditions of the people of our continent.

Far better, it seems to me, to return to the source from which that Convention originated, which is the Categorical Imperative. For this puts duty before right, and acknowledges no human rights which do not stem from the duties of others to respect them. The police officer, who sees the effect of bad legislation in action, will understand that a law is bad by sensing a conflict of duty in himself or herself.

A case in point (admittedly controversial) is the legislation banning hand-guns, enacted in the wake of the Dunblane massacre, on the strength of emotion and with scant regard to reason or to the interests of those who stood to lose. The police were in a position to see the oppressive effect of this law on the people who handed in their guns. These were innocent citizens, whose weapons were their hobby, their enthusiasm and in some cases their life, and who had no more intention of using them to commit a crime than the average person has an intention to commit murder with his kitchen knives (which are, nevertheless, just as lethal). The police were also in a position to indicate that crimes using fire-arms are committed, as a rule, with illegally owned weapons, and that the law would therefore have no beneficial effect. In these circumstances, I believe, the Categorical Imperative spoke much more clearly than the Convention On Human Rights. It told us that, by passing such a law, politicians were treating a class of their fellow citizens as means to their own self-opinion. To sacrifice others to one's own career, without regard for their interests and without proof of fault, is to treat them as means, and not ends.

This does not mean that the officer should actively defy such a law or refuse to apply it. Attending to the Categorical Imperative, the officer discovers that he or she has a duty to apply the law, but also a duty to speak out against it. To display this conflict is not to sacrifice one's authority. On the contrary, it is to enhance that authority, by making clear that one's motive is not interest but duty.

That is just one example of a stance that, were it to be widely adopted, would bring great confidence to both police and public, in the task of confronting the social and moral disorder of our society. You do not have to be a Kantian to adopt this stance; but Kant showed us that, in adopting it, we are obeying what is most worthy of respect in our nature—namely, the faculty of Reason itself. Contrary to what many journalists imagine, there is still great confidence in the police force in this country. In all the very great difficulties that now confront us—drugs, hooliganism, vandalism and street crime—the public look more to the police than to priests or politicians for guidance. And I believe they are right to do so. It is the police who have to face these things. And the police know that we need a source of law that is neither political nor tribal nor religious. This source is the Categorical Imperative of Kant.

REFERENCES for *Chapter 5*

Acquinas, St Thomas (1964-1973), *Summa Theologiae*, 60 vols. London: Eyre and Spottiswood; and New York: McGraw-Hill.

Bodin, Jean (1962), *The Six Books of Commonweale*. Translated by Richard Knowles in 1606. Republished Cambridge, Mass: Kenneth D McRae.

Gilby, Thomas *et al.*, *Translators* (The 'Blackfriars Edition, Latin and English).

Hobbes, Thomas (1981), *Leviathan*, London: Penguin Books.

Kant, Immanuel (1983), *Perpetual Peace and Other Essays on Politics, History and Morals*, Hackett Publishing.

Kant, Immanuel (1997), *Groundwork of the Metaphysics of Morals*, Cambridge: Cambridge University Press.

Kant, Immanuel (1998), *Critique of Practical Reason*, Cambridge: Cambridge University Press.

Locke, John (1967), *Two Treatises on Government*, Cambridge: Cambridge University Press, second edition.

Rousseau, Jean-Jacques (1998), *The Social Contract*, Wordsworth Editions.

Scruton, Roger (1967), *Kant*, London: Fontana.

CHAPTER 6

Justice, Integrity and Corruption: Lessons for Police Leadership

Sir Robert Bunyard

Sir Robert Bunyard completed a long and distinguished police career, beginning as a constable in the Metropolitan Police and rising to be Chief Constable of Essex and then Her Majesty's Chief Inspector of Constabulary, as well as Commandant of Bramshill Police Staff College—where both editors of this text worked for him. Sir Robert focuses upon what is to some extent the Cinderella of police leadership studies—the role of supervision. An historian by academic training, he makes an historical investigation into police corruption as a result of inadequate or in some cases non-existent supervision, and suggests a number of ways to improve the situation. He recognises that junior officers must be able to trust their seniors if they are to be able to confide in them when necessary, and that this cannot occur in a punitive culture. Knowledge is the key, and there can be no good reason for the leader not to know what is happening.

THE PRINCIPLES OF POLICING

The British police service is unique in the way it fits into the constitution of the country. All police officers are sworn in as constables and have powers to enforce the rule of law and maintain order. The police are not above the law, but subject to it like any other citizen and are answerable for their actions if they overstep their legal powers. They are also required to be strictly impartial and to administer the law without fear of favour, whatever the political, religious, racial or social complexions of the people with whom they are dealing. The system is totally dependent on public support and this is at its strongest when police are seen to be effective and dependable. When incidents occur in which the police conduct has been negligent, aggressive or dishonest public approval declines rapidly.

Anyone who has worked in a police force following a *cause célèbre* will be very aware how honest police officers can find themselves tarred with the same brush as those who have transgressed. Suddenly, the whole police service can find itself dubbed dishonest, racist, sexist or violent depending on the nature of the incidents that caused the furore. Isolated cases of police misconduct are inevitable but good leadership can reduce their number and prevent malpractice and corruption from becoming institutionalised. The aim here is to consider the causes of police misconduct and how it can be minimised by leadership and supervision. The starting point is police malpractice within the criminal justice system, then corruption, the role of police cultures and finally a case study that illustrates the features of leadership that help to determine the integrity of a police organization.

Police and criminal justice

When police forces were created in England and Wales, they were responsible for·prosecuting offenders. In 1977, a Royal Commission on Criminal Procedure registered concerns about the police being both the collectors of evidence and the prosecutors. One source of alarm was the declining conviction rate which it was assumed was due to poor police decision-making and case preparation. The Police and Criminal Evidence Act 1984 introduced mandatory rules governing the police in dealing with law enforcement. The Prosecution of Offences Act 1985 introduced the Crown Prosecution Service.

Then, in 1991, a Royal Commission on Criminal Justice (RCCJ) was set up following the decision of the Court of Appeal to quash the convictions for murder of the 'Birmingham Six'—six men who had been convicted following bomb explosions in public houses in Birmingham in November 1974 and who had in consequence served over 16 years in prison. This case, together with others where there had been successful appeals against conviction for serious criminal offences, undermined confidence in the criminal justice system. The RCCJ was given the task of reviewing the criminal justice system from the police investigation stage right through to the point at which a convicted person has exhausted rights of appeal. There were eight specific areas to be addressed, the first of which concerned the police service (HMSO, 1993, p. iii):

> To consider whether changes are needed in the conduct of police investigations and their supervision by senior police officers, and in particular the degree of control that is exercised by those officers over the conduct of the investigation and the gathering and preparation of evidence.

The reason for this topic was that inadequate police supervision had been identified as the cause of many convictions being overturned, particularly those for violent crime. In the eyes of the public, police incompetence or misconduct had either caused innocent people to be sent to prison or had allowed guilty ones to escape punishment. Such cases did not always involve Irish terrorism. For example, Stefan Kiszko was convicted of murder in Leeds in 1975, after signing a confession. He was released in 1990 when a semen test showed that he could not have been the murderer. A particularly notorious case, and one that will be discussed later, occurred in 1985 when three men were convicted of the murder of Police Constable Blakelock in North London and the prosecution conceded an appeal in 1991.

Both of these cases occurred before the Police and Criminal Evidence Act 1984 (PACE) introduced new safeguards for suspects but there were already post-PACE cases where an appeal had succeeded on similar grounds. For example, in South Wales two men, Paul and Wayne Darvell, convicted of the murder of the shop manageress Sandra Phillips in 1985, were released in 1992 after irregularities were found in police records of evidence. From 1989 onwards appeals were allowed in cases originally based on evidence gathered by members of the West Midlands Police Serious Crime Squad. Clearly there were still problems with the integrity of police investigations and evidence despite PACE.

There were eleven members of the Royal Commission on Criminal Justice, one each from the different constituencies involved in the criminal justice system.

For me, it was a chastening experience because, as the police representative, I was so often asked how serious cases of police malpractice could happen without senior officers knowing. This chapter is, perhaps, a belated answer to that question. The police explanation for malpractice was that the police are hampered by over-restrictive rules in dealing with criminals who are bound by no rules at all. Their critics felt that as the police were misusing their existing powers they should be constrained still further. In Britain, as in America, past attempts to regulate police malpractice had imposed additional safeguards for suspects and constraints on the means of obtaining admissible evidence but without additional means whereby the police could lawfully do their job. The RCCJ approach was summed up in this way:

> The manner in which police investigations are conducted is of critical importance to the functioning of the criminal justice system. Not only will serious miscarriages of justice result if the collection of evidence is vitiated by error or malpractice, but the successful prosecution of the guilty depends on a thorough and careful search for evidence that is both admissible and probative. In undertaking this search, it is the duty of the police to investigate fairly and thoroughly all the relevant evidence, including that which exonerates the suspect. If they are to meet this objective, police officers conducting investigations must be properly trained and supervised, and must have available to them the necessary scientific and logistic aids.
>
> Furthermore, they must operate within a set of rules and procedures which not only affords the necessary protection to witnesses and suspects but also guarantees that records are properly kept, mistakes so far as possible detected, and the lessons to be learned from completed investigations, whether or not they end in a conviction, disseminated in such a way as will improve the quality of investigations in future. At the same time such rules and procedures must strike a reasonable balance between the need to protect the suspect and the need to leave the police free to do the job they are called upon to do. A set of safeguards which prevented the police from bringing large numbers of offenders to justice would be unacceptable.

In evidence to the RCCJ, police witnesses sought an amendment to the 'right of silence' whereby if a suspect remained silent during questioning, no inference could be drawn during a trial from that refusal to answer questions. Many professional criminals evaded justice by taking advantage of this right. I drafted a proposal and supporting arguments for reform but the majority of the members of the RCCJ (HMSO, 1993, p. 50) took the view that:

> There is the risk that, if the police were allowed to warn suspects who declined to answer their questions that they faced the prospect of adverse comment at trial, such a power would sometimes be abused.

The police service was widely perceived as lacking integrity and this illustrates how such a perception can prevent progress towards making the police more effective in dealing with crime and criminals. Fortunately, another member supported my arguments; the government accepted the two to nine minority view, and the law was amended.

It is impossible to overestimate the effect of the failings of a small minority of police officers on the effectiveness of the service in its role as part of the criminal justice system. Our whole system of trial and punishment depends on the quality of the police input; it cannot provide justice if the raw material supplied by the police is contaminated by error or malpractice. Police identify and interview suspected offenders; they produce various forms of evidence which form the basis of all subsequent transactions; and they identify the prosecution witnesses whose evidence is assembled in statements subsequently used in court. Courts do not deal with reality; the police convert the reality of what occurred into evidence and it is that which forms the raw material of trials. Producing a cogent file of admissible and probative evidence from confused and unstructured transactions represents a substantial challenge and one for which many police officers are inadequately equipped, trained or supervised.

Because they operate with much more freedom of action and the ratio of sergeants and inspectors to constables is usually higher, it might be thought that detectives would be more closely supervised than uniformed colleagues but it is not usually so. Detective sergeants and inspectors are, for the most part, operational detectives who deal with more serious cases but provide little by way of supervision for junior staff. A research project studying CID supervision in a number of police forces (Baldwin and Molone, 1992, p. 59) found that:

Officers were uncertain and uneasy about our use of the word 'supervision' to describe their role. Officers repeatedly went out of their way to coin alternative descriptions of what their role entailed. These alternatives suggest an important phenomenon: other than the few high-ranking officers leading major teams of investigators, police officers on the whole shy away from seeing themselves as supervisors, preferring instead to regard supervision in terms of 'teamwork' or 'partnership' or 'coordination' or simply as a 'joint venture.' Although in this report we shall describe the officers in charge of cases as 'supervisors', it is nonetheless important to recognize that this is our description and is not necessarily the one that the officers themselves would accept as appropriate.

Another research project (Maguire and Norris, 1992, p. 86) found much the same thing; supervision does not have the same connotations for detectives as elsewhere in the police:

Officers did not see supervisory mechanisms as relevant for ensuring compliance with legal or procedural rules which might lead to a miscarriage of justice: Rather, it was felt that the safeguards built into PACE were sufficient.

However, [this should not] be taken to imply that there are not other controls in place to prevent 'rule bending' or malpractice. It is merely to point out that 'supervision' is not generally seen as the way to achieve this.

Unsurprisingly, left to apply their own individual principles to their work, the ethical standards of the detectives studied varied, as did their ability to prepare a case file. Their performance and reputation tended to be gauged according to their success in solving crimes, arresting suspects and completing the paperwork. The obvious temptation this provides caused the RCCJ to recommend specifically that police performance should not be measured by results of this kind. The effect of not providing adequate training, support and guidance for CID officers has been to undermine their standing as professional evidence gatherers. Research showed that much of what appears to courts and juries as malpractice is, in fact, human error. An examination into CID investigations found and classified 111 ways in which errors can arise from the tasks a police officer may have to perform. In the absence of monitoring and guidance by a supervisor, a significant number of errors can get past the Crown Prosecution Service and into the Court. (Irving and Dunnighan, 1993, pp. 47-54). If it is in the interests of the defence to do so, errors can readily be made to look like malpractice in the eyes of a jury. This is a feature of adversarial trials that police officers find most irksome and it causes some of them to cover up genuine errors rather than have to admit them in court. Error thereby becomes malpractice.

Although most research has focussed on the work undertaken by detectives, all police officers and other personnel engaged in law enforcement face the same problems whether prosecutions are for public disorder, traffic, drugs or criminal offences. The possibility of error or malpractice in obtaining or presenting evidence is no less, although supervision may be more overt, in the uniformed branch. Uniformed police officers are especially at risk of engaging in malpractice when they are employed on 'task forces' set up to produce numbers of prosecutions. Some other police posts are also particularly vulnerable. The Royal Commission saw some worrying examples of poor supervision in custody offices where it was evident that custody officers receive very little support and are often placed in invidious positions by their peers and senior officers. Pressure can be applied to them to make false entries on custody records, usually in relation to the times at which transactions have taken place or when illegal 'welfare' visits by investigators have been made. The most worrying feature was a belief on the part of many sergeants and inspectors that they were expected by their senior officers to ensure that records produced in court looked as though PACE was complied with to the letter, even when this was not possible.

Ever since they were created, police have had an ambivalent relationship with judges and lawyers, many of whom regard the police in a somewhat condescending way as difficult artisans who cannot be trusted to do their work properly without supervision by legally qualified professionals. For their part, police officers, along with victims, witnesses and even jurors, resent the off-hand manner in which they are sometimes treated within the criminal justice system and deplore the dubious behaviour of some lawyers. Police officers and victims frequently suffer the additional frustration of hearing a trial conducted on the basis of 'relevant and probative evidence' that excludes substantial parts of what really happened and which, if known to the jury, would ensure a guilty verdict. Most victims seek something akin to what Francis Bacon in his essay 'Revenge' of 1625 described as 'a kind of wild justice, which the more man's nature runs to it, the more ought law to weed it out'. Police officers may empathise with a victim's feelings and perceive criminal courts to be places where lawyers play arcane games with no concern for the feelings of the people involved. Faced with the reality of some criminal behaviour it is not easy to remain professionally detached.

In evidence to the RCCJ it was claimed by a number of police officers, including some very senior ones, that malpractice was often committed under the influence of what was termed the 'Noble Cause Syndrome' whereby police officers, frustrated by being unable to get 'guilty' persons convicted of crime, use unlawful methods to obtain evidence. Malpractice is defended on the basis that they are protecting the public from criminals because the criminal justice system fails to do so.

One of the most significant cases involving an element of a 'Noble Cause Syndrome' was referred to above, the murder of Police Constable Keith Blakelock at the Broadwater Farm Estate in North London. The background to the murder on 5 October 1985 was a large-scale riot that took the police several hours to quell. A shop was set alight and the fire brigade came under attack from a mob. PC Blakelock was part of a group of officers in riot gear who went to assist the fire brigade. They were overwhelmed by the mob and PC Blakelock slipped and fell; he was hacked to death by masked rioters, having sustained 40 separate wounds before he could be rescued. An experienced detective chief superintendent and detective inspector conducted the investigation into his death but they faced an impossible task while being subjected to intense pressure from the media and police, against a background of allegations of racism and a refusal of witnesses to give evidence. They secured the conviction of three men using written confessions that were subsequently proved to contain alterations. In 1991, the prosecution counsel, in conceding the appeal of the men, said:

> We say unequivocally we would not have gone against ... any of the ... defendants having learned of the apparent dishonesty of the officer in charge of the case. I say that because the Crown has to depend on the honesty and integrity of officers in a case, especially when [the officer in charge] has close control of the case.
>
> (Morton, 1993, p. 194)

The two investigating officers were charged but acquitted at the Central Criminal Court; one retired when the investigation started and the other was reinstated and retired later. This is a good example of the police organization putting unreasonable pressure on police officers to produce results that could not be achieved honestly. The question as to how senior officers could have allowed this to happen is very relevant here. The two investigators should have been working within a chain of supervision into which they felt free to report that the desired result, convictions for PC Blakelock's murder, could not be achieved within the law. A decision should have been taken at strategic level to accept that fact and take appropriate action. The outcome of this case was that the reputation of the Metropolitan Police Service was damaged more by the fall-out from the successful appeals than it would have been by an admission that the refusal of people to give evidence had prevented a group of savage murderers from being brought to justice.

It is very dangerous to accept the proposition that a 'Noble Cause Syndrome' can lessen the culpability of police who tamper with evidence, entrap suspects, and obtain confessions by illegal means. It was such behaviour that resulted in courts and juries rejecting police evidence during the second half of the twentieth century. Illegal acts done in the name of 'justice' can extend to malpractice to improve statistics, to justify the continued existence of a specialist squad, for personal ambition, or for personal greed. There is no hard line between malpractice, for whatever reason, and corruption.

Corruption

A familiar and useful starting point for any discussion about police corruption is the New York City Police Department that was founded in 1843 and, from the outset, suffered from corruption. By 1970 there were serious concerns about its widespread and highly institutionalised nature and some serious cases of criminality, including the sale of large quantities of drugs the police had seized, some of which came from the famous 'French Connection' case. A two-and-a-half-year investigation resulted in the Knapp Commission Report on Police Corruption (Knapp, 1972). For the first time, it was documented how a culture of routine malpractice could create a climate in which serious corruption could flourish.

The Commission divided corrupt police officers into two groups: 'meat eaters' were actively corrupt in that they sought and obtained bribes, engaged in illegal drug trafficking and operated protection rackets. They were few in number. The far more numerous 'grass eaters' were passively corrupt in that they accepted free meals, drinks or services, 'discounts' , free entry into places of entertainment, and gratuities for services rendered. 'Grass eaters' were seen as the heart of the problem, their greater number tending to make corruption seem a perk of the job and 'respectable'. Their existence also created the climate of conspiratorial silence and sanctions that branded anyone who exposed misconduct as a traitor. The Knapp Commission argued that only within a culture of routine malpractice could more serious corruption flourish. The problems of New York could well have been imported with the original design from London.

Sir Robert Peel established the Metropolitan Police in 1829 and it became the prototype for all urban police forces subsequently set up in Britain and was widely copied in cities around the world. It was originally conceived as a means of preventing riots: a common feature in Britain that has often acted as a safety valve at times of social discontent, and only more recently has become a by-product of sporting events. A large corps of disciplined and unarmed men to deal with public disorder and control crime was very cost-effective. Colonel Rowan, one of the prospective joint Commissioners, designed a mobile sentry system of beats and, as with soldiers, the 'New Police' were governed by a rigorously enforced discipline code by supervisors who were the equivalent of non-commissioned officers and who were controlled by an officer class at the top. To gain public approval, police constables were exhorted to regard themselves as 'servants of the public', to remain calm even when provoked and to refrain from interfering in legitimate public activities. Rowan had invented 'the bobby on the beat' who became the future answer to all public fears of crime and violence.

Uniformed police were accorded the social and economic status of a shop worker, servant or labourer in a class-structured society. Constables had to be physically fit, at least five feet nine inches tall, and able to take care of themselves in a fight. They had to be able to read and write (although many were almost illiterate) and work long hours for three shillings a day (15 pence) at a time when skilled workers received five shillings. The pattern of low-paid police was set for the whole country. The supervision system survived until the second half of the twentieth century in many police forces; it was facilitated by constables walking at a steady pace along fixed routes and making 'points' with supervisors at set times. Other supervision was *post-facto*, achieved by demanding that every movement and incident be scrupulously recorded, thereby creating the notebook beloved by discipline authorities and defence counsel.

The belief that supervision was about checking entries in official documents created a tradition in which what was written in official documents was more significant than what had actually happened. Making false entries became an art form and was often done with the tacit approval of supervisors as, for example, when justifying an unlawful arrest. Despite the apparent close supervision of uniform patrols, there was a lot of 'grass-eating'. In towns this could include obtaining free beer from publicans, food and drink from cafes, costermongers and domestic servants 'below stairs' and coming to arrangements with prostitutes; in rural areas police officers could receive useful contributions to their larders. Poorly paid and working very long hours, with the discipline code and threat of dismissal on one side and a critical, demanding and sometimes hostile public and courts on the other, police officers developed a strong police culture of mutual support governed by informal rules, one of which was not informing on one's colleagues.

Misconduct among detectives had started in London even before the Metropolitan Police was created. The Bow Street Runners were employed to catch criminals, receiving rewards for successful convictions; a system always calculated to produce corruption. Some of them became part of Peel's 'New Police' in 1842 when a detective branch was set up to deal with major crimes; the rest came from the uniform branch. Detectives had higher status, they were known by name and not a number and they had a glamorous image. Supervision was largely a matter of controlling their expense claims. When other forces introduced detectives, they followed the tradition of selecting them from the uniform branch but often promoted detectives into uniform and vice versa. There is no evidence that this system produced less malpractice.

Few constables recruited during the nineteenth and early twentieth centuries had the potential for duties such as detection or supervision; nonetheless virtually all detectives and supervisors came from their ranks except in London and county forces where 'gentlemen' were recruited from outside the police to be chief officers. The quality of recruits improved a little after a police strike in 1919 brought about better pay and conditions, but physique was still considered more important than brains in recruits. The absence of knowledgeable and literate people created supervisory problems within the police for over 100 years as men worked their way up the ranks and then selected people in their own image to become the next generation. For most of police history, the service was led by chief officers with no experience of policing who relied on subordinates with many years of police experience but of uncertain ethical standards.

In 1934, Lord Trenchard, concerned about the paucity of leadership at superintendent level, set up the short-lived Metropolitan Police College. As Sir Robert Mark commented, 'The Hendon College, founded by Trenchard in the 1930s, produced some very good policemen and some very bad policemen' (Mark, 1978, p. 85.) A large number of Hendon graduates were amongst those men who became chief officers in the 117 police forces in England and Wales after the 1939–1945 war, and dominated the scene when that number was reduced to 43 police forces by amalgamations after 1966. Robert Reiner wrote (Reiner, 1992, pp. 73 and 100):

> Most chief constables have come from manual working class backgrounds, but performed far better than the norm for their class of origin ... Underlying the whole career pattern of the successful there is a blend of luck, effort, drive, and self-confidence which I labelled 'the first to ... syndrome'.

This was the era of chief officers who joined the police as ordinary recruits and achieved promotion, often in a large urban force, and were groomed by the Police College, Bramshill. An accelerated promotion system started in 1962 followed by a graduate entry scheme in 1967 (against opposition from the Police Federation) that led to a more representative cross-section, in terms of educational qualifications, of people choosing the police as a career.

Police cultures

All groups of people who live or work together evolve unwritten rules whereby members of the group co-exist in relative harmony. The culture of police groups has always been particularly strong, partly because the police occupy a unique and ambiguous role in society but also because they feel the need to defend themselves against what is seen as a hostile world. The Knapp Commission (Knapp, 1972) concluded:

> Two principal characteristics emerge from this group loyalty: suspicion and hostility directed at any outside interference with the department, and an intense desire to be proud of the department. This mixture of hostility and pride has created what the Commission has found to be the most serious roadblock to a rational attack on police corruption: a stubborn refusal at all levels of the department to acknowledge that a serious problem exists.

The problem is not the existence of groups *per se*; policing is based on teamwork and supervision is about leading a team and being part of the team at the level above. The Knapp Commission was commenting on way in which group loyalties can extend to concealing misconduct and opposing efforts to uncover it. Groups can develop aberrant standards and patterns of behaviour that, for example, can enable them to apply their own concept of 'justice' in defending society's quality of life. This can result in violence against perceived criminals, disorderly factions or even public nuisances.

A Leeds detective sergeant and former detective inspector were imprisoned in 1971 for assaulting David Oluwale, a harmless Nigerian vagrant who had been subjected to a prolonged campaign of police harassment during which officers had beaten and kicked and urinated on him and taken him miles into the countryside before abandoning him. It took 18 months before the offences for which the two policemen were convicted came to light. To cover up, police notebooks and other station records had been doctored, for which the complicity of several officers was necessary; indeed, during trial several other policemen said they had seen Oluwale assaulted but had failed to report anything. All 16 policemen accused of disciplinary offences in connection with the case remained in the Leeds force. But standards are contagious: in two years, eleven members of the Leeds force were convicted of criminal offences (Whitaker, 1979, p. 279.)

Group norms have in the past countenanced 'instant justice' being meted out to troublemakers on the streets; men arrested for injuring police officers and for committing offences against women and children. One downside of loyalty to the group is that people may find themselves bound to dishonest or violent colleagues. This is why otherwise honest people sometimes get involved in a cover-up and tell lies. There is also a bond of loyalty to the police force and to its supervisors, provided such loyalty is perceived as being justified. Loyalty should also work in the other direction; many cases of misconduct have become crises because senior officers have failed to take appropriate action out of loyalty to members of their police force.

The supervisory problems for groups of uniformed personnel are much the same as for detectives. The 'cop culture' can be no less strong and although individual police officers are often required to work alone, they are usually part of a shift or other work group. Special teams, divorced from a normal police station culture, are particularly prone to deviant cultures, which, as we saw in the Leeds case, can involve or even be led by supervisors. In London in 1983, some of the occupants of a police van assaulted four youths whose injuries required hospital treatment. An enquiry failed to identify those responsible although only three police vans were in that vicinity. Nearly three years later, an offer of immunity to prosecution encouraged four officers to come forward and give evidence. A sergeant and four constables received terms of imprisonment for offences arising out of this incident. As a member of Home Office Police Appeal Tribunals, I encountered cases in which members of mobile groups had behaved in aggressive, racist, sexist or bullying manner towards members of the public or colleagues. In some of those cases sergeants and constables, who were present at the incident, declared they saw and heard nothing. These cases often illustrated the dilemma faced by decent police officers whose loyalty to the team and fear of sanctions from colleagues and senior officers caused them to become passive co-conspirators.

People who are aggressive, racist or sexist may intimidate or harass anyone they assess as being vulnerable, whether they are colleagues or members of the public. Supervision requires a detailed understanding of the nature of the person being supervised, including their attitudes and behaviour towards other people. The original nineteenth-century supervisory system was based on sergeants closely regulating constables, inspectors keeping a watchful eye on sergeants and so on up the supervisory chain. Underpinning it was the fear of being disciplined. Nearly all police forces remained like this until the second half of the twentieth century but, as more police constables began to patrol in vehicles and conditions in the police service began to equate more closely with other types of employment, such close monitoring of individual constables became impracticable.

Supervisors became increasingly involved in bureaucratic procedures and the concept of supervision became less structured. Apart from those occasions when police officers are employed on public order duties, the appropriate form of supervision is closer to that needed for professional groups. The supervisor provides the link between his or her group and the level of supervision above and supports, trains, encourages and counsels group members. There is also a requirement to exercise controls and, if necessary, discipline group members. It is these last two duties that can be the most difficult, especially when the relationship between leader and group has become so close that the supervisor has accepted or taken part in previous misconduct.

There is no doubt that high quality leadership greatly improves the ethos and effectiveness of individual units within a police organization as well as producing such benefits as a lower sickness rate and reduced vulnerability to error and misconduct. The worst examples of violent or corrupt behaviour emanating from deviant police cultures have been associated with weak or non-existent supervision or where senior officers appear to encourage or acquiesce in what is happening. Such an appearance can stem from a lack of accurate information flowing through the organization

The flow of information

It is obvious that leaders have to be clear about their aims and objectives and that there needs to be an effective way of communicating values, policies and strategies down through the organization. Of equal importance is a constant flow of reliable and relevant information upwards so that policies and strategies can be adjusted and new ones formulated. In passing through supervisory hierarchies information tends to become distorted and, while it is possible to use alternative methods to send information down through an organization, it is much more difficult to ensure that important information travels upwards without distortion. For example, few supervisors relish giving their boss news that may reflect badly on them. In a large police force, there is a long supervisory chain through which information may have to pass and leaders at the highest level can easily become isolated from the reality of what is happening on the ground.

Even a specially commissioned report may not be objective and accurate. In 1993 a young man named Stephen Lawrence was killed in south London. The crime remained undetected and the Commissioner ordered an internal review of the case, the report of which concluded that the investigation had made sufficient efforts to trace those responsible. Subsequently, an inquiry chaired by Sir William Macpherson (1999) criticised this report because it had not identified the inadequacies of the original investigation which was described as being 'marred by a combination of professional incompetence, institutional racism, and a failure of leadership by senior officers'. What started as a poor piece of police work became a major *cause célèbre* that affected the reputation of the entire police service.

Cleaning up

One of the most difficult tasks for any leader is to take over responsibility for an organization with a long history of endemic corruption and poor leadership. It is made all the more difficult for leaders when they do not know whom to trust against a background of expectations that reforms can be made quickly and without pain. Five years is a short period in the life of a police organization in which careers are based on a 25 to 30 year cycle; it can take that length of time just to obtain the evidence and follow the procedures to remove corrupt staff.

For example, the New South Wales Police, the largest force in Australia, suffered from inherited long-term problems with dishonesty dating back to the days when Sydney was a penal colony. Matters reached crisis level in the last decade of the twentieth century. Its supervisory problems were apparent 15 years earlier when I was asked to advise on promotion systems. At that time assessments were performance related but, because there was no litigation-proof way of measuring performance, everyone received maximum points so that, in effect, promotion was based on seniority. The absence of any incentive or opportunity for more able supervisors to progress through the ranks created a *laissez-faire* environment in which leadership was ineffectual. To change the system against the opposition of police officers who were content with the status quo would have required more commitment and leadership skill than was then available.

Unsurprisingly, problems derived from a lack of supervision and leadership reached a critical level, and a chief officer from England, Peter Ryan, was appointed Commissioner of the New South Wales Police to 'clean up its tarnished image'. Five years later, in 2001, the Police Integrity Commission, following a three year under-cover enquiry, announced that 25 people had been arrested on 60 charges and dozens of officers in the force were facing accusations that they colluded with criminals or took thousands of pounds from drug dealers in return for shelving or reducing criminal charges. The Commissioner's supporters pointed to these arrests as evidence that he was being successful in weeding out the bad apples amongst his officers. The opposition police minister demanded the Commissioner's resignation, because the police force was in a state of 'absolute turmoil' and cited rising crime rates and a series of damaging dismissals of senior officers by Commissioner Ryan over the past few months (*Sunday Telegraph*, 21 October 2001, p. 32).

This is a typical state of affairs when police corruption is being seriously addressed. There are close parallels between this Australian case, the Knapp Inquiry in New York, and attempts to address and remove corruption in the Metropolitan Police Service.

A short history of police corruption in London

When Robert Mark became Commissioner of the Metropolitan Police in 1972 he told Police Federation representatives of the CID (1978) 'that they represented what had long been the most routinely corrupt organization in London.' How such a state of affairs came about contains useful pointers for police leaders.

In 1878, following serious corruption for which three senior detectives were imprisoned, the Metropolitan Police established a Criminal Investigation Department with its own selection, promotion and discipline procedures. This separated detectives from the rest of the police force and created a self-perpetuating closed system. The 'enabling' environment within which major corruption could flourish was a culture that encompassed unlawful methods of obtaining evidence and confessions, making deals with criminals and 'improving' evidence. Many members of the CID were not corrupt at the 'meat eater' level, but in the name of loyalty and commitment to the CID they would not take action against less scrupulous people.

Formal training for detectives was minimal and they learned the ropes alongside more experienced colleagues who inducted them into the prevailing culture. Dissent would mean a 'return to uniform'. There were strong bonds between detectives, cemented by codes of silence and mutual support and reinforced by their frequent socialising together and sometimes their joint membership of external social organizations whereby they might also meet criminals on equal terms. By the second half of the twentieth century women could become part of this culture but normally only on the men's terms otherwise they would be sidelined or harassed out of the department.

Complaints and allegations of corruption against detectives were investigated by other detectives who might well be former colleagues or fellow members of the same social organization. The aim would be to write a report exonerating the accused officer; as most complainants were criminals, it was seldom difficult to cast doubt over their characters, veracity and motives. It was impossible for uniformed senior police officers to initiate action against corrupt detectives, even those under their nominal command; as I discovered as a divisional chief superintendent.

'London policemen in bribe allegations. Tapes reveal evidence'
In 1969, under the above headline in *The Times*, two detective sergeants and an inspector were exposed as corrupt. It was during their trial that a detective giving evidence referred to the CID as 'a little firm within a firm', and the term 'firm within a firm' has come to denote police units which develop group norms at odds with those of the parent organization. This case was merely part of a wider malaise within the CID but a massive cover-up prevented even one of Her Majesty's Inspectors of Constabulary from establishing the truth; hardly surprising considering that Commander Drury, who headed the enquiry, was himself later imprisoned. This case was followed by a scandal involving the Drug Squad that belatedly reached trial in 1973 when three detectives were imprisoned for perjury.

By then, in 1972, the *Daily Mirror* had exposed large-scale corruption at senior levels in the CID which resulted in Commander Drury receiving a sentence of eight years imprisonment alongside a fellow Commander who received 12 years (later quashed on appeal) and a detective superintendent who received 12 years. Police corruption was shown to be big business; pornography in the West End of London was virtually controlled by senior police officers under the aegis of the Obscene Publications Squad. Large sums of money were extracted from pornographers and seized pornography was recycled.

At the trial in 1976, evidence was given that £100 'transfer-fees' had been demanded from honest police officers who wanted to leave this corrupt squad. Some paid; they could not 'blow the whistle' because they did not know how far corruption extended up the hierarchy of the Metropolitan Police. The inquiry team who dealt with this case 'investigated 74 police officers and saw 40 of them leave the police force … 13 were charged with offences and sentenced to a total of 96 years' imprisonment' (Ascoli, 1979, p. 223).

The extent of corruption within the CID had been revealed and, during his five-year term of office, Sir Robert Mark with his deputy Sir Colin Woods rid the force of over 450 officers by shot-gun resignations and dismissal—a rate more than ten times that of his predecessors' (Whitaker, 1979, p. 263). Sir Robert Mark estimated that at that time five out of six detectives were reliable. No wonder he made the quip, 'A good police force is one that catches more crooks than it employs' (Fido and Skinner, 2000 p. 305).

Despite the purge conducted during Mark's reign as Commissioner, malpractice and corruption did not cease; there were people serving as junior officers who had already adopted the standards of their supervisors. Like 'The Times Enquiry' of 1969, another large scale outside investigation into London's problems again failed to penetrate through to the truth in 1978. 'Operation Countryman' was an inquiry overseen by the Chief Constable of Hampshire into allegations of corruption involving gangs of armed robbers in the City of London and Metropolitan Police; the provincial officers claimed they did not receive enough cooperation from London senior officers and the case ended in mutual recriminations that did nothing to enhance the reputation of the police service. In 1980, a detective superintendent attempted to bribe another CID officer into releasing a robbery suspect and received a three-year prison sentence. In 1991, a large inquiry was conducted into allegations of drug dealing, theft and conspiracy to pervert the course of justice at Stoke Newington.

Mark's solution to preserving the integrity of the CID was to intersperse every detective's career path with periods of uniform work. Sir Paul Condon, Commissioner from 1993 to 2000 who shared Mark's abhorrence of corruption, went a stage further by introducing a maximum tenure policy and, in 1998, increasing the resources available to investigate allegations of misconduct.

The failure to act

Sir Joseph Simpson was Commissioner from 1958 until 1968, a crucial period of social change. He joined the Metropolitan Police as a constable, was selected for the Hendon Police College and served as Chief Constable of two provincial forces before rejoining the Metropolitan Police as an Assistant Commissioner, becoming Deputy Commissioner in 1957. He should have been ideally qualified to sort out the CID during his ten years in office. An examination of possible reasons why he did not do so provides useful pointers for all leaders. The reasons fall into three groups: a) the effects that uncovering corruption can produce; b) structural problems within the organization; and c) personal factors relating to the person who must make the decision.

Uncovering corruption

Setting up a large-scale investigation into police corruption would have produced a public scandal and severe loss of confidence at a time when the police service was trying to cope with the social change and organized crime was on the increase. As in New South Wales, tackling corruption does not necessarily increase confidence in the police and its leaders. In general, corruption in the police has only been seriously addressed when it has already come to public attention; many corrupt police officers have been, and continue to be, allowed to resign rather than face a prosecution with all its attendant publicity.

Structural problems within the organization

There is also the possibility that Simpson did not realise the extent of the corruption in the CID because that knowledge was systematically kept from him and possibly even from the Assistant Commissioner (Crime). Although the Home Secretary appoints assistant commissioners, the Commissioner clearly has a say in who is appointed. At one stage, all of his assistants were, like Simpson, graduates of the Hendon Police College. This was probably to surround himself with people he knew, a common practice amongst leaders who are uncertain as to whom they can trust to support their aims. Below the Assistant Commissioners were a number of dissident senior officers who believed they had been overlooked for promotion. These people formed a barrier between the Chief Officer ranks and the rest of the force. In 1964 'a number of senior superintendents and ex-superintendents' primed an MP to raise questions about the management of the Metropolitan Police. An inquiry conducted by a QC (Mars-Jones, 1964) brought out the tensions and animosity between senior police officers but produced no solutions.

The structure of the top echelon of a police organization can significantly affect its effectiveness and colour leadership styles below it. Under Commissioners prior to and including Waldron, the Assistant Commissioners headed their departments as autonomous organizations, each protecting its own territory. Most well-led modern organizations are run by a top team within which genuine interaction can take place between members who have complementary skills, attributes and experience. It is the top team that sets and reinforces the ethical standards by which the service is to be governed, operating through a hierarchy of interlocking teams, the number of levels depending on the size of the organization. In this way standards can permeate the whole organization and create a leadership climate in which members of the top team can empathise with the people they lead. Such concepts would have been foreign to Simpson, as indeed they would to many other chief officers both prior to his time and since. In 1990, over 20 years after Simpson's death, Robert Reiner conducted a survey of all 43 chief officers in England and Wales and wrote (Reiner, 1992, p. 247):

> As the directors of complex organizations their role had more in common with senior administrators in any large modern bureaucracy than with the policemen [sic] they managed. Being professional managers they believed they knew what was right for the organization. Consultation was a subtle tactic for managerial control rather than a supplement for limited know-how at the top.

An unwillingness to supplement their knowledge about what was happening on the ground and engage in genuine consultation is very common and it makes even the most able chief officers liable to be caught unawares when corruption surfaces.

Personal factors

As to the extent to which his personal characteristics influenced Sir Joseph Simpson's failure to stem CID misconduct, again there are some indicators of general interest to all leaders. As the first Metropolitan police constable to become Commissioner, he is often regarded as the first of a new breed of 'coppers' who became chief officers. In fact, he was one of the last of the old tradition. His operational service was short and did not include CID. Within six years of joining, one of which was spent at Hendon Police College, he became the Assistant Chief Constable of Lincolnshire.

Cultured but not learned, he attended a public school and technical college but did not obtain a degree; in his early years he was a noted athlete and rugby player. As Commissioner, he was a popular figure, irreverently referred to as 'Joe' by members of the force who appreciated his concerns for their welfare; he was proud of their achievements and enthusiastically followed police sporting activities. Unlike some of his successors, he was not a charismatic speaker, he did not like meetings and he was not easily approachable. Prompted by the Police Federation, he was the first British chief officer to introduce 'man-management' (i.e. group leadership) training into the police in 1966.

Having given me the job of setting this up, he gave me his personal support and visited classes where I was teaching inspectors who would run the courses, but he never sought information from or entered into a dialogue with these inspectors, nor was he interested in what was being taught. For him, it was enough that it was being done because that was what the Police Federation had asked for.

Just as Trenchard despaired of the senior officer material available to him and created the Hendon Police College to produce better leaders; so Simpson strongly advocated Bramshill Police College for the same reason. His greatest policing achievements were with large-scale public demonstrations; his last great victory followed several years of protests, marches and riots in London —it was a sort of police Battle of Agincourt.

The climax came on Sunday 17 March 1968 when the committee of the Vietnam Solidarity Campaign launched a full-scale assault on the United States Embassy in Grosvenor Square. It was by far the most violent demonstration yet seen in the metropolis, and in something of a pitched battle 145 policemen were injured. The television cameras provided a visual commentary. The public was deeply shocked. The civil libertarians uttered cries of indignation. Three days later (Ascoli, 1979, p. 298) Joseph Simpson died of a heart attack.

His ethical standards were high and he assumed others shared his values; he was poorly supported by people who, had they been more able, could have lessened the weight of responsibility he carried. His personal attributes and the tradition to which he belonged made him vulnerable to things happening below him of which he was unaware. As a result, malpractice and corruption continued to thrive.

CONCLUSIONS

Police malpractice has always been a problem for the leaders of police forces; but in Britain it only became a major issue in the second half of the twentieth century when the mores of society changed and police malpractice to deal with crime and criminals was no longer tolerated. Because the police were slow to adapt, additional procedures and independent agencies were introduced to regulate their conduct in pursuing their law enforcement role. The fundamental problem still remains; police officers still find themselves convinced that someone committed a crime but they have insufficient evidence to prove it beyond reasonable doubt.

Most resist the temptation to commit perjury to secure a conviction; others do not and create the situation in court where defendant and police officer are both lying but, unlike the defendant, the police officer has to make the lies fit complex legal procedures. A defence counsel can often exploit inconsistencies in an honest account; it can be even easier if there has been malpractice. The outcome can be a public *cause célèbre* and damage to the standing of the police. Leadership plays an important part in determining the levels of police honesty. Pressure from above for results increases the temptation to fabricate evidence or extract confessions illegally.

Patently incorruptible leaders support and emphasise the need for honesty and integrity. They deal positively but fairly with allegations of dishonesty. They provide supervisory support. And they do not make unreasonable demands for 'results'. By these means, they can produce an ethos in which honest people are less likely to be tempted into malpractice and less tolerant of misbehaviour in their midst.

The vast majority of police officers do not want to commit perjury, forge documents or become accessories to harassment. Better training and supervision can also reduce the risk of error and malpractice; most police officers are woefully ill-equipped to deal with the demands of an adversarial criminal justice system which puts the police on trial in every case.

The desire to get something for nothing or 'at a special discount' is deeply ingrained in human beings and police officers face many temptations to obtain money, goods or services illegally. Left unchecked, corruption can become endemic. The type of leadership required to reduce malpractice will do the same with corruption and for similar reasons. Once corruption has become prevalent, supervisors seeking to eradicate it face a real test of leadership. Often they do not know whom to trust yet they have to identify the honest police officers to work with them in transforming the climate that allows corruption to exist. For supervisors to feel confident in initiating action, they must be assured that senior officers will support them and provide the expertise that will be required.

Dealing with criminally corrupt police officers is much the same as with any other professional criminal but a corrupt police officer knows how the system works, can take full advantage of any procedural error and may have allies within the service. In criminal cases there is irony in the fact that, as one sage remarked, 'Juries do not believe police officers when they are in the witness box but they do believe them when they are in the dock'; many corrupt police officers have escaped justice when juries have acquitted them despite overwhelming evidence of guilt.

As we have seen, impressing ethical values on a large organization requires more than statements of intent. The structure and culture of the organization has to be such that information flows through it without people fearing repercussions for telling the truth. Leadership groups need to operate as genuine teams in which information, ideas and proposals are shared and openly discussed. Leaders at all levels need to be in touch with service provision to be aware of the reality of what is happening on the ground rather than accept general assurances that all is well. All leaders need a touch of healthy scepticism.

Now that police authorities are on the same footing as other local government agencies and the police are subject to performance indicators purporting to measure their effectiveness, there will be pressure on chief police officers to provide the quantitative outcomes needed to satisfy governmental demands. Supervisors will face increasing problems in balancing the need to achieve greater efficiency with the need to ensure they do not encourage rule breaking.

Errors can be forced on subordinate officers by career-motivated pressure from above or by individual officers trying too hard to please superiors for the same reason. But if overall quality of performance was the overriding consideration in appraisal then this career-generated conflict would be less likely to arise. In fact it is not currently feasible for junior officers to resist, for example, time pressure from above on the ground of quality assurance. And the junior officer seeking promotion still has to show his or her worth on relatively crude indicators which may well conflict with measures of total quality performance (Irving, 1993, p. 56). As the RCCJ (RCCJ, 1993, p. 190) wrote:

> Police performance should not be based on the basis of arrest or conviction rates. A far as possible performance measures should be based on the quality of the work performed.

Finally, as a corrective to the unflattering portrait of the police painted here, it must be emphasised that the police service has not become more inefficient, corrupt, racist or sexist than previously; quite the contrary. Changes in the structure and standards of society, the growth in communications technology and media coverage has resulted in a public that has become more (but not necessarily better) informed, more prepared to take issue with authority, and increasingly litigious. Under close scrutiny, police officers have to conform to ever more detailed procedures in dealing with suspects with the result that their skills are being tested as never before.

Like it or not, the police are being forced out of their artisan origins into the world of the trained professional. Leadership will need to be responsive to that change because it requires a closer and more involved style of supervision. Concerns about the integrity of the police have increased alongside increasing complaints about the quality of service they provide. If a shortage of resources prevents members of the public receiving the policing they demand, at least the police service should be able to ensure that when they do meet police officers their ability and integrity can be taken for granted.

REFERENCES for *Chapter 6*

Ascoli, D (1979), *The Queen's Peace: The Origins and Development of the Metropolitan Police 1829-1979*, London: Hamish Hamilton.

Royal Commission on Criminal Justice (1993), *Report*, London: HMSO Cm. 2263.

Bacon, F (1625), *Of Revenge : From Essays or Counsels, Civil or Moral*, London.

Baldwin, J and Moloney, T (1992), *Supervision of Police Investigation in Serious Criminal Cases*, Royal Commission on Criminal Justice Research Study Series, No. 4, London: HMSO.

Fido, M and Skinner, K (2000), *The Official Encyclopaedia of Scotland Yard*, London: Virgin Books, second edition.

Irving, B and Dunnighan, C (1993), *Human Factors in the Quality Control of CID Investigations*, Royal Commission on Criminal Justice Research Study Series, No. 21, London: HMSO.

Macpherson, Sir William of Cluny (1999), *The Stephen Lawrence Inquiry*, Cm. 4262, London: HMSO.

Maguire, M and Norris, C (1992), *The Conduct and Supervision of Criminal Investigations*, Royal Commission on Criminal Justice Research Study Series, No. 5, London: HMSO.

Mark, R (1978), *In the Office of Constable*, London: Collins.

Mars-Jones, W, QC (1964), *Report of Inquiry*, London: HMSO, Cm. 2526.

Morton, J (1993), *Bent Coppers: A Survey of Police Corruption*, London: Little, Brown.

Knapp Commission, The (1972), *Report on Police Corruption*, New York: George Braziller.

Reiner, R (1992), *Chief Constables: Bobbies, Bosses or Bureaucrats?* London: Oxford University Press.

Whitaker, B (1979), *The Police in Society*, London: Eyre Methuen.

CHAPTER 7

Authority, Leadership and Character in Policing

Seumas Miller and Michael Palmer

In this chapter the authors outline the proper goals of policing, consider the professional autonomy of all police officers, review the general virtues and vices of police leaders and managers in terms of both discretion and original authority, and offer an account of good management and leadership in the contemporary policing context. They reject the performance management culture that has now spread to Australia as shallow and unhelpful. They believe in appropriate virtue:

> Policing ... inescapably deploys methods which are harmful [and] which are normally considered to be morally wrong ... To be effective a police leader must have, and clearly demonstrate, an understanding of the reality of this complex environment before exercising authority over it. This requires sensitivity as well as decisiveness, compassion as well as strength, and the courage to protect and share blame as well as the preparedness to punish. It also requires the enthusiasm to celebrate the success of others, as well as one's own.

INTRODUCTION

Good leadership and good management are relative to the nature and goals of the occupation or organization to be led or managed. Good managers facilitate the successful pursuit of the proper goals of the organizations they manage. By contrast, bad managers impede or undermine the successful pursuit of such organizational goals. But there are important differences between institutions and between occupations. Police services are not, and ought not to be assimilated to, business corporations or educational institutions. It might be an important goal of a business corporation to make a profit by providing whatever goods and services will best meet consumer demand, but this is not a fundamental goal of a school. Rather, schools ought to have as a fundamental goal the provision of education. So if a school simply provided a diet of light entertainment because it was cost effective and in keeping with what children desired, that school would be failing in its fundamental institutional purpose. Again, police services to not exist for the purpose of making a profit, nor do they exist principally for the purpose of providing education.

Good managers not only facilitate the proper purposes of an occupation or organization, they also understand and respect the nature of the occupational and organizational roles and tasks undertaken by those who comprise that organization or occupation. In particular, good managers understand and respect the degree of professional autonomy that ought to accorded to those whom they manage. Clearly, the level of autonomy that the manager of a sandwich shop should accord to a casual sandwich hand is different from that a headmaster needs to accord to a senior school teacher. And the degree of autonomy that individual police officers ought to have relative to their managers is going to be different to that of a sandwich hand relative to their supervisor, and perhaps different also to that of a teacher relative to a headmaster.

So good leadership and good management are relative to the proper goals of an occupation or organization, and relative also to the degree of autonomy that the occupants of the occupational and organizational roles in question ought to have. But good leadership and good management are also relative to the specific features of the organizational and wider context. What might be good economic management practice in a time of abundance, might not be so in an economic depression. Similarly for police leadership. Management practice in the Royal Ulster Constabulary in the nineteenth century might have needed to be quite different from contemporary police management best practice. Accordingly, if we are to provide a coherent account of good leadership and good management in policing, we need to do four things. We should provide:

- an outline of the nature and proper *goals* of policing;
- a description of the *professional autonomy* of police officers;
- a description of the *general virtues and vices* of police leaders and police managers; and
- building on these first three points, an account of what might count as *good management and good leadership* in the contemporary policing context.

THE PROPER ENDS OF POLICING

The ultimate justification for the existence of fundamental human institutions such as government, the education system and the criminal justice system is their provision of some moral or ethical good or goods to the community. The existence of universities is justified by the fact that the academics that they employ discover, teach and disseminate the fundamental human good, knowledge. The existence of governments is justified by the fact that they provide the fundamental social good, leadership of the community, and thereby contribute to prosperity, security, equitable distribution of economic goods, and so on. In short, the point of having any one of these institutions is an ethical or moral one; each provide some fundamental human or social good(s).

In times of institutional crisis, or at least institutional difficulty, problem solving strategies and policies for reform need to be framed in relation to the fundamental ends or goals of the institution. That is to say, they need to be contrived and implemented on the basis of whether or not they will contribute to transforming the institution in ways that will enable it to provide, or better provide, the moral good(s) which justify its existence. However, in relation to policing, as with other relatively modern institutions—the media is another example—there is a lack of clarity as to what precisely its fundamental ends or goals are. Indeed it is sometimes argued that there can be no overarching philosophical theory or explanatory framework that spells out the fundamental nature and point of policing, and that this is because the activities that police engage in are so diverse. Certainly the police are involved in a wide variety of activities, including control of politically motivated riots, traffic control, dealing with cases of assault, investigating murders, intervening in domestic and neighbourhood quarrels, apprehending thieves, saving people's lives, making drug busts, shooting armed robbers, dealing with cases of fraud, and so on.

Moreover, police have a number of different roles. They have a deterrence role as highly visible authority figures with the right to deploy coercive force. They also have a law enforcement role in relation to crimes already committed. This latter role involves not only the investigation of crimes in the service of truth, but also the duty to arrest offenders and bring them before the courts so that they can be tried and—if found guilty—punished. And police also have an important preventative role. How, it is asked, could we possibly identify any defining features, given this diverse array of activities and roles?

One way to respond to this challenge is first to distinguish between the activities or roles in themselves and the goal or end that they serve, and then try to identify the human or social good served by these activities. So riot control is different from traffic control, and both are different from drug busts, but all these activities have a common end or goal, or at least set of goals, which goal(s) is a moral good(s). The human or social goods to be aimed at by police, will include upholding the law, maintaining social order, and preserving human life.[1]

Policing seems to involve an apparent multiplicity of ends or goals. However, some ends, such as the enforcement of law and the maintenance of order, might be regarded as more central to policing than others, such as financial or administrative goals realised by (say) collecting fees on behalf of government departments, issuing speeding tickets and serving summonses.

But even if we consider only so-called fundamental ends, there is still an apparent multiplicity. For example, there is the end of upholding the law, but there is also the end of bringing about order or conditions of social calm, and there is the end of saving lives. Indeed Lord Scarman relegates law enforcement to a secondary status by contrast with the peace-keeping role.[2] Moreover, the end of enforcing the law can be inconsistent with bringing about order or conditions of social calm. As Skolnick says: 'Law is not merely an instrument of order, but may frequently be its adversary'.[3]

Can these diverse and possibly conflicting ends or goals be reconciled? Perhaps they can by recourse to the notion of moral rights.[4] The first point here is that the criminal law is fundamentally about ensuring the protection of basic moral rights, including the right to life, to liberty, to physical security, to property and so on. The moral rights enshrined in the criminal law are those ones regarded as fundamental by the wider society; they constitute the basic moral norms of the society. Naturally, some of these are contentious, and as society undergoes change these moral norms change—for example, in relation to homosexuality—but there are a core which there is reason to believe will never change or ought not to change e.g. right to life, freedom of thought and speech and physical security.

The second point is that social order, conditions of social calm and so on, which are at times contrasted with law enforcement, are in fact, it might be suggested, nothing other than conditions in which basic moral rights are being respected. A riot or bar room brawl or violent domestic quarrel is a matter for police concern precisely because it involves, at least potentially, violation of moral rights, including the rights to protection of person and property.

So the general human and social good which justifies the institution of the police is arguably the protection of moral rights, and in particular those moral rights which are fundamental moral norms, and thus enshrined in the law, and especially—though not exclusively—the criminal law. But policing has further distinguishing features.

Bittner has propounded a very different theory of policing to the one suggested here. However his account is insightful. Bittner focuses attention on the means deployed by police to secure those ends. He has in effect defined policing in terms of the use or threat of coercive force.[5] Bittner defines police-work as: 'a mechanism for the distribution of non-negotiable coercive force employed in accordance with the dictates of an intuitive grasp of situational exigencies'.[6]

Bittner's account of policing is inadequate because it fails to say anything about the goals or ends of policing. Moreover, coercion is not the only means deployed by the police. Other typical means include negotiation, rational argument, and especially appeal to human and social values and sentiment. Nevertheless Bittner in drawing attention to coercion has certainly identified a distinctive feature of policing and one that separates police officers from, say, social workers or criminal lawyers.

Further, Bittner in stressing the importance of coercion draws our attention to a fundamental feature of policing, namely, its inescapable use of what in normal circumstances would be regarded as morally unacceptable activity. The use of coercive force, including in the last analysis deadly force, is in itself harmful. Accordingly, in normal circumstances it is morally unacceptable. So it would be morally wrong, for example, for me as a private citizen forcibly to take someone to my house for questioning or because I felt like some company. Use of coercive force, especially deadly force, requires special moral justification precisely because it is in itself harmful and therefore in itself morally wrong. Similarly, locking someone up deprives them of their liberty, and is therefore considered in itself morally wrong. It therefore requires special moral justification. Similarly with deception. Deception, including telling lies, is under normal circumstances morally wrong. Once again use of deception requires special moral justification because it is in itself morally wrong. Intrusive surveillance is in itself morally wrong—it is an infringement of privacy. Therefore intrusive surveillance requires special moral justification. And the same can be said of various other methods used in policing.

The point here needs to be made very clear lest it be misunderstood. Coercion, depriving someone of their liberty, deception and so on, are harmful methods; they are activities which considered in themselves and under normal circumstances, are morally wrong. Therefore they stand in need of special justification. In relation to policing there is a special justification. These harmful and normally immoral methods are on occasion necessary in order to realise the fundamental end of policing, namely the protection of moral rights. An armed bank robber might have to be threatened with the use of force if he is to give himself up, a drug dealer might have to be deceived if a drug ring is to be smashed, a blind eye might have to be turned to the minor illegal activity of an informant if the flow of important information he provides in relation to serious crimes is to continue, a paedophile might have to be surveilled if evidence for his conviction is to be secured. Such harmful and normally immoral activities are thus morally justified in policing, and morally justified in terms of the ends that they serve.

The upshot of our discussion thus far is that policing consists of a diverse range of activities and roles the fundamental aim or goal of which is the securing of those moral rights regarded as fundamental by society—and therefore for the most part enshrined in the criminal law—but it is nevertheless a profession which inescapably deploys methods which are harmful; methods which are normally considered to be morally wrong. Other occupations which serve moral ends, and necessarily involve harmful methods are the military—soldiers must kill in the cause of national self-defence—and politicians—political leaders may need to deceive, for example, the political leaders of hostile nations.

POLICE AUTONOMY

Thus far we have sketched an account of the proper ends of policing. We need now to turn to a consideration of the autonomy of individual police officers, and specifically to their individual power and authority.

On any account individual police officers have a significant measure of legal power.[7] They are legally empowered to 'intervene—including stopping, searching, detaining and apprehending without a warrant any person whom [the police officer], with reasonable cause suspects of having committed any such offence or crime'[8]—at all levels of society. Moreover in exercising this authority they interfere with the most fundamental of human rights. Arresting someone is necessarily depriving the person of his liberty. And should a suspect attempt to evade or resist arrest that person can under certain circumstances lawfully be deprived of his or her life by a police officer. For example, in many jurisdictions around the world police officers are legally entitled to shoot fleeing suspects.

These substantial legal powers are to a large extent discretionary, for at least four reasons. First, the law has to be interpreted and applied in concrete circumstances.

Second, the law does not, and cannot, exhaustively prescribe. Often it grants discretionary powers or has recourse to open-ended notions such as that of the 'reasonable man' or 'reasonable suspicion'. Accordingly, a number of police responses might be possible in a given situation, and all of them might be consistent with the law. Police discretion is involved at most stages of their work. It may be involved in the decision to investigate a possible crime; to arrest or not to arrest; and whether or not to lay charges.

Third, upholding and enforcing the law is only one of the ends of policing. Others include maintaining of social calm and the preservation of life. When these various ends come into conflict, there is a need for the exercise of police discretion.

Fourth, policing involves unforeseen situations and problems requiring an immediate solution. It is therefore necessary to ensure that police have discretionary powers to enable them to provide such immediate solutions.

The original authority of the police and its relation to discretion

Regarding the concept of original authority, we first need to distinguish compliance with laws from obedience to the directives of men and women (including especially one's superiors). Thus according to the law an investigating officer must not prosecute a fellow police officer if the latter is innocent. On the other hand he or she might be ordered to do so by their superior officer. Now individual police officers are held to be responsible to the law, as well as their superiors in the police service. However it is claimed that their first responsibility is to the law. So a police officer should disobey a directive from a superior officer which is clearly unlawful.

However, the controversial doctrine of original authority evidently goes further than this. It implies that there are at least some situations in which police officers have a right to disobey a superior's lawful command, if obeying it would prevent them from discharging their own obligations to the law.[9]

According to the doctrine of original authority, there are at least some actions, including the decision to arrest or not arrest (at least in some contexts), which are ultimately matters for the decision of the individual officer and in respect of which he or she is individually liable. Accordingly, a police officer may be entitled to disobey their commanding officer to the extent of refusing to arrest someone, although not to the extent of refusing to assist the superior officer in the officer's attempt to arrest a suspected offender. Here the point is not that the superior officer has issued an obviously unlawful directive. Rather *in some contexts* the authority of the superior officer to direct is overridden by the authority of the individual police officer in respect of the police officer's power to arrest.

The notion of individual police officers' responsibility to the law, as opposed to their superior officers, and the concomitant legal liability of individual police officers, is known as 'original authority' in order to differentiate it from mere delegated authority. This notion of the original authority of individual police officers also needs to be distinguished from the notion of the quasi-judicial independence of police forces from other institutions, including especially government. Police forces have traditionally in liberal democracies jealously guarded their independence from government on the grounds that they exist to uphold the law and not to implement the political policies of the government of the day. This notion of the institutional independence of the police from political control has obvious resonances in places such as apartheid South Africa or the former communist regimes of Eastern Europe.

At any rate, the legal situation in relation to the doctrine of original authority in those countries in which is has been claimed to exist, namely the UK and Australia, seems unclear. While there is in law this notion of the individual police officer's original authority, there is also some legal support for the opposite view. For example, there is some legal support for the right of police commissioners to order their subordinates to arrest or not arrest people, irrespective of whether it is desirable or otherwise problematic for the subordinates to make those arrests.[10]

As far as the factual situation of a police officer's exercise of this original authority is concerned, it can be argued that there is a contradiction between this notion of the individual officer's independence on the one hand, and the reality of the hierarchical and militaristic structure of actual police forces and the powerful strictures of police culture, on the other. Notionally individual police officers might have original authority but in practice, it is sometimes suggested, they do what their superiors tell them, and they conform to conservative police cultural norms, including the norm of not reporting a fellow officer's misdemeanour.

In addition to the legal and factual questions, there is a normative or value question concerning police original authority. Here the question is whether it is desirable for individual police officers to have and to exercise original authority.

This question amounts to asking whether it is desirable:

- for individual officers to have the legal right to make decisions on the basis of their judgment of what the law requires—and to do so, at least in some circumstances, even in the face of the commands of superior officers;
- for individual officers to be legally liable for the untoward outcomes of these judgments, and;
- for the administrative structures and cultural norms within the police services to be such that individual police officers in fact act on that original authority in a significant number of situations.

This is a vexed and complex issue. On the one hand, if the police officers in the lower echelons are in fact the most competent to make decisions in a variety of circumstances—more competent than their superiors—then establishing original authority may be for the good. For when there is a clash between the judgements of such officers and their superiors or external authorities, it is likely that acting on the judgements of lower echelon police officers will lead to the best outcomes. On the other hand, since authority brings with it power, giving individuals authority enables the possibility of abuses of power. It also enables the possibility of bad consequences flowing from the poor judgements of inexperienced junior officers.

In conclusion, it is clear that where it applies the notion of original authority provides for a substantial degree of autonomy for individual police officers relative to their superiors, notably in relation to their powers to arrest, and to use coercive and deadly force.

VICES AND VIRTUES OF POLICE LEADERS

Let us now turn to the question of the matter of the specific character traits and qualities that police managers need to have if they are to facilitate the proper ends of police organizations, and suitably respect the autonomy of their subordinates.

We begin our moral analysis with police officers in general. Many of the moral principles which govern the actions of individual persons are universal; they apply to individuals at all times, both in their private life and in their public roles. For example, the moral principle prohibiting murder is universal.

The different purposes and activities of different professions and roles generate differences in required moral character. It is because the police officer must track down and arrest criminals that he or she needs to have a disposition to be suspicious, a high degree of physical courage, and so on.

Moreover, what may be virtuous in one occupation will not necessarily be so in another. For example, to deceive others is in general morally wrong: but it is necessary for some professionals, such as undercover police operatives, to engage in deception and to do so as a matter of routine.

There is a further point in relation to moral character that might follow from the nature and purposes of the profession of policing. Perhaps the minimum standards of integrity, honesty, courage and so on, demanded of police officers ought to be higher than for many, even most, other professions and roles. After all, police have extraordinary powers not given to other groups, including rights to take away the liberty of their fellow citizens. Yet police are subject to moral temptations to an extent not typically found in other professions. Consider detectives working in drug law enforcement who are exposed to drug dealers who are prepared to offer large amounts of money to bribe police. This conjunction of extraordinary powers and moral vulnerability justifies higher minimum standards of moral character for police than for members of many other professions.

Thus far we have been speaking in general terms of the virtues and vices of police officers in general. We now need to focus on a particular species of police officer, namely, police managers. What are the appropriate virtues and unacceptable vices of police managers? As argued above, what counts as virtue or vice will in large part be determined by the ends and means of police organizations, and, more specifically, by the role of police managers in realising those organizational ends by recourse to those means.

Presumably, a police manager who is unduly preoccupied with his own career and with self-promotion fails the first test for a virtuous police manager. When it comes right down to it, it is the collective and properly focused abilities of the men and women engaged in street-level policing that he ought to be centrally concerned to promote. The problem for officers in charge is to learn how to support that cohort' s endeavours, rather than pursuing his or her own professional self interest.

This failure to understand and submit oneself to the proper ends of the profession and organization, and therefore to facilitate the activity of subordinate police officers in their pursuit of those same ends, is one vice that has been prevalent within some police services.

Another vice of some police managers is negligence in respect of performing actions and framing policies that realise proper policing ends. For example, suppose a police manager who allows the manpower levels to run down to the degree that an area cannot be properly policed.

Another dimension of managerial or supervisory negligence concerns the tolerance of dysfunctional or corrupt behaviour among subordinate officers. Again, corrupt or incompetent police officers are problematic because they undermine the proper ends of policing, and accordingly it is the responsibility of police managers to ensure that the corrupt and incompetent are (at least) removed.

A related vice to that of wilful negligence is that of negligence by dint of psychological incapacity. Consider a senior police officer in the sphere of operations who is probably psychologically unable to take control of the situation he or she confronts; being too fearful to manage such stressful situations properly. Knowing this, the senior officer ought never to have accepted this kind of position of responsibility, or at the very least finding oneself incompetent in this position they ought to have resigned from it.

Another dimension of police management relates to the preparedness not only to take on the responsibility of managing others in the pursuit of the ends of policing, but also to accept blame for the failure to achieve those ends; or at least failure to discharge one's management responsibilities in relation to the pursuit of those ends. As we have seen, 'Captain of the ship' notions of responsibility are a common feature of police organizations everywhere.[11] However, when things go wrong, police managers and senior law-enforcement bureaucrats may attempt to shift or spread responsibility through a range of devices. Amongst the rank and file of the service also, junior members may endeavour to evade responsibility by failing to volunteer information, exercise their autonomy or take initiatives unilaterally.

These two varieties of the evasive instinct can generate profound problems both upwards and downwards within a police bureaucracy.

Thus far we have spoken of police managers and police leaders as if there was no distinction to be made between these notions. However, this seems incorrect. A good manager is presumably someone who achieves the *de facto* and explicit aims of the organization efficiently and effectively by working within the framework of the rules and procedures, and by following instructions from above. The virtues of the good manager include:

- knowledge of the stated aims of the organization, and of its rules and procedures, as well as of the latest relevant technology;
- the ability to delegate in accordance with the job specifications of subordinates; and
- the capacity to communicate and to promote civility. Budgets are balanced, good relations prevail between the manager and his or her superiors, and the trains run on time (so to speak).

However, the virtues of leadership go beyond these qualities, and might on occasion come into conflict with them. A good leader generates, or stimulates other to generate, new ideas; he or she questions, and at times seeks to replace, given rules and procedures; a good leader supports subordinates when they are in the right, even at personal cost; a good leader interprets the rules and the explicitly stated aims of the organization not only in the light of political realities, but especially in the light of fundamental ethical values that ought to guide the organization and its constitutive activities; and a good leader energises and mobilises subordinates as members of a team in a collective enterprise to which all can contribute and from which all can derive kudos.

POLICE LEADERSHIP IN CONTEMPORARY SETTINGS

Thus far we have elaborated a highly general account of police leadership, and done so within a normative theoretical framework that emphasised, on the one hand, the goal of policing to protect moral rights, and on the other, the importance of an appropriate degree of autonomy for individual professional practitioners. It is now time to look specifically at police leadership in contemporary settings. What are the challenges for contemporary police leaders? Or, at least, what are the challenges for contemporary police leaders who are seeking to fulfil, as they ought to be, the fundamental normative aims of policing, and doing so in a manner that respects the legitimate autonomy of the individual police officers under their command?

Contemporary policing remains an intrusive and demanding profession. It places an unusually high burden and public responsibility upon its more inexperienced and junior members—both in terms of the discretion they are expected, even required, to exercise, and the nature and diversity of the work that they are tasked to perform.

As argued earlier, the reality of the operational policing environment is that, unpredictably and frequently with little or no warning, police practitioners may find themselves involved in any of a wide range of activities for which no amount of training can properly prepare them. Attending a violent domestic disputation involving people old enough to be their parents; dealing with a multiple road fatality in which the vehicle occupants have been horrifically injured; resolving a drunken fracas between people of their own age and with whom they may, not infrequently, associate in other circumstances; maintaining the peace at a demonstration in support of an issue to which they themselves are deeply committed; delivering a death message to a distraught mother; and determining the exercise of discretion in a drug overdose situation are just some examples. In today's world in each of these situations the practitioner's actions are likely to be subject to post-event analysis; in many they will be subject to contemporaneous public and media scrutiny.

Moreover, these activities occur against an organizational background in which high emphasis is placed upon quantitative results—such as clear up rates and response times—the financial cost of operations and investigations, and adherence to general orders and guidelines. They also occur in an environment of behavioural expectation in which there is little tolerance for error.

Added to this diversity of ends and functions is the stringency and ubiquity of internal and external, formal oversight and review, and the fundamental dichotomy between the independence and autonomy of the 'office of constable' on the one hand, and on the other, the restrictive, rules driven, autocratic structure of most police organizations.

To be effective a police leader must have, and clearly demonstrate, an understanding of the reality of this complex environment before exercising his or her authority over it. This requires sensitivity as well as decisiveness, compassion as well as strength, and the courage to protect and share blame as well as the preparedness to punish. It also requires the enthusiasm to celebrate the success of others, as well as one's own.

This challenge is accentuated, some may say aggravated, by the continuously increasing levels of accountability which apply to policing and its performance. This is not to deny that similar expectations are held of many other organizations, but rather to emphasise that within policing the journey has been more recent, yet faster and longer than for most organizations. Police leaders and governments must share the blame for the delay in departure. Moreover, the increasing demands of accountability have become such that there is a real danger that police performance will be measured only in narrow and superficial ways.

On the other hand, many of the changes in policing, including the recognition of the need for accountability, are to be welcomed. As David Bayley said,

> A new form of professionalism is emerging. This is professionalism that accepts accountability, that accepts the desirability of performance publicly evaluated. Whether the objective is enhanced effectiveness, efficiency or rectitude, police are beginning to collect the information that will show whether they are entitled to the expertise they claim. This might be called 'verifiable professionalism'. [12]

Although Bayley's comments were made some seven or eight years ago they hold true today.

Policing, particularly over the past decade, has taken on a new dimension. Senior police managers are no longer simply field commanders, but people who are responsible for large and complex organizations and substantial public money; people who are expected to anticipate emerging trends and needs, to reshape their organizations and to upskill their people to meet new goals and objectives.

But, as Bayley said (see above), 'unless the public plays very close attention to what often seems like a technical discussion, the promise of 'verifiable professionalism' may be still-born'. [13]

The Australian experience

Accountability for performance depends on the selection of measurement criteria. It seems highly probable that: 'Unless the public insists on the right criteria, the police might become more accountable but for matters that do not make an important difference'. [14] In the Australian experience of the past decade there are arguably two areas to which this concern most importantly applies: funding and behaviour.

The adoption by most Australian governments of accrual accounting principles, and the consequent emphasis on achievement over activity; on output and outcomes, rather than input and on the 'cost of doing business', has markedly changed the equation for policing and police leadership. Historically, policing in the western world has been carried—probably driven—by the commitment of its members. Even members with little respect for police management or their organization have almost invariably applied themselves with dedication and sacrifice—particularly in emergency—to 'the job'. That is their individual job rather than the organizational job to which they belong. Even at the height of industrial unrest police services are rarely significantly disrupted; and in the investigation of serious and violent crime—the protection of the most central of human moral rights—it has been common for police to work without any expectation of payment. The focus on cost-efficiency and outcomes rather than on activity and effort, whilst overdue, fully understandable and largely appropriate, has the potential to undermine morale overall operational effectiveness, unless properly led and managed.

Policing is a 'people business'. As a profession or occupation it sinks or swims on the back of the quality and endeavour of its people, regardless of legislation, rules and regulations, technical support or government imperatives. Never has policing been in better shape to allow its practitioners to exercise the individual discretion and original authority vested in the 'office of constable' but, arguably, never has it been under so much pressure to retreat to an environment of autocracy and prescription.

Over the past 15 years or so, as Australian police services, both individually and collectively, have aggressively moved to improve the professionalism of policing in all its dimensions. A number of features have emerged. Recruitment and in-service education and academic qualification levels have increased markedly; the quality and wider relevance and sensitivity of training and development programs has improved *(inter alia* through greater emphasis on skills and qualities such as conflict resolution, cultural awareness and negotiation skilling), internal audit and professional standards and review processes have been dramatically advanced, and levels of accountability extended both vertically and laterally to an extent unlikely to have been seen a few years previously.

Whilst the models have varied, in keeping with these developments Australian police organizations have modified structures and autonomy levels to better reflect modern work practices and the quality and potential of contemporary police practitioners.

In many jurisdictions the scope of uniform patrol work has been significantly widened as more strategic, intelligence driven patrol and problem solving initiatives are introduced. Budgetary accountability has been devolved, in many cases to the district, even local station level, with district and station officers accountable for the results achieved with the money allocated to them. In the case of the Australian Federal Police, budgets are frequently allocated to individual investigations with the team leader of the investigation, regardless of 'rank', responsible for its expenditure and the results achieved.

As an example of structural and cultural change, the Australian Federal Police abolished its traditional rank structure for all national operations personnel, replacing them with a generic rank of 'Federal Agent', and virtually abolished all divisions and branches and implemented a flexible teams approach to all operational and operations support work. The team model is based on the ingredients of work, people and money. Basically, the competing importance of work is assessed and people and money applied to the work according to this assessment. While obviously initial decisions are frequently reviewed as an operation progresses, the approach allows the best mix of available skills—from the general workplace—to be applied, with the size and composition of the team varied according to competing demands and operational developments. As the team leader has responsibility for the operational budget the team has real ownership of its own work, decisions made and the results achieved.

A range of not dissimilar structural and cultural reforms are occurring in police organizations worldwide. The challenge of leadership in this environment is to achieve an appropriate balance between organizational flexibility, preparedness and capacity *and* organizational accountability and cohesion which will ensure the trust of the community, properly develop, skill and use police practitioners, and improve operational effectiveness.

This challenge requires, among other things, a commitment to, and proper understanding of, risk management by police leaders. It also requires an understanding of risk management on the part of governments and other critical stakeholders. A narrow fixation with accountability, driven simply by cost efficiency and a commitment to risk minimisation (e.g. through maintenance of corporate autocracy as a safeguard against autonomy and the resultant risk of corruption) has the genuine potential, we suggest, to render policing in the current century impotent. Accountability without context, it is suggested, is a recipe for failure.

The twenty-first century always promised to offer an environment of unpredictability, global interactivity, dynamism and diversity. The terrorist events of 11 September 2001 in the USA have simply—but dramatically—added to this already dangerous cocktail. In law enforcement terms, issues of security, social disorder and heightened ethnic tensions will take precedence over the challenges posed by organized criminal groups and electronic crime. This is occurring at a time when, it seems, criminal groups are operating increasingly in loose coalitions and partnerships, which are both mobile and international, in an environment of unprecedented opportunity, variety, profitability and potential for power.

If law enforcement is to remain credible and relevant it must direct every effort to improving individual and collective effectiveness in relation to the fundamental goals of policing. Police leaders and their organizations must become more flexible, imaginative, clever, patient, resourceful, co-ordinated and influential. Teamwork has always been important to police work. Now it is essential; and the size and structure of the necessary teams has changed. While local knowledge of the patch remains important, law enforcement practitioners now must recognise that their patch is part of a global patchwork quilt—a quilt of many cultures and languages, of many governments and systems. Whilst it is probably true to say that most police administrators are cognisant of these needs, it will take courage in the current environment to implement and maintain the strategies necessary to effect real change.

For despite the reforms occurring in most police services around Australia, we suggest more needs to be done. Certainly, in the terms of David Bayley's definition of 'verifiable professionalism,' policing in most parts of the western world would struggle to identify a positive connector between accountability and results. Police leaders need to set minimum standards and ensure compliance and accountability.

However, police leaders must also continue to strive, we suggest, to create organizational arrangements which properly empower and personally enrich their people, and which facilitate and enable good performance and good results. For one thing, ethics in policing is not simply about compliance with minimum legal and moral standards, it is also about enhancing individual and collective virtues, and striving to improve one's professional performance.

For another thing, it is only by the good performance of individual police officers, and the good results of teams of police officers, that the fundamental moral purposes of police organizations will be realised in contemporary policing contexts. If these goals or purposes, notably the protection of the moral rights of citizens, are not realised, then the existence of police institutions ceases to have any point. The virtues of a good leader are inextricably linked to these purposes. One such virtue is trust. With devolution and autonomy goes trust in others, as well as accountability. Another virtue is the ability to communicate. For example, the effectiveness of the communication of the organizational directions and strategies is an important determinant of the level of ownership of those directions and strategies by those under their command.

The quality of the policies and decisions of police leaders is a fundamentally important contributing factor to the success of police organizations in achieving the moral purposes that ultimately justify their existence.

REFERENCES for *Chapter 7*

1. Different theorists have seen one of these goals as definitive. See, e.g. Skolnick, J and Fife, J (1993), *Above the Law: Police and the Excessive Use of Force*, New York: Free Press.
2. Scarman, Lord (1981), *The Scarman Report*, London: Penguin.
3. Skolnick, J (1966), *Justice Without Trial*, New York: Macmillan.
4. For more details in relation to this theory of police work see Miller, S and Blackler, J (1997), *Police Ethics*, Sydney: Allen and Unwin, *Chapter 3*; and Miller, S and Blackler, J (forthcoming), *Ethical Issues in Policing: Contemporary Perspectives and Problems*, Aldershot: Dartmouth Press.
5. Bittner, E (1980), *The Functions of Police in Modern Society*, Cambridge, Mass.: Gunn and Hain.
6. Bittner, E, *op. cit.*
7. On general issues of autonomy and accountability in policing in Australia see Moore, D and Wettenhall, R (eds.) (1994), *Keeping the Peace: Police Accountability and Oversight*, Australia: University of Canberra. An earlier version of this and the next section is to be found in Miller, S, 'Authority, Discretion and Accountability: The Case of Policing' in Charles Sampford, S and Noel Preston, N (eds.) (1998), *Public Sector Ethics*, Federation Press/Routledge.
8. *NSW Crimes Act* (1990), No. 40 section 352 sub-section 2(a).
9. Two relevant legal cases here are *R v. Metropolitan Police Commissioner, ex parte Blackburn* (cited in Bryett *op. cit.* p. 43) in which Lord Denning considered the Commissioner of the London Metropolitan Police 'to be answerable to the law and to the law alone' and *Fisher v. Oldham* (cited in Bryett *op. cit.* p. 42) in which the court found the police service was not vicariously liable in virtue of the original authority of the office of constable.
10. See Hogg, R and Hawker, B (1983), 'The Politics of Police Independence', *Legal Service Bulletin*, Vol. 8, No. 4 and papers by Alderston, Goldring and Blazey, and Plehwe and Wettenhall in *Keeping the Peace, op.cit.*
11. See Blackler, J and Miller, S (2000), *Police Ethics*, Vol. 3, Case Studies for Police Managers, Canberra: Centre for Applied Philosophy and Public Ethics.
12. Edited by Bryett and Lewis (1994), *Un-Peeling Tradition: Contemporary Policing*, Macmillan Education Australia Pty.
13. *Ibid.*
14. *Ibid.*

CHAPTER 8

Leadership Myths and Realities

Robert Panzarella

Robert Panzarella lays bare the myths and realities of police leadership with surgical precision. Although police forces promote from within, many police leaders have climbed the bureaucratic ladder and have little operational experience. But lack of reality-based knowledge does not align itself with humility. Police leaders, politicians and the public are unforgiving in their expectations of those who do the actual work of policing. The quasi-military model of police command is outmoded even as a military model. The contemporary military may provide a more apt model for the necessary task of reinventing police leadership.

THE ORIGINS OF MODERN POLICING

Modern policing was created in London by Home Secretary Sir Robert Peel, who set up the Metropolitan Police in 1829 as a response to the urban disorder that accompanied industrialisation (Hobsbawm, 1968). Across the Atlantic, mob disorders gave rise to police departments based on the London model (Johnson, 1981). A delegation of New York City politicians went to London and brought back the plan for a new police organization, strongly influenced by military experience of organizing men to achieve a common task. Uniforms and ranks were introduced to facilitate large-scale deployments. Military-style roll calls were used as indicators of sobriety and fitness for duty. Like an army of occupation, the police sent out regular patrols to keep an eye on things and handle minor incidents. Back-up forces were maintained in fortress-like stations for deployment in larger incidents, and the entire force could be mobilized when necessary to put down major disorders.

Most importantly, a military ideology was imposed, more or less successfully, on the police. The essence of it was the understanding that superiors would make decisions and give orders, and that subordinates would obey orders without question.

That ideology is still alive today, and can be seen in the most professional of police-type organizations, such as the FBI. FBI agents do not wear a uniform or salute each other. But the FBI may be even more military in essence than other police organizations: by demanding greater faith in the organization's mission, greater loyalty, and more readiness to do whatever may be ordered by superiors.

Although police forces today are often referred to as 'paramilitary' or 'quasi-military' organizations, the military and the police have evolved along separate paths and as time goes by they resemble one another less and less. Both, however, have had to cope with changing notions of leadership. It will be the essence of this article to argue that the police service has yet to find an appropriate model of leadership, or cluster of models, to replace the military one which was first applied; and we shall approach this task in four stages.

Firstly, in order to chart what the police service has done, we shall need to say something about the progress of ideas on leadership in general. Secondly, we need to identify some of the myths upon which ideas of police leadership are based. Thirdly, we need to articulate some of the realities of police leadership. And finally, we need to offer some conclusions based on this analysis.

1. THE SEARCH FOR LEADERSHIP

In the United States, as elsewhere, notions about leadership have reflected the general values and prejudices prevalent in society at the time. The police service was founded on a military model, and the army had traditionally drawn its leadership from the aristocracy. However, this source of leadership was no longer viable in the twentieth century. Education replaced birth, and a college education became the normal requirement for leadership.

A small peace-time army could be commanded by a small, educated officer corps; but a mass army was another matter. The mass mobilization of draftees at the US entry into World War II produced far more soldiers than could be commanded by the limited supply of college educated inductees available. In this time of crisis, the problem was to find the leaders from a much broader spectrum.

At the outset of World War II the US War Department (since renamed the Defense Department) met the challenge of selecting officers by creating a staff unit of hundreds of social scientists whose mission was to find some way to pick out the leaders from among the recruits. This staff group worked on the task throughout the war. Faith in paper and pencil tests was still in its youthful vigour. They studied officers who were considered good leaders and they queried soldiers and officers about what they thought to be the traits of good leaders. They compiled a list of traits, constructed tests to measure the traits, selected officer candidates based on the scores, and beheld the results (see Jenkins, 1947).

Apart from the novel assessment exercises based on simulations, which were used with great success to select personnel for the extraordinary missions of the Office of Strategic Services, nothing seemed to work. High intelligence produced as many puffed shirts as excellent officers. The 'energetic' included as many impulsive bunglers as competent doers. The 'loyal' included mindless conformists to inept policies as well as ingenious protagonists of critical initiatives. The 'aggressive' included the fools who rush in as well as the determined and persistent campaigners. Down the list of traits thought to be the essence of leadership, one study after another yielded more complexities than conclusions.

At the end of the war these social scientists were discharged; but they remained united by founding the American Management Association. The supposed leadership traits, which had already proven useless, somehow found their way into personnel evaluation systems of American police departments, where they remain entrenched.

Changes in the military

When Dwight Eisenhower became President of the US he knew that the military was an anachronistic organization which succeeded more by its bulk than by its prowess (Moskos, 1970). In Eisenhower's new army soldiers were no longer interchangeable, soldiers became specialists, more extensive training was required, individual fitness and performance were assessed regularly, and new leadership concepts evolved.

What was expected from subordinates came to be called 'co-operation' more often than it was called 'obedience.' Superiors of specialists were trained to realize that their subordinates might be more competent than the superiors at particular tasks. Decision making was pushed downwards. Eisenhower created the virtually leaderless hybrid teams of specialists intended to operate away from the chain of command in poorly defined situations, which eventually became known as 'green berets.'

In the Vietnam War era, highly publicized atrocities by military personnel resulted in a new training module for officers on the legitimacy of disobeying improper orders. The Nuremberg trials had established the principle that obeying military orders should be limited to obeying orders that are legitimate and moral by international standards. It became an obligation of leadership to weigh the morality of operational practices.

However, this new ideology of qualified military obedience was conceived in response to public outcry, and it remains on the periphery of military consciousness. Day-to-day leadership is still a matter of faithfully implementing policies and procedures flowing down from the top of the organization. The rule applied in quasi-military agencies, such as police or fire-fighting agencies, is that orders are to be obeyed in an emergency situation and questions should be brought to the superior's attention later.

Social science models of leadership

Meanwhile, social scientists were continuing their leadership experiments. Some studies suggested that, at least in certain circumstances, supportive and facilitative leadership styles were more effective than autocratic styles (e.g. Likert, 1961, Berkley, 1971). They found that there is a variety of leadership 'styles' beyond the dichotomy between democratic versus authoritarian styles. For example, Owens (1973) distinguished five styles: autocratic, bureaucratic, diplomatic, participative and free-rein. However, little consensus has evolved on how many styles there might be or how to name them. There may be a virtually infinite number of leadership styles, and the names may be rather arbitrary.

A neater approach was to classify 'dimensions' of leadership, such as 'production-centred' versus 'employee-centred' leadership styles (Likert, 1961, 1967); or styles of leadership which focus on 'initiating structure' versus 'consideration' for employees (Stogdill, 1959, Bass, 1990). Tannenbaum and Schmidt (1958) conceptualized a continuum of leadership styles ranging from boss-centred to subordinate-centred styles. Blake and Mouton (1964) plotted management styles on a two-dimensional grid reflecting concern for people and concern for production. These various categorizations of leadership behaviour offer general agreement that some styles or dimensions seemed to focus on the tasks to be done, and some on the relationships between leaders and followers.

But there seems to be a nearly infinite way of describing and categorizing these leadership styles along the axes of various dimensions.

Charismatic leadership

Social scientists began to examine charismatic leadership (Bryman, 1993). Charismatic leaders arise in times of crisis. The charismatic leader is a person of great vision, with grappling hooks caught on the future. The charismatic leader cultivates ardent personal loyalty among followers, dissatisfaction with the present, and willingness to sacrifice for the future. Followers construct their own self-image on the basis of their dedication to the charismatic leader's cause. Charismatic leaders are often found in a political or religious context, but include people in business organizations and in social services who enter the stage at a time when renewal is urgently needed or new visions are required to meet future challenges.

However, in the everyday operations of most organizations charismatic leaders may be unnecessary, or too disruptive to be valued. Most police organizations do not want a leader whose style is built on a radically divergent view of what the organization should be doing, a programme of fostering discontent, and a demand for personal and unfailing loyalty. The cult aspects of charismatic leadership would render it incompatible with the ideology of policing in a democratic society even if the dangers were not already known from the US experience with J. Edgar Hoover's use of the FBI to aggrandize his personal power during his long reign.

Many top leaders lean in the direction of charismatic leaders, although they do not go so far as to demand self-sacrifice from subordinates but rather reward total loyalty. They tend to be strong-willed, intolerant individuals who expect their directives to be carried out without question. They have their own ideas about what needs to be done, seek minimal input from others, and are impatient with subordinates who challenge their assumptions.

They require as subordinates, in the organization's second level of command, a deputy or deputies whose only will is to carry out the imperatives of the top leader. Loyalty is the great virtue of these second level individuals. Their leadership role is faithfully to implement the directives of their superior, whatever their own opinions may be. A good second level leader may be a disaster in the top spot, and a person who might be right for the top spot might be a disaster in the second level position. This is in marked contrast to the idea that a person who is highly effective in the second level position would be the right person eventually to take over the top position.

Situational leadership

Researchers found that a style of leadership which is effective in one set of conditions may not be effective in another set of conditions (Hutchison, Valentino and Kirkner, 1998).

Fiedler's (1965, 1966) 'contingency theory' of leadership defined a typology of situations in which three factors were varied: the amount of trust and liking between the leader and followers; whether the structure for achieving tasks was clearly defined or ambiguous; and the amount of formal power possessed by the leader. For Fiedler, the interplay of these factors determined which type of leadership would be effective, and whether it should be geared towards task or working relationships. Fiedler believed that individuals were not capable of such adaptations, and that the organization should select leaders who were matched to the situation at hand—which could be seen as including and the political climate of the organization (McGregor, 1966).

In general, the idea that an individual leader could adapt to a great variety of tasks and subordinates seems to have been overly optimistic. Rarely is it said of an individual, by others, that sometimes this person is authoritarian and sometimes democratic. Possibly more amenable to training are the smaller components of leadership, and a plethora of management students began a continuing movement to describe and classify the 'habits' or ' practices' of effective managers, with the intent that these habits could be imitated (e.g. Drucker, 1966, Sayles, 1979, Blanchard, *et al.* 1982, Peters and Waterman, 1982, Fox, 1998, Strock, 2001).

One might expect it to be easier to teach and learn a specific behaviour than a 'style.' Empirical research for many years has indicated that actions are easier to teach than attitudes. (See a summary of research in Jones and Gerard, 1967.) When people are induced to act in some new manner, then however inconsistent it may be with their pre-existing attitudes, they are more likely to adjust their attitudes and beliefs to match their actions. Hence, management training has tended to rely heavily on simulations and role playing.

Summary
In contemporary practice the search for a leader in a particular situation has become a search for a particular type of leader, among the organization's available human resources, to handle a particular kind of work group or task. The quest for a generic leader, to the extent that such a creature may exist, has changed from a search to a manufacturing process. People can be trained in the specific skills and habits thought to be essential for leadership—although some will be more suitable for training than others.

Organizations vary in their demand for control and their tolerance for diversity in the workplace. Hence, management training programmes or leadership schools tend to have a bias toward a particular style of leadership, which may reflect their culture and traditions more than their contemporary needs, given the persistence of organizational norms and the perturbations of organizational needs. In the end an organization is likely to create its leaders, and to create them in its own image and likeness, whether they are effective or not.

2. LEADERSHIP MYTHS

The myth of command
The most constant and most active threat to the liberty of any people, whether in a despotic tyranny or in some sort of democracy, is the police. For the public, control of the police is more important than police effectiveness. One of the functions of the military veneer of the police is to create the impression among the public that individual police are under the effective control of superiors (Bittner, 1990).

Whether or not top police leaders would like to believe that they are in effective command of their organizations, they do not directly control the behaviour of those whom they officially command. Senior police officers are essentially bureaucrats, and it is as bureaucrats that they exercise leadership. They create the policies, set the priorities, assign the personnel, and allocate the resources to favour particular outcomes. To the extent that subordinates concur, those outcomes may occur. If subordinates do not concur, there are usually too many layers of command and too little direct supervision of police encounters for superiors to make a difference (see Reuss-Ianni, 1983).

Within a quasi-military organization, subordinates can make or break their superiors. The myth of command attributes outcomes primarily to the superior. Subordinates know this, and can use this knowledge to destroy or save the leader. Similarly, higher ranking superiors can terminate the career of a junior superior by putting the person in command of a unit with unskilled or reckless people operating on the edge of disaster. Or they can advance the career of a junior superior, however untalented, by putting the person in command of a unit of highly skilled and motivated people working in a tranquil area.

The myth of responsibility
The myth of responsibility confuses the authority of the leader with the power that achieves results, and fails to acknowledge that the power of a work group resides in the group.

Moreover, it fails to recognize that at least in the US police experience, the person who is officially in the leadership role may lack the professional experience to be an effective commander, having been promoted for other reasons.

Front-line operations can backfire or result in backlashes, destroying the careers of potential risers. Hence, it is not surprising that in a large police force the way to the top is through staff and support units, not through front-line operations. Thus, one sometimes finds that those who have become the leaders of the leaders are the least likely to be able to lead. The Mollen Commission investigating widespread corruption in the New York Police Department in the 1990s asked the Commissioner, who had been a member of the Department for over 30 years, whether he was aware of the widespread corruption. He answered that he was not, because very little of his career had been spent in the field.

For top-ranking officers like this one, sometimes experience on patrol or in investigations may be measured in weeks, even when time on the job is measured in decades.

The Two Cultures of Policing: Street Cops vs. Management Cops (Reuss-Ianni, 1983) was a report of an intensive study of the New York Police Department by sociologists Elizabeth Reuss and Robert Ianni. They found that superiors and police officers were barely in touch with one another except through formal, hardly understood and mostly ignored official communications. Street cops and management cops follow separate career paths, have different constituencies, have different attitudes, and practise different versions of police work. Officially it is clear who the leaders are. But in practice it is unclear where the leadership comes from, if there is any.

Police leadership in paramilitary operations

When large numbers of police respond to a situation, the result is often what some police call 'a circus.' (The analogy is misplaced, but we shall let it stand.) Individuals or sometimes pairs of police officers compete to handle the situation, unco-ordinated with one another and often working at cross-purposes. Police are trained to think and act mostly as individuals, not as a co-ordinated group. When brought together in large numbers for some special operation, they still act as individuals.

Bittner (1990) has noted that police are at their poorest when called upon to perform paramilitary operations. Most of the time tactical suggestions come from random individuals, not from superiors, although it is customary to get approval from a superior, e.g., 'Mike and I will go around to the back, okay, Sarge?' The sergeant nods approval. Superior officers on the scene provide a veneer of authority, but in practice individual police officers decide what to do.

The organization may sustain the myth of command by holding high-ranking operational persons responsible when bad things happen. But in large police forces, the mid-ranking people running front-line operations are in the risky spots, while the top-ranking people enjoy the safety of staff and support assignments. In a more logical world the staff and support units would be in the hands of mid-rank people (if not civilians) and the people commanding field operations would have the high ranks. The Assistant Chiefs would be commanding police stations while the superintendents or captains would be running personnel, budgeting and administration.

Leaders lead most successfully when they are urging subordinates to do what subordinates want to do anyway. One is reminded of the anecdote about Gandhi breaking off an interview with reporters by pointing to a marching crowd of demonstrators and explaining, 'I have to go and catch up with them. I am supposed to be their leader.' A leader who is able to grasp what people want or need and hold it up to them more clearly than they could see it for themselves is often characterized as a charismatic leader. Unfortunately, this is the kind of leader as likely to unleash evil as good. The most popular police superiors in US police folklore have been those who, according to the old timers, 'took the handcuffs off us' or 'unleashed us' (see Bratton, 1998).

If that is not enough, for a dubious enterprise in military or quasi-military organizations it is convenient to call for volunteers. In a large enough organization, which recruits from a broad spectrum based on minimum qualifications, it is not difficult to find some volunteers, especially if there are added inducements. The leadership role in these operations is to stay out of the way and to block others from snooping or getting in the way.

The old adage is that authority can be delegated but not responsibility. This is a maxim with no logical substance or empirical demonstration. In a military type of organization all authority flows downwards from the top. But responsibility nearly always gets stuck in the middle, at the level of precinct command rather than at the top.

Take, for example, the issue of police corruption. The Knapp Commission, to which we have already referred, discovered systematic and pervasive corruption in the New York Police Department. Under the logic of the myth of command, it would be sensible, whenever corruption is discovered, both to hold the relevant precinct commanders to account, and to put in new men or women to replace them and root out the problem.

In reality, after the Knapp Commission most of the time the precinct commanding officer knows nothing of corruption, because those involved take special care to keep the commanding officer unaware of it. After the commanding officer is removed, bringing in a new person as commanding officer means assigning a stranger to run the precinct who will barely understand anything in the precinct for the first year, thus allowing the corruption to revive more easily. But the myths of command and responsibility allow no other course of action. A new leader will be seen as a solution to the problem.

The doctrine of responsibility, and the recent example of its application, supposedly will make the new leader more diligent. In practice, when an organization assigns its best leaders to its most troublesome units it engages in systematic destruction of its best leaders. The problem situations are seldom controlled by the superior. The problems are rooted in the unit's history, personnel, customs and circumstances beyond the reach of a newly appointed superior stranger.

Disciplinary systems

In the police civil service systems of the US individuals are brought before hearing boards which, like the military, uphold the myths of the organization. But once the hearings and appeals inside the system have been completed, the individual defendant may appeal to an outside civil court. There, the rules change. Civil courts have not accepted the myths of leadership and responsibility. They tend to find that things may happen due to the actions of several people, and due to uncontrollable factors. They nearly always find that the police organization was unrealistic and overly severe in punishing superiors for actions they did not personally do, and the courts routinely overturn agency decisions in these cases. That is why police departments prefer to punish mid-level superiors without due process by blocking any further career advancement or by transferring them to punitive assignments rather than bringing any charges of negligence against them. Again, the career hazards of operational commands make it prudent for any aspiring officer to get transferred to a staff or support unit and rise from there.

Zero defects

Underlying the myths of leadership and responsibility in military and quasi-military organizations is the myth that these are zero defect organizations, perfect and without fault. Failures are not due to any problem in the organization itself. They are due to failure of individuals to do their duty and carry out the orders and policies of the organization. Although the FBI provides the extreme example of the zero defect myth in law enforcement, it is commonplace in police organizations.

The need for secrecy

The myth of the zero defect organization is one of the bulwarks of secrecy. Although secrecy is sometimes essential to successful operations, it is just as essential for maintaining the self-image of the organization as a zero defect entity. When corruption or an embarrassing incident poses dangers to the image of a military or quasi-military organization, it is not unusual to transfer involved individuals to thwart investigations or to accept resignations rather than pursue investigations. When investigations and reports are completed they are commonly classified as secret or confidential to protect the image of the organization.

Police superiors sometimes bemoan the 'blue wall of secrecy' surrounding subordinates. They realize that the code of secrecy is not a bond of friendship but a bond of mutual blackmail and intimidation (Westley, 1970). Yet superiors maintain the same code of secrecy at their own level, purportedly for the sake of the organization. They believe that secrecy about organizational defects is essential for effectiveness, so the secrecy itself acquires mythic status. The myth is that secrecy in just about everything is essential for the organization to achieve its mission. The myth does not acknowledge that a major function of secrecy is to conceal the organization's failures. The myth of secrecy unwittingly serves the myth of the zero defect organization.

3. LEADERSHIP REALITIES

Bureaucrats and entrepreneurs

Police organizations are a mixture of bureaucracy and entrepreneurship. This curious mixture is found even among recruits. Some recruits view the police job as a steady source of employment, at good wages, with excellent fringe benefits and pension. They believe that the main requirements of the job are fitting in, following procedures, and staying out of trouble. Many recruits of this type come from families already anchored in police or other civil service jobs. They know that the movie images of police are not true; and they see police as people who are not going to change the world. They begin with the cynicism which others acquire later.

In contrast, coming largely from non-civil service families, are the recruits who view police work as a mission and start out thinking that they will change the world. These people start off knowing less of the police organization, and have a greater estimate of what an individual police officer can and should accomplish.

Once ensconced within police work the bureaucrats do what is expected of them by superiors and peers, move towards assignments in low-profile units and areas, and do good police work, however routine (see Van Maanen, 1974). Muir (1977) has developed the theme that a police officer is a street corner politician, in the form of a mobile bureaucrat who takes reports and carries out certain routine governmental tasks in routine ways. For the bureaucratic police officer leadership comes from the bureaucratic system itself. The leaders, in the sense of those who decide what is to be done and how it is to be done, are the 'system leaders' who created the bureaucratic protocols, regardless of their rank, and regardless of whether they are still alive or long dead. Current appointed superiors of higher rank in the chain of command oversee the routine operations and paperwork, and highlight current emphases. Some bureaucratic police officers seek and achieve promotions within the hierarchy, moving from being the doers to being the overseers in the system. They are the rock-solid foundation of police organizations.

The entrepreneurs, on the other hand, are the ornaments of police organizations. They thrive in the streets, investigations or high-profile special operations. To them, police work is a chance to do things as an individual or small team player. Traditional police work is structured to be entrepreneurial. Traditionally, most investigators are assigned their own cases and given considerable freedom to go about the task in their own way. Uniformed police are assigned to beats or areas, the way sales people are, and are given considerable freedom to patrol and manage their beats in their own way. Unlike the military, there is usually no supervisor present when the assignment is being carried out. In training, police are drilled to assess situations, make decisions and take action as individuals. If they need and request assistance, it will come later. But most of the time the individual police officer must initiate some action immediately. It is in this sense, that police are ordinarily assigned tasks or work areas and mandated to handle them as individuals in whatever ways they deem appropriate, that police are entrepreneurs.

Customary work practices

No standard procedure or general mandate can provide specific instructions for any situation, no matter how novel and unpredictable. In fact, where it comes to practical advice for action, the procedural guide will at the crucial point simply advocate: 'Take appropriate action'.

In reality, however, police officers usually do know in advance how they will handle situations. They have customary ways of doing things. The customs are learned from one another and passed on from one generation to the next. Many of them are effective shortcuts. For example, in the case of a young teenager found in possession of an illegal knife, the custom may be to confiscate the knife and warn the teenager not to carry a knife like that again, with no record of the event whatsoever. In the case of a fight between a small number of drunken fans a few hours after a football match, the custom might be to send them their separate ways, again with no record of the event having occurred. These are work norms which police officers learn from one another. It would puzzle other police officers and might annoy superiors if these norms were not followed in ordinary circumstances.

The customary ways of doing police work cannot always be written down, because often they are difficult to explain logically, and sometimes they are difficult to justify legally or morally. For example, in disorderly situations police officers are encouraged by custom and sometimes by the instructions of trainers to take a 'forceful' approach to establishing their control over the situation. The approach may include, among other things, vigorously barking orders to people who may or may not have committed an offence; yelling at people to 'shut up' if they try to explain what happened, at least until some order has been established; brusquely ordering some people to move along, even if such an order has no legal foundation; or arresting people even if it is not clear why.

In ambiguous situations that involve no clear physical danger, the rule of thumb may be to take the person to the police station and sort out the matter there. If it is an ambiguous situation which appears to present an imminent risk of serious physical harm to a police officer, the rule of thumb may be to shoot first and figure it out later. These sorts of operational directives cannot be put in writing. But some of them may be inculcated in training, and all of them may be well established in the customs of a particular police force or unit. In short, police officers rely on local custom for guidance in doing their work, which is taught mostly by peers.

Peer and informal leadership

To the extent that a police officer's actions are determined by someone else, they follow the leadership of peers more than the leadership of superiors. It is from peers that police officers learn the practical lessons of what to do in various situations. Peers preserve, teach, and often enforce the customary and expected practices of police work. Superiors may be more or less aware of how police officers operate in practice, but often they are constrained from acknowledging this.

For example, a study of deception tactics in police work in the UK and the US found that varying but substantial numbers of police officers, and superiors as well, are in favour of such tactics as committing perjury to gain convictions and planting evidence on drug suspects to facilitate arrests (Panzarella and Funk, 1988). This may be expected behaviour in some police units, and failure to perform as expected may be punished informally by the group, or even by superiors. In this sense, leadership emanates from the work group, whether for good or for bad as with any type of leadership. This reality of leadership coming from peers has been encapsulated in such phrases as 'collaborative leadership' (Seifter and Economy, 2001) and 'side by side leadership' (Romig, 2001).

In a leadership contest between appointed superiors and peers, in police work peers generally win. The best laid plans of superiors are readily thwarted by disgruntled subordinates. In police forces, as in other bureaucratic organizations, the subordinates' ultimate weapon is the organization's own procedures. Subordinates seldom resort to the ultimate weapon except under circumstances related to their personal interests, e.g. long-stalled contract negotiations. Then a 'by the book' mode of operation is put into practice; all personnel follow all official procedures precisely and only as required in printed operational directives.

This 'job action' is virtually guaranteed to bring a bureaucratic organization to its knees, for the rules and procedures of bureaucratic organizations are not geared to make the organization effective. They are geared primarily to pinpointing responsibility and protecting the organization itself from liability. They deliberately sacrifice efficiency and effectiveness to blunt liability. Moreover, they rarely wipe outmoded rules or procedures off the books, counting instead on the prudence of personnel not to enforce what is no longer useful. The anecdotal literature of policing, especially its humorous chapters, is replete with victories of subordinates over superiors through officially required conduct (see Baker, 1985, *passim*).

Police unions may exercise more actual leadership than appointed superiors. Their leadership is visible and powerful in personnel matters, but they often play a major role in operational matters as well. Sometimes operational standards or tactics become embodied in contracts, which superiors are not free to ignore. In addition, unions act as the guardians of custom. When there is an overt contest between the police administration and a union, nearly all police officers do as told by their union. The informal disciplinary power of a union is far more certain and awesome than the formal disciplinary power of a police administration.

The worst that a police administration can do is try to take away someone's job and pension, in which case the union will step to the defence of the person if the person has been loyal to peers. The peer group can ostracize an individual, fail to assist in a dangerous situation, and pressure an individual into resignation more forcefully than management. If actual leadership is determined by who is calling the shots, the police union is a constant and powerful leader, and experienced superiors know that they can be most effective by working through the union.

Officially appointed leaders may also work through other natural or informal leaders, with expertise relevant to the situation in hand. Here, the function of the leader is to lead the leaders in a system which has been described as *The New SuperLeadership* (Manz and Sims, 2001).

Police organizations may try to pick out the informal leaders and make them the appointed leaders. However, there are obstacles to this, and special steps must be taken to transform informal leaders into appointed leaders. One obstacle, especially in UK police forces, is that promotion to superior officer ranks depends so much on written civil service exams. In these personnel systems the individual's leadership traits are not considered. Another obstacle, perhaps more marked in UK police forces which have more freedom in choosing individuals to be promoted, is that informal leaders may be too non-conformist. Being non-conformist may be part of their charisma as informal leaders. Non-conformity is a highly desirable trait in some organizations, especially in organizations in crisis and new organizations still seeking a direction. Interviews with about 80,000 executives about what makes an effective leader found that the single most signal rule for an effective leader is *First, break all the rules*, which became the title of the study by Buckingham and Coffman (2001).

However, police organizations tend to be old and not much inclined to pass the reins to people who break all the rules. They also need to preserve an appearance of maintaining tight control over the actions of subordinates. They are looking for a kind of leader who follows the rules, and will prompt subordinates to do the same.

The police officer as a leader

One might ask whether the individual police officer might be called a leader in some meaningful way. The fact that individual police officers make significant decisions on their own was not acknowledged by police administrators until well into the 1970s. The older texts on police administration maintained that there is no such thing as 'police discretion.' They stated that police officers do not make the law, but only enforce it. The early discussions of police discretion were shortened by the realization that there was no legal basis for an individual police officer, or even a chief of police, to suspend a law made by the legislators. Attempts to say that laws permitted but did not require police to act in criminal situations sputtered to an end. Denial of police discretion was the easiest way out. But increasing empirical data from social scientists looking at the police, particularly the extensive observational study of the police sponsored by the American Bar Association (1973), made continued denial impossible.

At that point, police administrators began to argue that police discretion was a practical necessity, regardless of legal or theoretical questions. The acknowledgment of discretion conferred upon the individual police officer the authority and duty to take command of situations in ways which went beyond the apparent meaning of existing laws, policies and procedures. To the extent that an individual police officer takes initiative and determines how a situation will be handled, the individual exercises some of the qualities of leadership.

One might speak of an individual police officer as a leader if the officer is trying to influence the behaviour of citizens in a non-coercive context. The ideology of 'community-based policing' redefines the role of the individual police officer to include efforts at leading citizens or members of other agencies in projects aimed at reducing crime and disorder.

The more specific ideology of 'problem-solving policing' (Goldstein, 1990) encourages police officers to take the lead in a broad range of social problem solving, although the qualifications of typical police officers for problem solving may be questionable and thus the kind of leadership they might exercise needs to be defined at some point.

Overall, there are many situations in which individual police officers may be considered leaders in the broad traditional sense of exercising initiative and directing the actions of others. In addressing the leadership role of the individual police officer, one could repeat most of what has been said already about the myths and realities of leadership.

4. ALTERNATIVE MODELS FOR POLICE WORK AND LEADERSHIP

Movements within policing such as community-based policing or problem-oriented police work raise the question of whether the quasi-military, bureaucratic model which has been applied to police work for nearly 200 years is still the appropriate model.

A contrasting model would be the professional work model. The professional model assumes that expertise lies in the hands of individual practitioners. Administrators manage only by co-ordinating support operations, not by telling the professionals how to do their work, nor by directly supervising them.

Attempts to apply the professional model to police work go back to before the 1920s (Fogelson, 1977). However, only the most tangential and questionable aspects of professionalism have been applied to the police, particularly the idea that actions by members of the occupation should be judged only by other members of the occupation, and not from outside.

The notion of specialization within the occupation has been disembowelled by the persistence of the belief that all members of a uniformed service should be interchangeable; and a general contempt for expertise. People are assigned to specialized tasks on very subjective grounds and it is assumed, in traditional military fashion, that people will quickly acquire through personal experience and association with more experienced personnel any skills necessary for the tasks to which they have been assigned by superiors.

Although general education requirements for police officers have risen over the decades, they have trailed behind the education level of the general population. The expertise which might be expected of a 'police science' has not materialized to the minimal degree necessary for a profession; at the university level the few existing programmes in 'police science' have been recasting themselves as 'police studies.' Perhaps most important, the public may not be willing to let individual police officers operate with the amount of discretion characteristic of professionals.

As police organizations evolve they may become more complex. A single model may not be applicable to the entire organization. Civilianization of some jobs, high and low, within the police organization forces some departures from the quasi-military model. It may be that certain aspects of police work require one model, such as professionalism, and other aspects of police work require a different model, such as the quasi-military model.

A professional model is more effective when work is ill-defined, people work alone, and oversight is difficult. A bureaucratic model works best when the organization is large, tasks are predictable, uniformity in work methods is required, records are essential and subordinates are more dutiful than creative. The quasi-military model with its emphasis on leadership may be more apt when there are few layers of command, unpredictable tasks, diversity in operations, skilled and active supervisors, minimally competent personnel, and a crisis or a great cause.

CONCLUSION

Despite the gulf between organizational myths and realities, the quasi-military model of the police with emphasis on leadership is likely to persist. However, the changing nature of police work will require police organizations to change as the military itself has changed. The quasi-military model of the police is outmoded even as a military model. The contemporary military may provide a more apt model for reinventing the police. In the area of direction, indirect leadership through systems planning has to be acknowledged as well as the direct leadership exercised by one individual upon another. Among leaders, the informal or natural leaders must be both acknowledged and utilized. The appointed formal leaders need to be freed from the myths of arbitrary responsibility and zero-defect organizations so that realistic responsibility can be practised and police organizations can improve. If leadership is to have a meaning today, it must mean a multiplicity of leaders, openness in the organization, and leadership erupting in the middle and at the bottom of the organization as well as at the top.

REFERENCES for *Chapter 8*

American Bar Association (1973), *The Urban Police Function,* Chicago: The American Bar Association.
Baker, M (1985), *Cops: Their Lives in Their Own Words,* New York: Pocket Books.

Bass, B (1990), *Bass and Stogdill's Handbook of Leadership: Theory, Research and Managerial Applications*, New York: Free Press.

Berkley, G (1971), *The Administrative Revolution: Notes on the Passing of Organization Man*, Englewood Cliffs, NJ: Prentice-Hall.

Bittner, E (1990), *Aspects of Police Work*, Boston: Northeastern University Press.

Blake, R and Mouton, J (1964), *The Managerial Grid*, Houston: Gulf Publishing Co.

Blanchard, D et al. (1982), *The One Minute Manager*, New York: William Morrow and Co.

Bratton, W (1998), *Turnaround: How America's Top Cop Reversed the Crime Epidemic*, New York: Random House.

Bryman, A (1993), 'Charismatic Leadership in Business Organizations: Some Neglected Issues', *The Leadership Quarterly*, 4, 289-304.

Buckingham, M and Coffman, C (2001), *First, Break All the Rules*, New York: Simon and Schuster.

Drucker, P (1966), *The Effective Executive*, New York: Harper and Row.

Fiedler, F (1966), *A Theory of Leadership Effectiveness*, New York: McGraw-Hill.

Fiedler, F (1965), 'Engineer the Job to Fit the Manager', *Harvard Business Review*, 43 (5), 115-122.

Fogelson, R (1977), *Big-city Police*, Cambridge, MA: Harvard University Press.

Fox, J (1998), *How to Become CEO*, New York: Hyperion.

Goldstein, H (1990), *Problem-oriented Policing*, New York: McGraw-Hill.

Hobsbawm, E (1968), *Industry and Empire*, Harmondsworth: Penguin Books.

Hutchison, S, Valentino, K and Kirkner, S (1998), 'What Works for the Gander Does Not Work as Well for the Goose: The Effects of Leader Behavior', *Journal of Applied Social Psychology*, 28, 171-182.

Jenkins, W (1947), 'A Review of Leadership Studies with Particular Reference to Military Problems', *Journal of Educational Psychology*, 44, 54-79.

Johnson, D (1981), *American Law Enforcement: A History*, St. Louis: Forum Press.

Jones, E and Gerard, H (1967), *Foundations of Social Psychology*, New York: John Wiley and Sons.

Likert, R (1961), *New Patterns of Management*, New York: McGraw-Hill.

Likert, R (1967), *The New Organization: Its Management and Value*, New York: McGraw-Hill.

Manz, C and Sims, H (2001), *The New Super Leadership: Leading Others to Lead Themselves*, New York: Bernett Koehler.

McGregor, D (1966), *Leadership and Motivation*, Cambridge, Mass.: MIT Press.

Moskos, C (1970), *The American Enlisted Man*, New York: Russell Sage Foundation.

Muir, W (1977), *Police: Street Corner Politicians*, Chicago: University of Chicago Press.

Owens, J (1973), 'The Art of Leadership', *Personnel Journal*, 52, 393.

Panzarella, R and Funk, J (1988), Deception Tactics in Policing in England and the United States, *Criminal Justice Policy Review*, 2(2), 133-149.

Peters, T and Waterman, T (1982), *In Search of Excellence: Lessons from America's Best Run Companies*, New York: Warner Books.

Reuss-Ianni, E (1983), *The Two Cultures of Policing: Street Cops vs. Management Cops*, New Brunswick, NJ: Transaction Books.

Romig, D (2001), *Side by Side Leadership*, Austin, Texas: Bard Press.

Sayles, L (1979), *Leadership: What Effective Managers Really Do and How They Do It*, New York: McGraw-Hill.

Seifter, H and Economy, P (2001), *Leadership Ensemble*, New York: Henry Holt.

Strock, J (2001), *Theodore Roosevelt on Leadership*, Roseville, CA: Forum Books.

Stogdill, R (1959), *Individual Behavior and Group Achievement*, New York: Oxford University Press.

Tannenbaum, R and Schmidt, W (1958), 'How to Choose a Leadership Pattern', *Harvard Business Review*, 36(2), 95-101.

Van Maanen, J (1974), 'Working the Streets: A Developmental View of Police Behavior' in Jacobs, H (Ed.), *Reality and Reform: The Criminal Justice System*, Beverly Hills: Sage.

Westley, W (1970), *Violence and the Police: A Sociological Study of Law, Custom and Morality*, Cambridge, Mass.: The Colonial Press.

CHAPTER 9

Three Types of Leadership

William C Heffernan

William C Heffernan is professor of Law, John Jay College of Criminal Justice and the Graduate Center, City University of New York.[1] He sets out to examine the contribution that policing can make in furthering the aims of a free and generally just social order. In doing so, he considers three styles of leadership—exemplary, reformist and counter-majoritarian, and concludes that police leadership needs on occasion to be capable of all three. He believes that even in a generally just society police leaders will be required to enforce specific laws that they consider morally unacceptable—an issue which John Alderson also debates in *Chapter 3* and Roger Scruton in *Chapter 6*, and of prime doctrinal significance he emphasises the importance of the proper application of discretion.

INTRODUCTION

'I would absolutely not take a job as a police chief,' John Diaz, an assistant police chief in Seattle, recently remarked during the course of an interview with a reporter for *The New York Times*. 'The politics of being a police chief have become so insane no one wants the job,' Diaz continued. 'I work an eleven-hour day, but our chief is here before me every day and doesn't leave until I'm gone, and all he gets is attacked in the media.'[2]

Diaz's claim that no one wants the job is clearly an exaggeration. Although neither he nor any other assistant chief in the Seattle Police Department applied for the top position after the city's chief resigned in the wake of rioting during the World Trade Organization meeting held in the city in fall 2000, others did. Unfortunately, the person selected, Gil Kerlikowske, formerly the police chief of Buffalo, New York, discovered quickly just how thankless the position can be. During the course of a Sunday afternoon jog not far from his downtown office, Chief Kerlikowske happened upon a woman lying on the street who, it was eventually established, had passed out as a result of a heroin overdose. While still in his jogging gear, the chief stopped to give her mouth-to-mouth resuscitation. When the woman began to breathe, he took her to the hospital. A short time later, once the nature of the woman's condition became clear, the chief had to return to the hospital, this time to get a hepatitis B shot for himself.

There is no reason to believe that Kerlikowske intervened to publicise himself or his department, but his good Samaritanism was nonetheless significant, if only as a reminder of the aid police officers frequently provide the vulnerable and destitute. Seattle's TV stations did indeed mention the rescue. However, they devoted only a few seconds to it. Their lead story was about a police chase of a stolen car that struck a pedestrian—and for this, they provided extensive footage, criticism of the police by eyewitnesses to the accident, and an interview with the accident victim. The lesson for Chief Kerlikowske was clear. It's nice to help someone in distress. But what really matters is avoiding bad publicity. Doing the right thing by people is at most a sideline in police work.

This is the dreary lesson many police leaders insist upon when talking to their subordinates. I shall not expand on it here, however. Rather, what is needed is an essay on what police leadership might be, an essay that combines structural analysis with the good heart that impelled Chief Kerlikowske to aid the woman who had passed out on the Seattle streets.

I begin by surveying the conceptual terrain. In these opening sections, I consider some definitional points about police leadership and also the distinction between leadership of police organizations in democratic and authoritarian societies. The remainder of the essay is devoted to an analysis of three types of leadership: exemplary, reform, and counter-majoritarian in democratic polities. My inventory of categories is not meant to be exhaustive. Other types of police leadership—crime fighting and crisis management for example—can readily be imagined. I have confined myself to the three just mentioned in part because, given my professional training, I am not confident I could make a meaningful contribution to discussion of other types of leadership, in part because the three I do consider are critical to an account of policing democratic societies. My concern, in other words, is with the contribution policing can make in furthering the aims of a free, generally just social order.

THE POSSIBILITY OF POLICE LEADERSHIP

At first sight, the term 'police leadership' may seem to be an oxymoron. Police officers, whatever their rank, are members of a bureaucracy, and bureaucracies, it could be argued, are defined by their members' adherence to rules imposed from the outside. On this account, police leadership is impossible. In conforming to their rules of office, this argument maintains, the police are not led; rather, they simply adhere to the law.

Appealing as it is because of its simplicity, there are a number of fundamental problems with this thesis. One has to do with the nature of leadership. Even if it were conceded that all police behaviour is rule-governed, an important role could be found for leadership with respect to the way in which the police behave. Officers can honour their rules of office in a surly, rude manner, but they can also be courteous and considerate.

Given the bias of academics in favour of analytically difficult questions, it is easy to dismiss this factor as unimportant. I don't. Just as the president of a college sets a standard for the proper treatment of its students, a police leader sets a standard for the way in which his or her subordinates should treat civilians.

But there are further difficulties with the oxymoron thesis, all related to the issue of police fidelity to the law. One difficulty has to do with the fact that police often violate—indeed, *knowingly and egregiously* violate—the law. Leadership is critical to ensure that they do not. I shall have a good deal more to say in a later section about the nature of this leadership. It is sufficient now, as we define the intellectual terrain, simply to note that police leaders are constantly confronted with the challenge of making sure that their officers adhere to the law.

And what about leadership in settings where the law *is* honoured? Here, too, the oxymoron thesis is unsatisfactory, for police officers aren't simply rule-followers. They also have discretion as to the meaning of rules and the way in which they should be enforced and because discretion is an inevitable feature of the police role, leadership is not only possible, but necessary, for the police. The term 'discretion' is sometimes used in a broad sense to refer to unpunished violations of authoritative legal rules. I shall avoid this usage here. My concern instead is with those instances in which the police can reasonably infer, in light of the rule of recognition within their legal system, that they are entitled to interpret the meaning of a term contained in a rule or that they may determine whether and how extensively to enforce a rule.

The opportunities for these different kinds of discretion are endless. Numerous rules contain ambiguous terms that have not been interpreted by courts. Think, for example, about an officer's decision as to how to classify a child riding a tricycle when a city ordinance prohibits vehicles in public parks. Moreover, there are many instances in which courts have signalled that they are willing to let the police determine whether to enforce non-criminal statutes (motor vehicle codes, for instance), and there are other instances in which the police can decide how much enforcement is appropriate for a given type of action (consider questions related to the protection of demonstrators outside buildings). Some of these examples raise discretionary issues appropriately resolved in on-the-spot decisions. All, however, are potentially open to resolution by police leaders. Indeed, in his influential *Discretionary Justice*,[3] Kenneth Culp Davis advances a strong argument for the value of publicly announced decisions by police commanders as to the way in which their officers will exercise discretion. This is not the place to evaluate the merits of Davis's position. It is enough to note that his entire line of reasoning underscores the possibility of police leadership arising out of the opportunities for discretion provided by a legal system.

LEADERS OF POLICE ORGANIZATIONS VERSUS POLICE LEADERS

One more point must be considered in defining the conceptual terrain. There are numerous leaders of police whom I (at least) would say exhibit no qualities of police leadership. The fictional Baron Scarpia of *Tosca* was the chief of Rome's police, but he was not a police leader in the sense I am using the term. The all-too-real Heinrich Himmler and Lavrenti Beria were leaders of national police forces (Himmler of the Nazi SS and Beria of the Soviet Union's NKVD, subsequently known as the KGB), but they too do not qualify as police leaders on my analysis.

What is the identifying criterion of police leadership, then? As I use the term, a police leader is someone who (1) holds a high-ranking position in a police organization that operates in a generally just society and (2) seeks to use his or her discretionary powers to further the just aims of that society. Needless to say, there will be disagreement about when a society is generally just. The examples just provided demonstrate, however, that the concept is not infinitely contestable. Nazi Germany was committed to monstrous social injustice; the Stalinist Soviet Union comes off slightly better on this score. Any official who abetted the aims of these regimes that rounded up Jews on behalf of the SS, or prevented starving peasants from leaving their collective farms in the USSR, cannot possibly be considered a police leader in the normative sense that I am using the term. Leadership, as I understand it, promotes human welfare. It may result in a setback to the welfare of some (a setback that can include death), but this setback is justified only when it occurs in the context of a political regime that, on balance, promotes justice.

What, then, can be said about police organizations that operate in generally just societies where the police are legally required to carry out monstrously unjust acts? In my opinion, genuinely difficult cases are possible in such a setting. Because I shall *not* assume in the remainder of this essay that the police leaders I am discussing are legally required to carry out specific unjust acts, let me pause for a moment to consider the dilemmas that arise when the law does impose such obligations on them. Think, for example, about the difficulties that confronted police officers in northern cities of the United States when they were called upon to locate and render up, as per the terms of the Fugitive Slave Act of 1850, African-Americans who had fled from their southern slave masters. It is reasonable to assume that, apart from slavery and its treatment of native Americans, the United States of the mid-nineteenth century was a generally just society *for the majority of its residents*. It clearly was not, however, for African-Americans. Even those who were not slaves were ineligible for American citizenship; or so the Supreme Court held in *Dred Scott v. Sandford.*[4] And slaves lived under legal rules wholly inconsistent with the statements about human equality contained in the Declaration of Independence.

What options were open to a northern police chief of the 1850s when confronted with an order requiring the return of a fugitive slave? Three responses to this dilemma are worth considering. One possibility was to adhere to the law. Believing American society to be generally just, the chief might have concluded that the order should be executed. To fail to follow the legal obligations *he* views as unjust, the police chief might have said to himself, would encourage others (southerners, for example) to refuse to follow the obligations *they* view as unjust, thus jeopardising the security of a generally just society. Indeed, in adopting this line of reasoning, the chief might conclude that adhering to the obligation could have the effect of spurring northern public opinion into an even greater frenzy about slavery and so hasten its end. Second, a chief could have resigned and in doing so he could have stated publicly that his motive was to avoid enforcing the law. Resignation would not prevent the law's ultimate enforcement. Someone else would surely be found to do the job. But it would have found ways to ensure that the African-American in question was able to escape, thus frustrating the law while pretending to honour it.

I have no problem with either of the first two options. The second seems particularly attractive to me; it is the bureaucrat's equivalent of civil disobedience. However, the first option may actually do more to shape opinion, for enforcement of a patently unjust law in a generally just society can spur the public to consider change. In this instance, there is no doubt that questions about enforcement of the law not only influenced public opinion about the Fugitive

Slave Act but also about slavery itself. As the Boston textile magnet Amos Lawrence remarked after witnessing the scene in his city while federal marshals led a fugitive slave back to bondage, 'We went to bed one night old fashioned, conservative, compromise Union Whigs and waked up stark mad Abolitionists.'[5]

The third option is more problematic. It bears some resemblance to jury nullification in that a government official sworn to uphold the law frustrates a specific law while continuing publicly to champion the rule of law. But it is likely to be even less effective than jury nullification, which itself is usually haphazard in its effect, for the simple reason that stronger forces can be ordered by higher authorities on subsequent occasions to make sure that an odious law actually is enforced. Moreover, the third option blurs the central issue of injustice. It is certainly tempting, however, and this third option is likely to be particularly attractive in instances where the police are called upon *to* enforce laws that do not involve outrageous injustice. What this discussion makes clear, then, is that even in a generally just society, there will be occasions when leaders will be required to enforce specific laws they consider morally unacceptable.

EXEMPLARY LEADERSHIP

Let us now banish the moral cloud of unjust laws in generally just societies. This cloud can appear at any time and must be taken seriously indeed, but there are other issues of leadership that merit attention, and these are best addressed without having to consider the complications just mentioned. In thinking about what police leaders who accept the aims of a generally just society can do to further those aims, it is best to begin with leadership by example with the way in which a police executive demonstrates by means of his or her own conduct to those in the department how they should comport themselves.

Leadership by example matters in any organization. An executive who places personal interests ahead of the organization's takes a substantial step toward demoralising subordinates. But while this much is true across the board, there are three reasons why exemplary leadership is particularly important in a police bureaucracy. One has to do with the rule of law. Much as discretion matters in policing, there are many areas in which the law is sufficiently clear that the police must adhere to it. A leader who violates clear mandates of law or who even tests discretionary ones by interpreting ambiguous rules in his or her own self-interest helps to undermine subordinates' commitment to the rule of law.

Second, exemplary leadership matters because some police officers are routinely called upon to engage in acts of courage while all officers must live with the knowledge that they may, at some point in their careers, be called on to act courageously. In the former category, one would have to place members of a bomb squad or a hostage negotiation team. Elite units such as these tend to develop an *esprit de corps* of their own. But the strength of this spirit in turn often depends on the way in which department leaders comport themselves. These leaders must of course show respect for acts of courage. But they must also display courage within the bureaucracy that complements that of their squad members. As for the latter category, of which patrol officers are the best example, it must never be forgotten that routine police work can suddenly, and unexpectedly, require acts of great courage. On being summoned to a family quarrel, a patrol officer may witness an explosion of rage that places the officer in danger as well as others in the room. On stopping a car missing a headlight, an officer may find, on walking up to the driver's window, that someone has a gun pointed right at his or her head. Exemplary leadership establishes the context in which street officers accept the risks associated with encounters that can lead into the unknown.

Third, exemplary leadership can set the stage for courteous relationships between the police and the public. In a generally just society, the key to social order must lie in most citizens' willingness to refrain from self-interested violations of the law. The majority of citizens in a generally just society thus do not require repressive police measures. Rather, their encounters with the police will involve problems of co-ordination (making sure that traffic lanes are maintained, for example) and service (providing information to pedestrians and drivers, locating stray pets, and so on). A central, though often overlooked, question about policing in a free society is this: do the police perform these functions in a courteous manner in a manner that emphasises their role as public servants? Confining my observations to the police force I know best, the New York City Police, my answer to this is 'Sometimes'. I hope my answer errs on the side of pessimism; I hope that observers in other cities can deliver more positive reports about their police officers. To the extent I am right, though, there is surely a good deal of work to be done by exemplary police leaders. Good leaders will show by their example that the police need not be insular and suspicious, that they can instead be open and friendly. New York City Police Commissioners have been almost uniformly dour and unforthcoming in their remarks to the public; it is small wonder, then, that patrol officers are officious and often downright rude in their dealings with everyday New Yorkers.

How is exemplary leadership possible? What kind of bearing should a police executive have if he or she is to inspire subordinates to be law-abiding, courageous, and courteous? There are as many possibilities here as there are different types of human personality. One example, drawn from military rather than police history, will perhaps help to illustrate how someone can lead by example. Although plagued, at least to a degree, by alcoholism throughout his tenure in the Union army, Ulysses Grant was not only a formidable strategist but also an inspiring leader of troops.

According to Charles Dana, an observer sent by Secretary of War Edwin Stanton to report on Grant's unexpected victories in the Mississippi Valley at a time Union armies were being defeated in Virginia, the soldiers appreciated Grant's lack of 'superfluous flummery', his tendency to wear a plain uniform 'without scarf, sword, or trappings of any sort save the double-starred shoulder straps.' Grant, Dana asserted, was not a 'great man except morally, not an original or brilliant man, but sincere, thoughtful, deep and gifted with a courage that never faltered.'[6]

Grant, it should be noted, displayed these traits in a way that his subordinates found attractive and accessible. A private in Grant's army stated that the men 'seem to look upon him as a friendly partner of theirs, not as an arbitrary commander.'[7] Rather than cheer as Grant rode by, his soldiers would usually 'greet him as they would address one of their neighbours at home. '

"Good morning, General", "Pleasant day, General," and like expressions are the greetings he meets everywhere ... There was no nonsense, no sentiment; only a plain businessman of the republic, there for the one single purpose of getting that command over the river in the shortest possible time.'[8]

There is no formula for producing 'thoughtful, deep and gifted' leadership that simultaneously inspires subordinates to act while remaining accessible to them. It is not even clear that people possessing such traits are randomly distributed among eras and countries; it may be that certain cultural factors—a particular concern for the cultivation of virtue, for example—must be present for such traits to emerge in young men and women. I can thus suggest only that those charged with selecting leaders should try to identify these traits. What can be expressed in more formulaic terms are the rules organizations should impose on their leaders. The first rule is that police organizations should (and, as far as I can tell, largely do) operate on the basis of a strong presumption of promotion from below. By recruiting through the ranks, police organizations provide incentives to younger officers, solidify morale and ensure that executives have experiences in common with line staff.

Standing alone, though, this rule is hardly sufficient to ensure strong leadership, for police executives promoted from below can all too easily forget their early days. There are many factors that can induce this type of moral amnesia: frequent contact with elite members of the community, a desk-bound work schedule, the development of a technocratic world-view, and, in particular, the sweet perquisites of office. Taken together, these can cause *nomenklatura syndrome,* a disorder that has the potential to afflict leaders of all organizations, in particular those who have risen from below. In the Soviet Union (where the term *nomenklatura* was first used), it was a mark in someone's favour that he hailed from the working classes. But working class origins often blended poorly with the special privileges available to the party elite. The result was a *nomenklatura* that was resented not simply for its unequal access to primary goods but also for the hypocrisy with which it defended its special position. A similar threat of hypocrisy is possible among police executives.

Our second rule for police organizations is designed to counter this syndrome: in selecting people for promotion, organizations must consider carefully whether someone's prior career indicates that the person will inspire subordinates to act as police officers should. Some cautionary words are needed about this rule. I am not suggesting that the value on which it is based is the only one that should be taken into account when promotion is at stake; analytic intelligence is certainly important as well. Nor am I suggesting, even when intellectual issues are set to one side, that leadership potential can be gleaned simply from an officer's performance in a subordinate position. Rather, I am arguing the rather obvious point that past performance is the best indication available of the likelihood of future achievement. I am also maintaining that high quality past performance can serve as an example to officers as to how they should conduct themselves while still in subordinate roles. And finally, I am maintaining that the logocentric civil service perspective should be revised to ensure that exemplary conduct is considered as well as intellectual ability. In particular, leadership positions should be limited to those who have served in line positions, faced the hardships typical of those positions, and performed well when confronted with those hardships.

This approach can be made concrete only by focusing far more carefully than most police departments now do on the quality of service an officer has rendered while serving in line positions. During their first two to three years of service, officers should be rotated out of different line positions on an annual basis, thus providing them with opportunities to serve in various capacities for their departments. Their superiors should carefully evaluate officers' performance in these positions, and these evaluations should receive substantial weight in promotion decisions. Frequent rotation of officers will reduce the likelihood that friendship and favouritism between subordinates and superiors will influence evaluations undertaken by the latter.

And how is *nomenklatura* syndrome to be prevented among those who have already been promoted? A third rule is needed here: police executives, we may hold, should have access to special perquisites only to the extent these are necessary to further the public interests their agencies are charged with pursuing. This rule does not prohibit limousines, secretaries, carpeted office floors, special cell phones, and so on. Rather, it enjoins the use of these and other special advantages of office in settings where they don't further the organization's legitimate aims. It thus prohibits *expensive* limousines and prohibits completely the use of a limousine for personal business. It prohibits luxurious carpeting and office furniture—and so gives no heed to the argument that a fancy office is necessary if a police executive is to mingle on equal terms with other members of the community's elite. Given the ubiquity of personal computers and laptops, the rule also alerts to the problem of redundancy associated multiple secretaries: one is usually enough to keep track of appointments and print the documents the boss has generated by typing on his or her own computer. It may sound as if the 'no unnecessary perquisites' rule is one that Cincinnatus would devise for modern police forces. I would accept that characterisation were someone to offer it. Cincinnatus embodies the simplicity, self-discipline, and exemplary leadership that propelled the Roman Republic to greatness. Police leaders who adopt this manner will earn the respect of the public at large and also their own subordinates.

But how is this rule of Cincinnatus to be administered? I see no way in which it can be imposed from above; after all, police leaders are the 'above' in a law enforcement organization. I of course hope that the politically accountable officials who appoint police chiefs will take it seriously. But although mayors and governors will almost surely derive political benefit from police chiefs known for their republican simplicity, it seems unlikely that politicians will make this a high priority in the selection process. The rule of Cincinnatus thus must be *self*-imposed. Moreover, only if police leaders *do* adopt it for themselves is it also likely that the leaders will adopt an approach that emphasises character among line officers.

Is everything I've advocated with respect to exemplary leadership unlikely to be achieved, then? I think not. The story about Chief Kerlikowske's rescue effort for a woman who had fainted on a Seattle sidewalk reminds us that many chiefs already practise what I am advocating. If I am right about this and right as well in assuming that exemplary leadership is likely to increase public satisfaction with the police, then it seems reasonable to assume that more and more police chiefs will adopt this strategy on their own as a sound way to do business. In this case, the right thing to do is also the one that is politically wise.

REFORM LEADERSHIP

Exemplary leadership is needed at all times. I turn now to leadership styles suited to particular problems—first to the leadership appropriate for a department demoralised by allegations of corruption and brutality, then to the style appropriate for police violations of civil rights. The former style I call 'reform leadership', the latter 'counter-majoritarian leadership'.

It is not entirely clear why reform leadership is of perennial importance in policing. Other government agencies are routinely beset by charges of corruption—think, for example, about the frequency with which building inspectors are alleged to take bribes. Charges of brutality are also lodged against officials other than the police—against prison officers, for example. In trying to identify why reform leadership has mattered so much in policing, we must consider the confluence of many different factors. Many agencies have to take one or two of these factors into account. Only the police have to consider all of them.

One factor has to do with the freelance nature of police work. Like building inspectors, police officers operate on their own, acting beyond the gaze of their superiors. The opportunities for self-dealing increase under such circumstances. Another factor is that police work is not accorded high status. There are, of course, elite units within police organizations, but police work is best classified as 'dignified blue collar' rather than 'white collar' labour. Because few police officers think of themselves as members of an elite occupation, they also lack the sense of themselves as being under a special obligation to refrain from self-dealing. Related to this is the grim nature of police work. Like those who work in hospital emergency rooms, police officers spend a vastly disproportionate amount of their time on the job with the most troubled members of society. Unlike hospital emergency workers, however, the police are charged with using force. These last two factors are particularly combustible. The officers who are worn down by the grimness of the encounters they have to endure on a daily basis are more likely than their peers to use excessive force in heated street encounters. In discussing the factors that contribute to corruption and brutality among the police, I am not of course advancing an excuse for officers. Most officers resist the temptations associated with money and with the vengeful use of force. I am simply noting why corruption and brutality are problems particularly associated with the police.

What can a police leader do about these problems, given the impossibility of modifying the factors just mentioned? The answer is that steps can be taken to prevent them in most instances and that other steps are possible in the few instances when they do. A necessary condition is exemplary leadership. If officers don't believe that their own leaders refrained from such wrongdoing while in line positions and don't see their leaders as now committed to the public interest, they are unlikely to act properly themselves. But this is hardly sufficient for reform leadership. What is needed, both for purposes of prevention and redemption, is a system of carefully measured accountability that constrains mid-range executives while still allowing them the flexibility to act creatively.

The key to this system of accountability is a principle of reasonable foreseeability. A mid-level executive should not be able to avoid censure simply by arguing that he or shedid not know about wrongdoing on their shift. On the other hand, such an executive should not be censured for every act of wrongdoing within their command. The principle of reasonable foreseeability holds that an executive is accountable for those acts of subordinates that a person well acquainted with police organizational behaviour can anticipate under circumstances that assume the executive is using proper standards of performance. The 'proper standards of performance' criterion holds mid-level executives to the review standards set by the leader of a police organization; given this criterion, a mid-level executive cannot deviate from the review standards established by a police leader and then avoid responsibility for the wrongdoing of subordinates. The criterion of acquaintance with a police organization limits blame to those acts that insiders are likely to anticipate given proper standards of performance review. It thus rejects blame for freak occurrences.

There will always be debate about when misconduct is freakish. Even here, though, a 'going rate' can be established. As time passes and decisions accumulate under the reasonable foreseeability standard, executives will understand fairly well the degree of supervision they are expected to undertake. Systematic corruption and brutality should always be detected; the executive who fails to detect practices by subordinates that have been underway for a substantial period of time—say, six months or more—will invariably by sanctioned under this standard. Random, unpredictable misconduct by a subordinate will not lead to an executive sanction. The hard cases will be those that fall between these extremes. Modest over-deterrence is, in any case, desirable in this context. That is, whenever an executive is uncertain about whether his or her failure to exercise oversight will lead to a sanction, it is surely desirable that the executive engages in such oversight.

COUNTER-MAJORITARIAN LEADERSHIP

Police leadership is counter-majoritarian when a chief takes politically unpopular steps to further the legitimate aims of policing in a generally just society. Although the distinction is not hard and fast, most reform leadership does not involve politically difficult measures. The public usually welcomes the steps leaders take to reduce corruption and brutality. An exception to this is found in cases where brutality is directed at unpopular minorities. If, for example, officers routinely engage in physical abuse of members of an unpopular ethnic group, a leader may antagonise the public by taking steps to eliminate this abuse. But while this problem is certainly real (consider, for example, the torture southern police officers routinely applied to African-Americans during the first half of the twentieth century), it seems fair to say that brutality and corruption are *generally* disfavoured by voters in modern democratic societies and that these central problems for reform leadership are therefore not central problems for counter-majoritarian leadership.

What, then, is the central problem? Not brutality (or at least not brutality in today's political climate, though this statement is subject to revision) but rather the petty indignities associated with stops and frisks. There is practically no randomisation associated with stop and frisk in modern democracies. If someone is white, middle-aged, and moderately well dressed, that person has virtually no chance of being subjected to a stop and frisk. By contrast, if someone is identifiable by sight as a member of an ethnic minority and is also young and shabbily dressed, the chances of an intervention are substantial. These chances are not always the result of arbitrary public policy. For law-abiding members of ethnic minorities, however, they are the result of an arbitrary fate. It is not arbitrary public policy for the police to concentrate their attention on young members of ethnic minority groups; sadly, this is just the part of population the police must consider given the crime trends. But it is nonetheless a mark of cruel, arbitrary fate for law-abiding, young members of ethnic minority groups to have to be subjected to stops and frisks. No one chooses their race or age; to be subjected to routine police intervention —to intervention that has a degrading effect even when carried out politely—is to be reminded of the cruelty underlying the birth lottery.

Unfortunately, illegal stops and frisks provoke little outcry from the electorate in democratic societies. They thus pose a classic counter-majoritarian problem for proponents of human rights. The practice serves a useful social function and so is tolerated, if not applauded, because it places a burden on an ethnic minority segment of the population and provides a benefit for the majority segment. Courts perform an important role in trying to limit the practice. The legal systems of all western democracies offer monetary damages to victims of illegal stops and frisks. Some go further. Frustrated by the inefficacy of tort sanctions to deter police illegality in this context, some high courts (America's is the prime example) have also required suppression of the fruits of illegal interventions. But even this is far from foolproof. The suppression threat doesn't require return of illegally seized contraband, so officers often engage in what they know to be illegal stops and frisks in the hope of securing illegally possessed guns or drugs. And, in any event, suppression is required only in settings where trial courts find that officers acted illegally. If officers perjure themselves about an intervention—sometimes only modest shading is needed— then courts can uphold the officers' conduct and admit evidence.

If we step back from this, we can readily see that courts have adopted measures such as the exclusionary rule precisely because the police have been so reluctant to discipline themselves. And police reluctance in turn is understandable in light of the incentives democracies offer them. Politically elected officials appoint police leaders; the appointments are usually provisional; moreover, even when the appointments are for formally stated terms of office, they can often be terminated at the pleasure of elected officials. It is no wonder, then, that police illegality against ethnic minorities is a persistent problem in western democracies. The wonder is that police leaders are ever willing to take counter-majoritarian stands against such illegality.

How is it that counter-majoritarian leadership can be effective? In particular, how can police chiefs continue to survive in their positions when they are answerable to elected officials? The answer is to be found in the connection chiefs can forge with the courts. By reminding both their subordinates and the public at large that the police derive their authority from the law, chiefs can make it clear that adherence to judicially imposed limitations on stop and frisk is the price that must be paid in supporting the rule of law. 'The courts made me do it' is a refrain that may have limited resonance among the general citizenry. It has stronger resonance, however, among both the police and citizens-as-consumers-of-police-services once a chief makes clear that police illegality undermines the source of police authority. Needless to say, exemplary leadership is critical here as elsewhere. A chief who has risen to prominence by taking legal shortcuts will be in no position to guide his or her own officers in a different direction. But exemplary leadership is insufficient by itself in this context. A chief also must constantly reiterate that because officers are creatures of the law, they cannot use their authority to subvert it.

CONCLUSION

The typology of police leadership provided here is not proposed as an exhaustive one. As noted earlier, the list might be expanded to include crisis management and crime-fighting leadership. But important as these types of leadership may be, they do not, in my opinion, capture the moral seriousness associated with the three categories discussed in this essay. A Utopia can dispense with the police. I have reasoned in terms of the non-Utopian category of a generally just society. Police are essential to such a society. It is because policing is not a mechanical job that leadership of the kind I have discussed must be provided to further the aims of such a society.

REFERENCES for *Chapter 9*

[1]   Acknowledgements are also due to John Laffey, a doctoral student at City University of New York and also a police leader, who provided helpful comments on an earlier draft of this chapter.
[2]   Butterfield, F (2001), 'City Police Work Losing its Appeal and its Veterans', *New York Times*, 30 July 2001.
[3]   Davis, K C (1969), *Discretionary Justice*, Baton Rouge: Louisiana State University.
[4]   *Dred Scott v. Sandford* (1857), 60 US 393.
[5]   McPherson, J (1989), *Battle Cry of Freedom: The Civil War Era*, New York: Ballantine Books.
[6]   Dana, C K (1902), *Recollections of the Civil War*, New York: Shamrock Hill Price.
[7]   Catton, B (1960), *Grant Moves South*, Boston: Little, Brown.
[8]   Foot, S (1963), *The Civil War: A Narrative*, Vol. 2., New York: Random House.

CHAPTER 10

The Real Business of Policing

Terry Mitchell

Terry Mitchell is a chief inspector with the British Transport Police. He has served as a tutor on the Accelerated Promotion Course at Bramshill. In this article he delineates the emergence of the performance ethos in the public service and demonstrates the distortions it has created in police work. He believes that police leaders must return to a proper ethical basis for police work. We quote:

> Kant's moral philosophy, which is essentially egalitarian, implicitly discounts instrumental concepts such as economy and efficiency, and intimates that the humanity of every individual must be respected as an end rather than merely as a means.
>
> It may be argued that the business ethic, far from being dependent on a purely instrumental philosophy, has given rise to enlightened management techniques and practices, such as participative management, quality circles, and building and maintaining teams, that collectively rely on the stability and growth of human relations through the 'empowerment' of the individual. However, Kant might well ask what the essential motive is for adopting such practices. If enlightened 'human resource' techniques are seen merely as the means to contribute to and sustain the economic value of the organization, then the use of such techniques is akin to Machiavelli's contemplations in *The Prince* on the situational application of cruelty or kindness in order to enable a leader to maintain power.

THE CURRENT PERFORMANCE ETHOS IN THE POLICE SERVICE AND ITS UNETHICAL CONSEQUENCES

Police leadership has always had what Adlam (1998: 17; Adlam, 1998: 162) refers to as 'blurred edges', but ethical boundaries have been increasingly transgressed in more recent times. Ignoring the more demonstrable forms of police corruption and dishonesty, which, though tarnishing the professional image of the service, can hardly be considered a recent phenomenon, the evangelical promulgation of a business-oriented performance creed within the service since the late 1980s has witnessed a more insidious, less discernible but equally pernicious form of sophistry infecting the police leadership ethic.

The pressure on the police organization to produce demonstrable results has, during the last decade, increased in proportion to an increasingly honed and more focused performance regime, championed by government, and given an irresistible impetus by the increasing awareness and expectation of the public, in whom consent and ultimately legitimacy immutably resides. As the cultural roots of the performance ideology have taken hold, organizational and personal trajectories have become intertwined. Careers at all organizational levels are forged on conceptions of effectiveness, efficiency, economy and 'value' attuned to the dominant performance ethos.

The ethical predicament that may be seen to have affected the service most recently, and which is transferable to the domain of personal practice, is contained within organizational and individual responses to this new regime. Auditors of police activity, such as HMIC (1999), have chronicled a growing institutional tendency to 'integrity lapse', substantiated by examples of practice which entail the construction by some of an artificial and pejorative illusion of performance, characterised by individual and/or institutional expedience, manipulation, and image or 'surface' management, and designed to promote, foster and protect vested interests. There appears to be, in this regard, a disconcerting nexus between the latter-day evolution of policing and the values shift apparent in contemporary post-modern society, in the sense that police behavioural patterns are increasingly assuming an aspect that imitates the less attractive, more egregious features of the post-modern ideal, eschewing clarity and reality in favour of games, appearances, chimera and obscurantism.

TOTAL QUALITY MANAGEMENT

Total Quality Management (TQM), a philosophy that, in its purest manifestation, purports to guarantee 'business' excellence and continuous, sustainable organizational improvement, represents a rational form of expression of the new public managerialism. As Bendell, Boulter and Kelly (1994) maintain, central government has championed the school of thought enshrined in TQM, and, by means of the various instruments of authority at its disposal, TQM has insinuated itself across the spectrum of public service activity. TQM, at its best, is capable of synthesising the dualism that organizational typologists have identified. Organizations have been categorised as either: mechanistic, characterised by high formalisation, centralisation and complexity (Chapple and Sayles, 1981; Fayol, 1929); or organic, whereby (as an adaptation of Von Bertalanffy's work in 1950 on general systems theory in biology) the organization is thought of as intent on growth and survival, given to low formalisation and dependency on communication channels which are open in all directions (Burns and Stalker, 1961).

TQM should be capable of marrying the contradictory facets of organic and mechanistic organizations. A quality organization should have a low complexity: fewer layers and a 'flatter' infrastructure serve to reduce hierarchical rigidity and rule dependency, and to facilitate cross-functional teamwork and process-led, 'customer'-oriented operations. Tata and Prasad (1998) and Clemmer (1992) have correlated TQM success with organic organizational structures that de-emphasise status distinctions, minimise 'management by control' (Price, 1989) and correspondingly augment employee and customer involvement. However, contrary opinions (Spencer, 1994; Dean and Bowen, 1994) argue that TQM, most clearly manifested in the ISO 9000 concept, emanates from and resolutely adheres to Taylor's principles and practices of scientific management. Shewart, Deming, Juran, Feigenbaum and Ishikawa are some of the more famous proponents and exponents of quality philosophies and methodologies, the purpose of which was to achieve conformance by the reduction of variation in processes, thereby realising the synergistic effect of individual outputs and ultimately enhancing systemic effectiveness. The 'science' of quality intimates levels of control and formalisation that characterise the mechanistic organization.

There is, therefore, ostensibly a duality of incompatible goals underlying TQM: on the one hand, the determination of features of control and, on the other, the pursuit of empowerment and learning. For it to be successfully implemented, a critical balance must be achieved between 'hierarchies' of control and 'liberty' of individual action. The creation of such symmetry depends ultimately on the integration and deployment of 'principle-centred core values' (Edgeman, 1998: 190) and competencies, which serve to fashion and unify the ways of organizational working. The implicit need for unity of purpose has immense significance for leadership and the culture of organizations which pursue a quality ideology such as TQM, together with its associated systems, practices and techniques.

In a survey of European practice, Dahlgaard *et al.* (1997; 1998) identified six fundamental principles of business and performance excellence, viz:

- continuous improvement;
- commitment to creativity;
- customer focus;
- continuous learning;
- focus on facts; and
- empowerment and participation of all staff.

The strategic direction derived from these principles was seen to depend for its success on the congruency of the core values supporting these principles. Thus, for example, 'relentless pursuit and love of the truth' (ibid: 36) constituted a core value sufficient to guide the cultural development of all members of an organization, whilst further serving to fashion leadership and management practices and behaviours. Proponents of TQM (Juran, 1979; Deming, 1982; Crosby, 1992), who adhere to its central tenet that the overall effectiveness of the system is the synergistic effect of individual outputs, advocate and practise an advanced form of leadership that is inclusive and systemic. As opposed to traditional leadership systems, characterised by leaders who often maintain high visibility levels, display public charisma, and are 'progenitors of success with results that are personalised' (Edgeman and Scherer, 1998: 95), advanced leadership systems concentrate on interpersonal empathy, and the notion of leaders as guides, coaches or 'servants' to the organization, accessible to customers, employees and partners alike.

On the basis of the evidence so far provided, my own view is that the pursuit of quality in the police domain has been and continues to be governed and fashioned by the economistic, rationalist and generic policy framework constructed and refined by succeeding governments in the last 20 years. The current articulation of police quality doctrine represents an adaptation of the private sector philosophy of TQM, which views the total integration of quality in organizations as a precursor of business excellence and advantage, based on competitive and comparative practices. Its successful implementation depends critically on the existence of a unitary purpose and an organizational ethic which is consistently and congruently articulated in word and deed by leadership.

It remains to consider the impact of the cultural and leadership ramifications of the TQM ideology on the police service.

ECONOMIC VERSUS SOCIAL GAIN

The disparate motivating forces which drive the public and private sectors have, perhaps inevitably, engendered a polarity in the conception, intention and implementation of quality systems in the police service. Whilst the private sector manages for its own economic and competitive advantage, the *raison d'être* of the public sector revolves around management for 'social advantage' or 'social result'. The grafting of tangible economic gain (where gain = profit) onto aspirational social gain (where gain = benefaction) entails an actual or potential conflict between organizational, managerial and personal values which is liable to throw moral and ethical compasses into disarray.

The implantation of the business gene into police culture manifests itself in manifold forms which owe their conception to Johnson and Scholes (1998), including: the appropriation and adaptation of language redolent of new images and values; the creation of new symbols, logos, initiatives, artefacts and ceremonies; the personification of the new managerialist ideal in icons depicted as worthy of emulation; the orientation of training and personal development, acting as an incubator, in which new skills are hatched, and changes in perception of organizational and personal roles are nurtured; and systems and tokens of regard and sanction, which correlate performance with predetermined, quantifiable indices of productivity. The cumulative effect of this new cultural bearing has resulted in many positive benefits to police and society. As Farnham and Horton (1996) identified, organizational infrastructures have been critically examined and systematically rendered more efficient, productive, responsive and accountable. This has been engineered by police officials, at all levels, who are more cost conscious, and more skilled in planning, monitoring and evaluating operations, and more conservative in their use of resources.

Decentralisation, devolvement of responsibility, and the personalisation of actions, processes and results, have caused layers of obscurity and arcaneness associated with public administration to be stripped away. The rationality of systemic structures, exemplified by mission statements and business plans, enables police functionaries to be more precise and focused in their approach, more attuned to listening to and responding to 'customer' and 'stakeholder' need and expectation (Le Grand and Bartlett, 1993) and more prone to clarity about what is to be done, and how it is to be achieved. Finally, within the limitations of organizational constraints, a new-found capacity to innovate and to encourage the 'dynamism [of the] "enterprise culture" ' (Painter, 1991) counteracts traditional, anachronistic characteristics of bureaucratic inflexibility.

From a contrary perspective, the business-oriented performance culture also portends negative consequences which have significance for the direction of policing and the service's pursuit of quality. Emanating from policy determined and fashioned by central government, the new managerialism is steeped in an ideology which conceives a limited, formulaic and politicised model of management. Its rationalist mode is essentially 'directive and potentially authoritarian' (Farnham and Horton, 1996: 268), a feature prone to be accentuated in its application to the persistently hierarchical and militaristic structures and emblems of police institutions. Whilst ostensibly the performance culture supports employee participation in managerial processes, in practice it minimises involvement because it is a philosophy that is based on the 'right to manage' (ibid.: 269) and not on the search for and achievement of consent. If the validity of this argument is accepted, the underpinning ethic that supports the quality philosophy and embraces democratic values and requires leaders to invest their constituents and employees with the power of participation, is one that, in reality, is either not practised by police leadership, or, more perniciously, is merely affected or simulated.

The motivating factor for such affectation or dissemblance betokens another adverse consequence of cultural change identified by Farnham and Horton (ibid). Public sector managers, including police leaders, may be seen, to a greater or lesser extent, to have become agents of political and economic change, carrying out policy made by politicians. Police effectiveness and efficiency has been steadily personalised, by which is meant that the 'value' provided by the organization is, by recourse to mechanisms of quantification and standardisation, translated into the domain of personal practice. The correlation between high performance and systems of personal reward, which take limited form in police organizations and continue, in the absence of other forms of expression, to be deleteriously linked to promotion and personal advancement, suggests that, as the personal stakes continue to rise, there is little likelihood of the modern police leader relinquishing other than token degrees of authority. This suggests that the effectuation of the performance culture in the public sector may minister predominantly to the mechanistic tendencies and intentions of the total quality management doctrine, whilst denoting a corresponding institutional imperviousness to the pursuit of learning and empowerment which characterise the 'organic' model of organizations.

Finally, further concern with the nature and extent of management reform and its cultural impact on police leadership stems from the political stimulus for change. This has emanated from economic and social factors which have resulted, since the mid-1960s, in the reduction of real levels of public expenditure, and the concomitant imposition of measures to ensure more efficient use of existing public financial resources. The perceived 'fiscal crisis of the State' (O'Connor, 1997) caused commentators at that time to challenge Keynesian economic orthodoxies and social policy emanating from the Beveridge Report (1942), so that there developed a concurrent cultural 'revulsion against excessive [public] expenditure and a new emphasis on thrift' (Starks, 1991: 10). The economic, social and cultural legacy of the era of the New Right continues to inform the political policy of 'new' Labour, with the tenet of Best Value keeping the spotlight on ways to enhance public service consumerism and deliver ever greater efficiencies of service.

The concern is that the business trinity of 'economy, efficiency and effectiveness' may be little more than a euphemistic, political contrivance to cover up lack of investment in and the effective renewal of public service infrastructures. If such is the case, then the distinctiveness and capability of the police service as providers to the community is in danger of being eroded, as is its attractiveness to existing and potential members of the workforce. The often repeated assertions that morale in the service is diminishing as conditions of employment deteriorate and pressures for increased productivity increase, lowered further by a propensity for increasingly assertive and sometimes aggressive workplace management (Mason, 2000; Luzio-Lockett, 1995; Clarke, 1998), are worthy of deliberation by those with a claim to lead and manage others. Even if the police service may indeed be more efficient now than at any other stage in its history, the question remains whether it remains effective in achieving the social goals for which it was intended, amongst which are included the development, protection, and sustaining of a societal (as well as a correlative organizational) fabric that is 'fit to house the human spirit' (Pedler, Burgoyne and Boydell, 1991).

In summary, the police service has been osmotically impregnated with social market orthodoxies which, whilst beneficial in some of their implications, may be construed, in the main, to have had an ambivalent and disorientating effect on police exponents. The demands of police 'business', which have been ascribed paramountcy by the political will of government, have yet to coalesce with the traditional police ideal to provide a public service which contributes to the good and strength of society, and is unencumbered by political artifice and manipulation. The ethical conundrum created by this confusion is manifested in the phenomenon of 'process abuse' that has been the repeated focus of attention in recent years, particularly within the domain of police leadership.

CONFUSION OF ETHICS

In view of the executive powers vested in them and their evolutionary role as trustees of a social contract (Alderson, 1998), developed in order to protect inalienable human rights to life, liberty and property, and expressed in a national liberal democratic political order, police officers in the United Kingdom are subject to more stringent rules and controls than their counterparts in other areas of public service. Moreover, far from the assertion made by Artur Nebe, head of the German criminal police and of the Gestapo under Hitler, that, 'there are no such things as principles, only circumstances' (Hohne, 1972: 81), there is, as Kleinig (1996) perceives, a moral onus on the police service, derived from the same liberal democratic design, to provide a justification for the limitations it imposes on the freedom of citizens. In other words, there are not only rules, by which police must abide, but also principles that provide a justificatory framework for the exercise of police authority and responsibility. Rules, including laws, may be passed and enacted by democratic processes, but, as Alderson (1998) avers, that does not mean that they are inherently just, fair or right. Furthermore, laws or rules may be interpreted and enforced in an unjust, and in an ethically and/or morally reprehensible way. My own view is that the propagation of the 'science' of management, and its articulation in the performance culture, has geared policing to the pursuit of efficiency, and, in so doing, has given rise to abuses of practice of either an illegal or unethical nature.

The performance regime obliges all police personnel to demonstrate continuously improving performance to disparate and increasingly knowledgeable and critical audiences. The increasing elucidation and personalisation of work processes and functions, and the scientific substantiation of results and their attribution to personal action, is contributing to changes in the organizational ethos which demand pellucidity of responsibility and accountability. This manifests itself in an admixture of well- but narrowly-focused and frequently confrontational behaviours and attitudes on the part of staff, particularly those in leadership positions, whose material gain or loss is often proportionate to their status. As O'Dowd (HMCIC, 1999) observes, Chief Officers will not hesitate to 'share' the weight of pressure and expectation with their senior managers, who, in turn, will inculcate into staff under their auspices the prepotent effect of tangible measures of performance which contribute to the achievement of goals.

The nexus between personal careers at all levels and demonstrable performance largely acts as 'a spur to properly directed effort' (ibid: 18). However, a growing tendency to exploit the rules as a means of self-protection or self-advancement, allied to a willingness to seize on opportunistic means to paint spurious pictures of performance which ultimately subvert the service's corporate responsibility to society, has revealed itself in multiple forms in the last decade. These were recorded in the recent HMIC thematic report *Police Integrity* (HMIC, 1999), and include: under-recording of crime, particularly in relation to cases unlikely to result in detection; the intentional misclassification of crime; 'soft targeting' or 'trawling the margins' of more easily detectable crimes, commensurate with a decrease in the application of resources to crimes or types of crime that offer less certainty in their outcome, based on the logic that a detection is a detection for counting purposes, irrespective of the relative gravity and social impact of the offence; and recourse to easy, post-sentence detections from prisoners serving custodial sentences.

These are all forms of malpractice, which a cross-section of police personnel at all levels of the organization have either consciously engaged in, assented to, or tacitly accepted and tolerated. They can be attributed to the influence of the performance culture which, as one CID officer has opined, 'forces you to operate at the edge of the ethical envelope' (ibid: 19). They are abuses of process that signify the pernicious effect that a performance culture, misconceived in its intent and execution, can have on ethics.

In the final component of this paper, I shall propound a model of leadership, based on Kantian moral philosophy, that might serve to reconcile the altruistic impulse of the police 'service' with the economic determinants of police 'business', and thereby imbue the 'science' of quality with qualities of benevolence and tolerance. Actions are seen not as driven solely by economic prudence, but out of duty born of respect for the dignity of individuals.

A PATH TO RECONCILIATION

In a business-oriented community, there is a distinctive pressure on its leaders to increase the 'value' of their organizations, measured in predominantly economic ways. This in fact devalues those organizations, if not supported by a backbone of ethical values and principles that constitute the fundamental basis of individual and organizational action. Although ethics has come more to the fore since 1990, in an effort to address the pressures associated with the performance culture phenomenon, HMIC found it to be 'a sad fact that all too often fine words are not translated into positive action' (ibid: 64).

Such dubious activities suggest also the propensity of some to adopt the perspective of the cynic, which, if not confronted, threatens to subvert the whole value system on which policing rests. The specious plausibility of the underlying rationale which prompts their action suggests a continuum, along which expediency, corner-cutting and rule breaking have the potential, to adopt a musical metaphor, to segue into the most malignant and degrading form of integrity loss, namely 'noble cause corruption'. As Ker Muir (1977) eloquently elaborates, cynicism denotes a disregard for the human condition and human suffering, a detachment from other individuals and an abnegation of mutual need, the presence of which Socrates viewed as intrinsic to human society.

The manipulation of followers by their leaders also has implications for specific models of leadership, according to Kantian moral philosophy. Fiedler's Contingency Theory of Leadership (Fiedler, 1967), in common with many other contingency or situational models (Hersey and Blanchard, 1977; Vroom and Yetton, 1973; House and Mitchell, 1974; Yukl, 1998), propound that individual leaders are distinguished by differing characteristics, and that leader behaviours should be matched to the needs and situational characteristics of their organization and followers. These are intrinsically instrumental methodologies that concentrate on resorting to the most efficient means available, and on the leadership style most suited to achieve situational requirements.

Whilst some models, such as Hersey and Blanchard, encourage the growth of autonomy in the follower, developed and nurtured by the leader, it remains that the follower, and indeed the leader, is instrumental to the demands of the situation and the end to be achieved. This is even more pertinent to those contingency-based models which advocate matching managers to the strategic needs of the organization (Leontiades, 1982; Szilagyi and Schweiger, 1984). Organizational strategy should purportedly determine the characteristics of the preferred leader— an exploitative theory which contravenes Kant's (1785/1990) assertion that 'man is not a thing, and thus not something to be used merely as a means'.

Kantian leadership essentially eschews connotations of hierarchy and élitism, regarding organizational members as subject and sovereign in equal measure. As Bowie (2000) asserts, the Kantian leader would insist on the participation of all followers, and would be committed to the protection of the interests of dissenting voices. This tends to contradict the view shared by many that the leader is the boss or the person who makes the decisions. The Kantian perspective is that the decision can often be at the expense of the intrinsic 'value' or uniqueness of the individual under the leader's aegis. The economic or business imperative is capable of affecting an organization's ethos, such that followers are seen and used as means to leadership ends. Kant's moral philosophy, which is essentially egalitarian, implicitly discounts instrumental concepts such as economy and efficiency, and intimates that the humanity of every individual must be respected as an end rather than merely as a means.

It may be argued that the business ethic, far from being dependent on a purely instrumental philosophy, has given rise to enlightened management techniques and practices—such as participative management, quality circles, and building and maintaining teams—that collectively rely on the stability and growth of human relations through the 'empowerment' of the individual. However, Kant might well ask what the essential motive is for adopting such practices. If enlightened 'human resource' techniques are seen merely as the means to contribute to and sustain the economic value of the organization, then the use of such techniques is akin to Machiavelli's contemplations in *The Prince* on the situational application of cruelty or kindness in order to enable a leader to maintain power. In other words, their use becomes manipulative and instrumental, and the notion of 'personal empowerment' they claim to embrace is, as Joanne Ciulla states (Ciulla, 1998), apocryphal or 'bogus'.

Leadership that concentrates on the ideas or qualities of one person would be anathema to the Kantian leader, whose style would militate against hierarchical, authoritarian and prescriptive philosophies which deny followers autonomy of choice and the right to endorse action in a manner that is consistent with reason. Other leadership theories that are ostensibly analogous in their rationale to the Kantian perspective would also be rejected. Transformational leadership, according to its leading exponent, James MacGregor Burns (1978), is more respectful, as well as being more concerned with the development of the follower than the more typically practised transactional leadership. However, whilst it repudiates indoctrination as a means to raise the moral development of followers, its aspiration towards unity of purpose, potentially at the expense of unanimity of interests, signifies its capacity to silence the voice of the minority and exercise the arbitrary tyranny of the majority.

Kantian leadership bears closer comparison with theories of the leader as educator and servant, although *caveats* apply in both cases. Greenleaf's (1977) conception of the servant–leader entails personal subjugation to the needs of the follower, which, though virtuous in its rejection of the superiority of leadership, tends to a notion of servility which Kant would regard as inimical to the sovereign status of every person, which includes the leader.

Bowie (2000) argues that Kantian morality would inform the construction by police practitioners of universal rules, governing human interaction both in the police organization and in society at large. Those laws would enshrine a central maxim that all its members and customers are autonomous beings alike, rational in a practical sense, and not to be treated as means to organizational ends. The organizational rules or norms that govern human behaviour, and form the basis for decision making, in order to be acceptable to all, must be self-legislated. This suggests that the Kantian police leader, without having to seek unanimity in respect of every single decision made, should heed certain principles in the decision-making process.

Most importantly, there should be commitment to take into account the interests of all those affected by leadership actions. Secondly, followers should contribute to the expression of the rules and policies that affect them. Thirdly, the interests of all parties should receive equal consideration, and individual humanity should not be traded or sacrificed for collective good.

In conclusion, it seems that contemporary police leadership faces a singular challenge, namely to syncretise police business with the business (or purpose) of policing, and to create an organizational ethos which instils a universally accepted and shared code of morality into the science of performance management. People today want police officers who are morally good and, at the same time, effective at doing their job. However, it is sometimes the case that both of these qualities cannot be found in balance in the same person or the same organization. It is the task of leadership to cement the good and the effective, so that followers and leaders alike are capable of doing the right things as well as doing things right.

Ethics is arguably more important to police leadership now than it has ever been. It is debatable whether present-day leaders are much different from their past counterparts, but followers and those whom the police serve most certainly have changed. The information revolution has redistributed power among leaders, followers and citizens. Society increasingly asserts democratic values, and demands police leaders who not only represent their individual interests and give employees and constituents a say, but also stand for values that they honour.

The quality doctrine has much to offer the police service as a means to achieve organizational excellence, but if it is to succeed it is imperative that leadership regards it as more than a 'pick and mix' guide to organizational survival, or as a mechanism of 'police science' to regulate, control and substantiate police activity and productivity. It is as much as doctrine of values and principles, which need to be woven into the fabric of police culture, if it is to be fully realised as a philosophy and 'total' in its organizational effect. It is pointless fashioning and redesigning mechanistic structures, systems and processes, if the concomitant cultural principle, that leadership should be relinquished and pushed all the way down the organization, remains unobserved or is merely simulated.

Systemic organizational change is predicated on and legitimated by empowerment of individual action and choice. Empowerment, as may be inferred from Kantian philosophy, demands recognition and enhancement of personal autonomy, the exercise of which is dependent on a moral ethos in which people are regarded as rational beings entitled to respect and dignity, allowing them to be subject and sovereign at the same time. This leads to the conclusion that the police leader most likely to prove effective transforms relationships in their domain of influence; creates a community or 'kingdom of ends' in which all members are subject and sovereign alike; repudiates élitist and hierarchical symbols and values of leadership based on notions of power or status, and is committed to teaching their followers to become leaders. That, it seems, is the right way to do business.

REFERENCES for *Chapter 10*

Adlam, R (1998), 'What Should We Expect from Police Leaders?', *Police Research and Management*, Spring, pp. 17-30.

Adlam, R (1998), 'Uncovering the "Ethical Profile" of Police Managers and the "Moral Ethos" of Police Organizations: A Preliminary Analysis', *International Journal of Police Science and Management*, Vol. 1, No. 2, pp. 162-182.

Alderson, J (1998), *Principled Policing: Protecting the Public with Integrity*, Waterside Press: Winchester/

Bendell, T, Boulter, L, and Kelly, J (1994), *Implementing Quality in the Public Sector*, London: Pitman.

Beveridge, Lord (1942), *Social Insurance and Allied Service*, Cm 6404, London: HMSO.

Bowie, N (2000), 'A Kantian Theory of Leadership', *The Leadership and Organization Development Journal*, Vol. 21, No. 4, pp. 185-193.

Burns, J (1998), *Leadership*, London: Harper and Row.

Burns, T and Stalker, G (1961) 'Mechanistic and Organic System', in *Classic Organizational Theory*, Brooks Cole: Pacific Grove, pp. 207-11.

Chapple, E and Sayles, L (1981), 'Work Flow as a Basis for Organization Design' in Jelenik, Litterer and Miles (eds.), *Organizations by Design: Theory and Practice*, Business Publications, pp. 386-406.

Ciulla, J (ed.) (1998), *Ethics: The Heart of Leadership*, Westport: Quorum.

Clarke, J (1998), *Office Politics: A Survival Guide*, London: The Industrial Society.

Clemmer, J (1992), *Charting the Journey to Higher Service/Quality*, London: Zenger Miller.

Crosby, P (1992), *Completeness: Quality for the Twenty-first Century*, New York: Dutton.

Dahlgaard, J, Nørgaard, A and Jakobsen, S (1997), 'Styles of Success', *European Quality*, Vol. 4, No. 6, pp. 36-39.

Dahlgaard, J, Nørgaard, A and Jakobsen, S (1998), 'Profile of Success', *European Quality*, Vol. 5, No. 1, pp. 30-33.

Dean, J and Bowen, D (1994), 'Management Theory and Total Quality: Improving Research and Practice Through Theory Development', *Academy of Management Review*, Vol. 9, No.3, pp. 392-418.

Deming, E (1982), 'Quality, Productivity and Competitive Position' cited in Pool, S (2000), 'The Learning Organization: Motivating Employees by Integrating TQM Philosophy in a Supportive Organizational Culture', *Leadership and Organization Development Journal*, Vol. 21, No. 8, 2000, pp. 373-378.

Edgeman, R (1998), 'Principle-centered Leadership and Core Value Deployment', *The TQM Magazine*, Vol. 10, No. 3, pp. 190-93.

Farnham, D and Horton, S (1996), *Managing the New Public Services*, second edition, Basingstoke: Macmillan.

Fayol, H (1929), *General and Industrial Management* (transl. Conbrough, J), Geneva: International Institute of Management.

Fiedler, F (1967), *A Theory of Leadership Effectiveness*, London: McGraw Hill.

Greenleaf, R (1977), *Servant Leadership*, London: McGraw Hill.

Her Majesty's Inspectorate of Constabulary (1999), *Police Integrity: Securing and Maintaining Public Confidence*, Swindon: Swindon Press.

Hersey, P and Blanchard, K (1977), *Management of Organizational Behaviour: Utilising Human Resources* (third edition), London: Prentice Hall.

Hohne, H (1972), *The Order of the Death's Head*, London: Pan.

House, R and Mitchell, T (1974), 'Path-Goal Theory of Leadership', *Journal of Contemporary Business*, Vol. 3 No. 4, pp. 81-97.

Johnson, G and Scholes K (1999), *Exploring Corporate Strategy* (fifth edition), Prentice Hall Europe.

Juran, J (1979), 'Quality is Free' cited in Pool, S (2000), 'The Learning Organization: Motivating Employees by Integrating TQM Philosophy in a Supportive Organizational Culture', *Leadership and Organization Development Journal*, Vol. 21, No. 8, 2000, pp. 373-378.

Kant, I (1990), *Foundations of the Metaphysics of Morals*, New York: Macmillan.

Ker Muir, W (1977), *Police: Street Corner Politicians*, Chicago: University of Chicago Press.

Kleinig, J (1996), *The Ethics of Policing*, Cambridge: Cambridge University Press.

Le Grand, J and Bartlett, W (1993), *Quasi-Markets and Social Policy*, London: Macmillan.

Leontiades, M (1982), 'Choosing the Right Manager to Fit the Strategy', *Journal of Business Strategy*, Vol. 3 No. 2, pp. 58-69.

Luzio-Lockett, A (1995), 'Enhancing Relationships Within Organizations: An Examination of a Proactive Approach to Bullying at Work', *Employee Counselling Today*, Vol. 7 No. 1, pp. 12-22.

Mason, G (2000), 'Soul Destroying', *Police Review*, 7 July, pp. 18-20.

O'Connor, J (1973), *The Fiscal Crisis of the State*, London: Longman.

O'Dowd, D (1999), 'Perdition to Probity: Four Steps Towards Ethical Policing', speech given at the New South Wales Police Service Eighth Annual Internal Affairs Conference, NSW Aust, 2 September 1999.

Painter, C (1991), 'The Public Sector and Current Orthodoxies: Revitalisation or Decay?', *Political Quarterly*, 62.

Pedler, M, Burgoyne, J and Boydell, T (1991), *The Learning Company*, Maidenhead: McGraw Hill.

Price, F (1989), 'Out of Bedlam: Management by Quality Leadership', *Management Decision*, Vol. 27, pp. 15-21.

Spencer, B (1994), 'Models of Organization and Total Quality Management: A Comparison and Critical Evaluation', *Academy of Management Review*, Vol. 9 No. 3, pp. 446-471.

Starks, M (1991), *Not For Profit, Not For Sale: The Challenge of Public Sector Management*, Bristol: Policy Journals.

Szilagyi Jr, A and Scweiger, D (1984), 'Matching Managers to Strategies: A Review and Suggested Framework', *Academy of Management Review*, Vol. 9 No. 4, pp. 626-637.

Tata, J and Prasad, S (1998), 'Cultural and Structural Constraints on Total Quality Implementations', *Total Quality Management*, Vol. 9 No. 8, pp. 703-708.

Von Bertalanffy, L (1950), 'The Theory of Open Systems in Physics and Biology', *Science*, Vol. 3, pp. 23-9.

Vroom, V and Yetton, P (1973), *Leadership and Decision Making*, Pittsburgh: University of Pittsburgh Press.

Yukl, G (1998), *Leadership in Organizations* (Fourth edition), London: Prentice-Hall: London.

CHAPTER 11

The Need for a Paradigm Shift in Police Leadership[1]

Milan Pagon

> Never in the history of America or of the world has the need for police leaders of probity and sophistication been greater. (Delattre, 1996: xxx)

Milan Pagon has held a series of international conferences in Slovenia on aspects of policing, each of which has resulted in a substantial publication. Dr. Pagon has a comprehensive knowledge of police research, a clear idea of the reforms in police leadership which need to take place and an easy pen with which to express those ideas. He is convinced that the police need to move away from paramilitary policing in the service of the state, to community policing—for which a wholly new style of leadership is required and which is incompatible with the performance management culture which has now been superimposed even where community policing has been tried. He believes that the police service will have to look outside its own ranks to find the right people for this paradigmatic shift. Although his comments are set in the context of a formerly Communist central and eastern Europe, they fit a wider context.

INTRODUCTION

Developments in policing and criminal justice all over the world, research findings, anecdotal evidence, writings of theoreticians and visionaries and the new rhetoric are all sending signals that a new paradigm shift in this area is inevitable. Although some authors caution against too liberal and careless use of this expression (e.g. Punch *et al.*, 1998), a careful analysis of both the existing and the advocated systems of policing in particular and criminal justice in general, suggests that the differences are so fundamental, so far reaching and so drastic, that the usage of a term 'paradigm shift' is justifiable in this context (Pagon, 1998: 3).

Faced with the increasing crime rates (especially in serious and violent crimes), overcrowded prisons, increasingly violent acts and gang activities, a lowering of the age of first-time offenders, a widespread use of illegal drugs by younger and younger populations, budgetary constraints for criminal justice institutions, an increased fear of crime among large segments of the society and so on, both the public and the criminal justice communities have started to

---

[1] Parts of this paper were published in 'Organizational, Managerial and Human Resource Aspects of Policing at a Turn of the Century'in Pagon M. (ed.) (1998), *Policing in Central and Eastern Europe: Organizational, Managerial and Human Resource Aspects*, 3-14, Ljubljana, Slovenia: College of Police and Security Studies.

realize that most of what we were doing to stop or even revert these trends was unsuccessful. The strong judicial orientation of the past, based on criminal law and the law of criminal procedure, does not seem to be an effective solution for a myriad of the above-mentioned problems (Pagon, ibid.). Consequently, new approaches to the old problems have started to emerge, gaining in popularity over the last decade. These approaches, comprising the so-called proactive justice system, are community policing, community-based corrections and restorative justice (Hahn, 1998). From the standpoint of police leadership, the most important part of the new system is community policing and its sharp contrast with the traditional, paramilitary, philosophy of policing.

COMMUNITY POLICING VERSUS TRADITIONAL PARAMILITARY POLICING

The police used to be (and still are in some environments) servants of the political elite and an instrument of the ruling party. They quite often served as the instrument of discrimination, depriving people of the protection of the law because of their race, ethnicity, citizenship, or political beliefs (cf. Murphy, 1996). The ruling party determined the goals of the police.

In some environments this was followed by the development towards the politically independent professional police, dedicated to crime fighting. Here the police themselves set their own goals. The public had no say in determining those goals; nor was the idea of providing a service to the community considered to be a concern of the police. Policing was built around the criminal law and the law of criminal procedure. In order for police organizations to function effectively, paramilitary and bureaucratic approaches to police organization were emphasized. Police organizations were highly centralized and managed on the assumption that police work is readily measurable and controllable. As that assumption was mainly wrong, it is not surprising that police organizations spent enormous time and efforts on themselves and their problems, which lead to an internal preoccupation, instead of dealing with problems in their environment.

Police work was mainly repressive and reactive in nature, characterized by its orientation to the past, because the majority of the things that the police dealt with had already happened. The police officers, reinforced by their commanders and the media, perceived themselves as 'crime fighters,' the 'thin blue line' between the rule of the law and general disorder, constantly in war with criminals, liberals and enemies of other sorts. Police subculture was, in turn, characterized by isolation, solidarity and silence.

Community policing, on the other hand, is characterized by orientation to the future, a stronger external orientation, professionalism, emphasis on the local arrangements (i.e. local issues and multiple stakeholders), rethinking alternatives to the enforcement of the criminal law and organizational development (Punch *et al.*, 1998: 98-102). It emphasizes prevention, project-oriented and problem-oriented policing and the better use of intelligence. (ibid.: 29). The defining feature of this new approach is the involvement of the community. Police officers have to be sensitive to the community needs. 'Real sensitivity to human beings consists of taking them seriously as individuals' (Delattre, 1996: 247).

However, if the community exclusively determined what the police should do, that would again put the police in the reactive role. Instead, we are talking about a partnership between the police and the community. As Punch and his colleagues (1998) argue, 'The public only partly defines what the police do. The police—and, of course, the authorities that exercise control over them—have their own professional responsibility in the discussion' (p. 67).

While there are still many unanswered questions regarding community policing, the general shape of this new approach to policing is crystallizing. Many solutions are yet to be found and what are so far general ideas have to be tailored to the specificity of particular environments. But one thing is certain: integrating the police into the community changes many assumptions about the police and police work (e.g., issues of secrecy, isolation, loyalty and solidarity within the police). This not only changes the organizational culture of police organizations, but—in the words of Hahn (1998: xi)—requires a whole new mind-set in entire departments and individual officers.

THE PATH FROM PARAMILITARY TO COMMUNITY POLICING

There is an obvious need to change the bureaucratic paramilitary structure of police organizations, so prevalent in the majority of police organizations around the world. While such a structure is supposed to be effective in managing routinized activities with limited subordinate discretion (Steinman, 1986), it has been frequently argued that it is not appropriate for police work (Jobson and Schneck, 1982, Steinman, 1986, Bruns and Shuman, 1988, Jermier and Berkes, 1979, Fry and Berkes, 1983). It is the nature of police work itself, characterized by its 'discretionary paradox' (Lefkowitz, 1977), the uncertainty in police technology and the ambiguity of police goals, that makes the paramilitary police model an 'organizational misfit' (Fry and Berkes, 1983).

Because of a belief that police performance can be measured quantitatively, as well as because much of their effort is directed towards establishing their formal authority, police managers under paramilitary policing develop performance appraisal and reward systems that reinforce outcomes which have nothing (or very little) to do with the effectiveness of police work. Such systems may 'affront the individual policeman's sense of autonomy and self-control that is required by the task of policing. People in this situation are alienated from the organization as a result of being subjected to an inappropriate control mechanism' (Fry and Berkes, 1983: 230). Furthermore:

> The use of a bureaucratic rational control system based on measurement of behaviour and outputs, when such measurements are not possible, is likely to reward a narrow range of maladaptive behaviour, leading ultimately to organizational ineffectiveness.
> (Van Maanen, 1978, cited by Fry and Berkes, 1983: 230)

We can argue that police officers within a bureaucratic paramilitary model are likely to be rewarded (and, thus, reinforced) for producing desirable statistics.

If a police officer were judged strictly on a numerical count of tickets or arrests and the officer wanted to improve his or her evaluation, it is obvious what must be done. Following this situation to its logical conclusion, there would be numerous tickets and arrests that would not hold up in court, thereby creating all sorts of delays and generating all sorts of complaints.

(Alpert and Dunham, 1986: 221).

In terms of leadership, the paramilitary organizational structure encourages an authoritarian approach (Bruns and Shuman, 1988). Jermier and Berkes (1979: 17)

challenge conventional wisdom and stereotypes about police organization and the police commander's role. Blanket justifications for obedience socialization and military command supervision across hierarchical levels appear to distort the nature of police work and to overlook the important costs to morale which accompany these management philosophies.

In addition to the above-mentioned pressure for producing desirable statistics, police officers within a bureaucratic paramilitary model are likely to be rewarded and reinforced for exhibiting obedience and conformity.

Since the established standards and the rewards for good behaviour relate almost entirely to matters connected with internal discipline, the judgments that are passed have virtually nothing to do with the work of the policeman in the community. (Bittner, 1970: 175)

As Walker (1992: 360) points out,

the authoritarian military command style is contrary to democratic principles of participation. The authoritarian style produces low morale and the rigid rank structure fails to provide sufficient job satisfaction for police officers.

One of the most important means of perpetuating the paramilitary philosophy and style of policing is police training. Ainsworth (1995: 153) notes, 'If the police service views itself as essentially authoritarian, this message will filter through to all recruits going through the training process'. Training centres operating under the paramilitary style of policing often use the so-called militaristic, high-stress approach (Ainsworth, 1995). Earle (1973, cited by Ainsworth, 1995) found out that officers trained using the high-stress approach tended to be more aggressive, less flexible, had difficulty with decision-making in crisis situations and were less able to consider appropriate options in situations requiring the use of force.

Supporters of this militaristic, high-stress approach believe that it has three main advantages: it builds up the recruits' tolerance for stress, it strengthens their ability to work as a unit when needed and it teaches officers to follow commands and orders without question. Such an approach does, however, fail to recognize the fact that most of the time the officers will be working independently and will exercise their powers using their own judgment and discretion. (Ainsworth, 1995: 156)

The most obvious consequence of the above-described issues is an adaptive behaviour which results in the misuse of police discretion. Police discretion is the capacity of police officers to select the appropriate option from among a number of legal and illegal courses of action or inaction while performing their duties (Davis, 1969, cited in Feldberg, 1989).

Discretion allows an officer to choose among different objectives (e.g., peacekeeping, maintaining public safety, enforcing the law), tactics (e.g., choosing to enforce traffic laws by patrolling or sitting at a stop sign) and outcomes (e.g., choosing to warn rather than cite a traffic violator) in the performance of his or her work. (Feldberg, 1989: 146)

Police officers can misuse their discretion in a sense that they deliberately avoid dealing with problems which are important but whose solution would not affect the officers' performance evaluation and, consequently, their reward. For that reason, supervisors, whose knowledge about a situation largely depends on the officers' reports, do not get the 'real picture' of what is going on within their jurisdiction.

The next consequence is development of the already-mentioned police subculture (characterized by cynicism, insularity, secrecy and defensiveness), which is adaptive from the standpoint of police officers' frustrations and stresses, but has many dysfunctional consequences (Fry and Berkes, 1983). According to Fry and Berkes (1983: 228),

The police system may be the most powerful predictor of police violence and other manifestation of the 'police problem.' Police officers may routinely evoke their internalized paramilitary command model in interaction with community elements, thus reacting violently to any challenge to their authority and the organization they represent.

A move away from the prevalent quasi-military ideology and internal management structure and process may provide models of interpersonal interaction helpful in reorienting authoritarian interaction between the police and the community' (Jermier and Berkes, 1979: 19).

Finally, the effectiveness of highly directive leadership was questioned on the basis of its consequences for subordinates' motivation, participation and interpersonal relationships (Bruns and Shuman, 1988). As Cronbach *et al.* (1980, cited by Steinman, 1986) noted, management tools used without the consent of subordinates often produce avoidance behaviour instead of control. Kelling (1983, cited by Steinman, 1986) went even further and concluded that police supervision was a fiction.

From the above descriptions, it becomes obvious that community policing could not be successfully applied within the bureaucratic paramilitary police organization. Community policing calls for a different approach, because it becomes obvious that:

The new philosophy of policing is a major change from the traditional understanding of the police function, its organizational design, its relationships to consumers, its measurement of outcomes, its tactics and technologies and a whole host of other elements of policing. Most notably, the organizational design shifts from being highly centralized to decentralized and the police function begins to be legitimized by community support as well as by the traditional sources of law, the political structure and professionalism. (Hahn, 1998: 95)

New forms of organizational design need to be adopted by the police, enabling decentralization of responsibility, authority, power and decision-making, as well as community involvement and inspection. Fry and Berkes (1983: 231) believe that the most appropriate form of organization for 'professionals practising an occupation that requires high degrees of socialization, training, autonomy and collegial control because of the highly uncertain and complex nature of the environment and technology surrounding and permeating the occupational role', would be a hybrid structure with characteristics of a professional bureaucracy and adhocracy. Punch and his colleagues (1998) believe that the police organization

needs to be turned around. Resources and knowledge should feed the base. At the bottom there ought to be self-confident, flexible, creative, autonomous police officers whose aim is to respond to what the public continually makes clear that it wants—a visible, recognizable, responsive and caring police presence.

These new forms of organization should, therefore, go hand-in-hand with a new understanding of police human resources and police management. Hahn (1998: 90-1) notes:

Under community policing, individual officers are valued for and evaluated on:

- communication skills;
- sensitivity to cultural diversity;
- abilities to engage in interagency networking, problem solving, mediation, negotiation and community organization; and
- a host of other skills that have not appeared in police evaluation previously . . .

Whereas formerly their discretion was rigidly contained as far as possible and their responses were to be as predictable as possible, now their ability to use discretion and develop new solutions is crucial to their performance. Input from the community becomes a primary source of guidance and direction, as far as possible and programmes mandated from headquarters become much less frequent and perhaps eventually almost non-existent.

Several authors believe that the only real alternative to paramilitary policing is its antithesis: police professionalism. Fry and Berkes (1983: 230) argue that professionalism would solve the previously described problems with organizing, managing and evaluating police work: 'Professionalized occupational control would be more appropriate than the paramilitary model because it is more suited to the environment and technology of policing'. The authors imply that the nature of police work is similar to the nature of work of doctors, lawyers and professors.

The first step in eliminating the paramilitary influence in policing would be

a movement to a more professionalized training programme that formally recognizes the social work element in the selection and training of police ... A professional model for police training would, like in other professions, emphasize a system of procedures that charts professionally responsible decision making under conditions of uncertainty.

Perhaps a clinical approach to police training through universities or some other occupationally controlled educational organization would be appropriate ...

The central issue in police professionalization is therefore not just what is the most appropriate type of control but also what is the best method for developing and disseminating knowledge on how to perform a vital and pervasive function ... Control is maintained by society bringing pressure on the professionals and their associations rather than the organizations containing them. (Bittner, 1970: 231)

It has to be noted, however, that in the United States, especially among practitioners, the expression 'police professionalism' sometimes has acquired a special meaning, different from what we are discussing here. They are using the term 'professionalism' in the context of bureaucratization. They consider the professional police departments as those that adopted Wilson's principles of police administration: specialization, hierarchy, clear lines of authority, written rules and policies and so on, in which officers perform their job 'by the book.' For them, professionalism in policing, unlike other occupations, means controlling rather than encouraging discretion (Walker, 1992). I would like to emphasize that this is not the kind of professionalism that we are discussing here.

Other alternatives to a paramilitary approach to policing can also be found. Some police organizations, especially the British police, tried to find a solution by introducing models of management drawn from the private sector. While some of these features were undoubtedly beneficial to police organizations, that approach ran into some of the problems that were mentioned earlier. Namely, management models from the private sector are characterized by a strong performance culture. In implementing those models, the British police quickly ran into problems of measuring police work, defining customers and so on (Savage and Charman, 1996). This calls for further efforts to adapt the existing management models to suit police organizations, as opposed to simply imitating the private sector.

While this is undoubtedly a challenge for management scholars working within police colleges, academies, or institutes, one has to agree with Punch and his colleagues (1998: 67), who argue that

a business-oriented approach should solely be utilized in a subordinate fashion. Efficiency and cost-consciousness are essential concepts these days for governmental organizations. Yet the danger is that such notions (which have the appearance of being handily 'measurable') will in practice begin to play a dominant role in relation to those ideas which are far more desirable although less ready quantifiable (the symbolic function of police, feelings of lack of safety).

A CHANGING ROLE FOR POLICE LEADERS

As Schulte (1996) points out, any changes in the broader social context lead to changes in the general framework for the police service and police work, which in turn affect the role of police leaders. From the above-described changes in policing it becomes obvious that the role of police leaders has been changing dramatically. The emphasis is shifting from the role of commander to the role of facilitator, motivator and change agent; from management by control to management by commitment. In the words of Bittner (1970: 180):

> If policemen can be induced to face problems in the community and to deal with citizens in ways that meet at once criteria of purposeful efficiency and will correspond to the expectations of the kind of public trust commonly associated with the exercise of professional expertise, then there will be no need to treat them like soldier-bureaucrats. Correspondingly, as long as policemen will be treated like soldier-bureaucrats, they cannot be expected to develop professional acumen, nor value its possession.

Topics such as employee influence, participation and motivation are gaining the central role in community policing.

Finally, the issues of ethics and integrity are playing an increasingly important role. Talking about ethics in policing, Delattre (1996: xxx) observed: 'Never in the history of America or of the world has the need for police leaders of probity and sophistication been greater.'

The question is, however, whether police leaders of this kind are readily available in the existing police organizations characterized by the paramilitary structure. Actually, the question is even broader. Is it possible simply to take the existing police organizations, with their current leaders and employees and transform them into the community-oriented and problem-solving oriented police organizations that are required? Or does community policing require a different kind of people, the kind that cannot be found in the existing police organizations?

While the answer to this question probably differs from one police agency to another, the fact remains that such a transformation is a long process that has to be led by strong leadership with a clear vision and backed up by carefully planned systematic changes. All managerial and human resource practices in police organizations will have to be re-evaluated and, most probably, changed. Employees will need to be treated differently. Any police organization that practises community policing should provide the benefits of this approach to its own employees, thereby ensuring that intolerance of diversity, illegitimate discrimination and sexual harassment become the issues of the past. Let us examine some of the challenges that these changes pose for police leaders.

CHALLENGES FOR POLICE LEADERS WITHIN THE NEW PARADIGM OF POLICING

To be able to achieve the desired transformation, the police leaders need to concentrate on three levels of change and meet the associated challenges:

- their own individual change;
- organizational change; and
- change in human resources.

Individual changes for police leaders

The first, and quite likely the toughest, challenge is to change one's own philosophy, values, attitudes, knowledge and behaviour. As Brion (1996: 1175) cautions, 'experienced managers ... only naturally are not about to change their way of managing subordinates, even if they accept the news about the gap, unless positive proof is given on what's wrong about what they're personally doing wrong and how to correct it'. In policing, it is hard to provide positive proof on what police leaders are doing wrong, especially when we are dealing with police leaders with substantial service under the traditional paramilitary philosophy of policing, who are typically sceptical of research findings. And even if proof is available, it is not easy to provide quick solutions to the problem.

The existing literature points to a conclusion that police leaders should give up their preoccupation with micro-management. Instead, they should focus on the mission and vision of their organization. When talking about new ways of leading corporations, Ghoshal and Bartlett (1997) suggest a fundamentally new approach to management, namely a move beyond strategy, structure and systems to purpose, process and people. Police leaders should expand their traditional roles of commanding, supervising and disciplining, to include all necessary role responsibilities, described by Brion (1996: 1079-87) as motivating, directing, coordinating, controlling, teaching, changing and representing.

To facilitate individual change in police leaders, in addition to providing well-documented research proofs on what is wrong about what they are doing, we need appropriate systems of education and training for police leaders. As of today, we still do not have an agreed system of education and training that would be the most appropriate for the preparation of police leaders under the new paradigm of policing. An analysis of systems of police education and training in 17 European countries (Pagon, *et al.*, 1996) showed a great variety among the surveyed countries. The authors made a case for standardization in the area of police education and training.

Another means of support for police leaders who want to change in order to meet the challenges of the new policing are professional associations. Through participation in these associations and their meetings and by receiving their publications, police leaders may gain not only additional knowledge, but additional motivation for change, as well. Other forms of local, regional and international cooperation among police leaders could also prove beneficial in this regard:

> We can all learn from each other, assuming that we are willing to admit that in certain matters others might have more answers, resources, knowledge, or ideas and assuming that we are willing to change when the change appears reasonable.
>
> (Pagon, 1996: 8)

Finally, in discussing an individual police leader's change process, we should mention its inevitable companion, namely the stress one is likely to experience. Understanding stress and improving one's abilities to cope with it should be an inherent part of becoming a successful police leader.

Organizational change

As we showed in the beginning parts of this chapter, the new paradigm of policing requires a completely different approach to police organization. The central themes of decentralization, citizen oversight and community involvement dictate a drastic change not only in organizational design and structure, but also in police subculture and values. We are witnessing a shift in emphasis from obedience and conformity to commitment, discretion and innovation; from isolation and secrecy to openness and public trust; from conservatism to open-mindedness. Police leaders have to be the agents of change, orchestrating the whole process of transition from the old to the new police organization. As they give up their obsession with micro-management, they can become fully engaged in the process of organizational change and development. Their main goal is to create a stimulating environment within which teams of empowered and motivated professionals of high integrity perform their duties in the best interest of the community, in accordance to the principles of police ethics. Police leaders should use team building and effective communication techniques to establish trust and openness, promote employee participation in decision-making and manage potential conflicts. Goldstein (1990: 156) notes:

> Police leaders committed to problem-oriented policing must be prepared to adopt a flexible management style that gives much greater freedom to command officers, supervisors and rank-and-file police officers. If they are to be effective in working on problems, officers must have sufficient freedom to make contacts in the community, to explore alternatives, to make some decisions for themselves and even to make mistakes. In this type of atmosphere, a high value is placed on fostering creativity, on mutual respect and trust among co-workers and on open communication regardless of rank. Supervisors, rather than devoting most of their time to controlling subordinates on behalf of top management, are encouraged to be facilitators, helping rank-and-file officers carry out their broadened roles.

Knowing that societal changes are perpetual, constantly facing the police with new challenges, police leaders should turn their organization into a learning organization. As an informed reader can imagine, all these organizational changes require a profound change both in a composition and the quality of police organization's human resources.

Change in human resources

Considering that 'each system tends to require, attract and produce people suited to that system' (Brion, 1996: 1054), it is not hard to conclude that the traditional paramilitary policing has required, attracted and produced quite different people to those required under the new style of policing. Leadership efforts in this area should be directed both at transforming the existing human resources and attracting different kind of human resources in the future. To that end, police leaders must inspire their followers for the above-described changes. This effort has to be supported by a simultaneous change in recruitment and selection systems. No longer should recruits be selected primarily on a basis of their gender, physical strength, or conformity, but rather on a basis of their education, as well as their communication, problem solving and negotiation skills. Instead of elaborate systems of 'screening out' applicants with potentially unwanted traits or behaviours, new selection procedures should focus on 'selecting in' the most appropriate candidates.

Police leaders have to be aware of a simple law of human behaviour, namely that those behaviours that are reinforced are repeated. Therefore, performance appraisal and reward systems also need to be redesigned to reflect the changing values and goals of policing.

In addition to performance appraisal and reward systems, one of the most powerful influences on police officers' conduct and behaviour is training. Police leaders should assure that both the content and the form of police training reflect the changing nature of police work and organization. Topics such as police ethics, integrity, discretion and the social work elements in policing should be included, along with different skills typical of the new policing approach. (For a discussion on training in police ethics, see Delattre, 1996 and Pagon, 2000.)

Finally, a new approach to managing police human resources calls for a new career management and career system in the police. A different set of promotion criteria is required for different roles within the police organization. Under the traditional policing system, there was typically a one-tier career path. It was a normal practice for a person to enter the police organization at the lowest level and work his or her way up through the ranks, some of them making it all the way to the top. If we used a medical analogy, that would be an equivalent to entering the hospital as a nurse, working one's way up to a position of doctor, then to an assistant director and finally to the director of the hospital. While we may laugh at this example from medicine, that is what was typically done in police organizations. Under the new paradigm of policing, leaders are faced with a challenge to create two- or three-tier career systems, with some possible crossovers.

While this will sound heretic to police leaders from a paramilitary camp, it is my honest belief that it is not necessary for a successful leader to start at the very bottom of the organization, nor is it necessary for a successful community policing officer to have long years of experience as a patrol or traffic officer. What is more important is to possess appropriate education, determination and skills.

CONCLUSION

Different times call for different people. In this paper I have tried to show how a new paradigm of policing requires a very different kind of police leader than did the traditional paradigm. It was not my intent to elaborate on how exactly the police leaders should do their job—a question which has yet to be fully answered. What I wanted to do was to point out some of the more salient challenges that the leaders will have to face if they want to lead their organizations successfully. This has never been an easy task and it has become more complex. Not only has police work changed; so have the public and the communities into which it is separated. No longer do people uncritically accept whatever the police are doing in the name of a war on crime. People identify problems and they want solutions. They want the police to be effective and accountable. To meet those demands, police leaders have to change themselves, their organizations and their people. Those who are either not willing or not capable of doing so should step aside and let others do it. We should, however, keep in mind that very few people are willing to step down of their own will. This is where the community and the politicians should play their role.

REFERENCES for *Chapter 11*

Ainsworth, P B (1995), *Psychology and Policing in a Changing World.*, Chichester: John Wiley and Sons.

Alpert, G P and Dunham, R G (1986), 'Community Policing', *Journal of Police Science and Administration,* 14(3), pp. 212-222.

Bittner, E (1970), The Quasi-Military Organization of the Police. Reprinted in Kappeler, V E (ed.) (1995), *The Police and Society: Touchstone Readings,* Prospect Heights, Il: Waveland.

Brion, J M (1996), *Leadership of Organizations: The Executive's Complete Handbook,* Greenwich, Connecticut: JAI Press.

Bruns, G H and Shuman, I G (1988), 'Police Managers' Perceptions of Organizational Leadership Styles', *Public Personnel Management,* 17(2), pp. 145-157.

DeLattre, E J (1996), *Character and Cops: Ethics in Policing* (third edition), Washington, D.C.: The AEI Press.

Feldberg, M (1989). 'Discretion' in Bailey, W G (ed.), *The Encyclopedia of Police Science,* New York: Garland Publishing, pp. 146-152.

Fry, L W and Berkes, L J (1983), 'The Paramilitary Police Model: An Organizational Misfit', *Human Organization,* 42(3), pp. 225-234.

Ghoshal, S and Bartlett, C A (1997), *The Individualized Corporation: A Fundamentally New Approach to Management,* New York: Harper Business.

Goldstein, H (1990), *Problem-Oriented Policing,* New York: McGraw Hill.

Hahn, P H (1998), *Emerging Criminal Justice: Three Pillars for a Proactive Justice System,* Thousand Oaks: Sage Publications.

Jermier, J M and Berkes, L J (1979), 'Leader Behaviour in Police Command Bureaucracy: A Closer Look at the Quasi-Military Model', *Administrative Science Quarterly,* 24, pp. 1-23.

Jobson, J D and Schneck, R (1982), 'Constituent Views of Organizational Effectiveness: Evidence from Police Organizations', *Aademy of Management Journal,* 25(1), pp. 25-46.

Lefkowitz, J (1977), 'Industrial-Organizational Psychology and the Police', *American Psychologist,* May, pp. 346-364.

Murphy, P V (1996), 'Foreword' to DeLattre, E J (1996), *Character and Cops: Ethics in Policing* (third edition), xiii-xvi, Washington, D.C.: The AEI Press.

Pagon, M (1996), 'Policing in Central and Eastern Europe: The Role and Importance of Cooperation, Training, Education and Research' in Pagon M (Ed.), *Policing in Central and Eastern Europe: Comparing Firsthand Knowledge with Experience from the West,* 3-8. Ljubljana: College of Police and Security Studies.

Pagon, M (1998), 'Organizational, Managerial and Human Resource Aspects of Policing at the Turn of the Century' in M Pagon (ed.). *Policing in Central and Eastern Europe etc.* (above).

Pagon, M (2000), 'Police Ethics and Integrity' in: Pagon M. (Ed.), *Policing in Central and Eastern Europe: etc.* (above).

Pagon, M, Virjent-Novak, B, Djuric, M and Lobnikar, B (1996), 'European Systems of Police Education and Training' in: Pagon M (Ed.), *Policing in Central and Eastern Europe etc.* (above).

Punch, M, Vijver, K van deer, Dijk, N van (1998), *Searching for a Future: Reappraising the Functioning of the Police,* Dordrecht: The Dutch Foundation for Society, Safety and Police.

Savage, S P and Charman, S (1996), 'Managing Change' in Leishman, F, Loveday, B and Savage S P (eds.), *Core Issues in Policing,* London: Longman.

Schulte, R (1996), 'Which Challenges will Police Managers have to Meet in the Future?' in Pagon M. (ed.), *Policing in Central and Eastern Europe etc.* (above).

Steinman, M (1986), 'Managing and Evaluating Police Behaviour', *Journal of Police Science and Administration,* 14(4), pp. 285-292.

Walker, S. (1992), *The Police in America: An Introduction* (second edition), New York: McGraw-Hill.

CHAPTER 12

Leadership that Learns

Ian Blair

Ian Blair read history at Oxford before joining the Metropolitan Police Service. He transferred to Thames Valley Police as an Assistant Chief Constable, joined Surrey Constabulary as Chief Constable, and has now returned to London as Deputy Commissioner. He is very much the thinking chief officer—and one who has little time for unnecessary traditions, assumptions and myths. In his view, police leadership is not essentially different from leadership in almost all other spheres of human activity, and most of the lessons are straightforward enough to delineate: if not always so easy to apply:

> The leaders of tomorrow will have to engender a culture which is less risk-averse, in which mistakes can be part of genuine learning, in which the learning available in one part of the organization is available to others. It is also vital that leaders continuously question their own adaptability to changing circumstances.

INTRODUCTION

During my recruit training and, if I recall it rightly, on my sergeant's pre-promotion course, we received occasional lectures from terribly senior officers about leadership. This was in the early 1970s. All that I recall was that the models that were being put forward were invariably military, such as Montgomery, Patton, and Viscount Slim.

To most of us in the room this was old-fashioned drivel. Old men in khaki, seen on countless newsreels in our childhood, were no models of leadership in a modern and permissive society. These were a reflection of what seemed to be the almost equally old men who were lecturing to us: these models were the heroes of their youth and the talk of their national service experience. Leading 'troops over the top' was going to be a far cry from the complex and morally shifting world which we inhabited. Police leadership was going to need to be different, unique unto itself.

I think I was wrong. Not wrong in that I considered the military analogy inadequate, but wrong in that I thought police leadership was going to be different, in some way unique. That is the central message of this contribution. I believe that police leadership is not essentially different from leadership in almost all other spheres of activity.

Police leadership is not essentially different from leadership in almost all other spheres of activity. As I write these words, I am aware that the Home Office is initiating research to compare police leadership with that in other parts of the public sector, and I imagine that other contributors to this book will be arguing as to the special nature of police leadership. I may therefore well be proved wrong. For now, though, I will stay with this contention.

Senior police officers need some specialist skills. In the current debate around police reform, one clear theme is the requirement to identify what the police should and should not do. There is such a thing as core police business, and police leaders should know how to do it. So, to take but three examples: police leaders need to be competent in managing complex and protracted criminal enquiries, perhaps involving different forces; they need to be able to control public disorder, effectively and even-handedly; and they need to be competent in controlling the scene of major disasters, co-ordinating the work of emergency services in extremely difficult and public conditions. There are certain skills which only the police bring to the party. Police leaders had better be good at doing them.

Beyond that, however, police organizations are like other organizations and police officers and civilian support staff are like other human beings. They respond to the same stimuli and react in the same way as other large and small groups. They will react to leadership in a similar way to others—and we know a lot about leadership. One of the preliminary papers coming before the newly formed Police Leadership Development Board is a relatively brief literature search on the topic of leadership by the Home Office. The list of references is very long indeed. The Cabinet Office is examining leadership, the *Harvard Business Review* scarcely has an edition without an article on leadership and many universities have leadership components within their schools of management. Theories and constructs of leadership abound; and almost all of them can be read across to police organizations.

Most of the lessons of leadership are very simple. Human beings need to be involved in decisions; they need to feel that leaders understand—and here the fact that all officers have beat experience is a significant advantage; they need to believe in the moral worth of their leaders; and they need to believe that those leaders are fair. So, for police leaders, communicating with staff, being visible, being people whose integrity is manifest and being fair are essential pre-requisites of being successful in leading subordinates.

But to take one example—visibility—the concept of 'managing by walking about' is not police specific; every management book talks about the need to get out and about on the shop floor and to have an open door policy. This, indeed, is neither rocket science nor police science.

Although it is possible to think of one or two leadership styles that would be inappropriate, there is a place for almost all types of leaders in the police service. Sometimes the style will be entrepreneurial and charismatic. Organizations, which are in or are recovering from crisis will need visible, vocal, high profile leaders in whom they can believe. At other times, other leadership and management paradigms will become necessary and will be displayed by police leaders, in the same way as they are in other organizations.

If the first proposal is therefore that police leadership is like other leadership, the second is that police officers can be and need to be taught leadership skills. The basic pattern of police leadership is broadly similar across all ranks, albeit the mixture of required competencies will change with seniority.

The third proposal is that police officers need to be taught those skills within the context in which modern public sector organizations find themselves. That context includes:

- the attempt to achieve joined up governance. In the words of Andrew Foster, Controller of the Audit Commission: 'We need to be a unified army for good rather than different battalions criss-crossing people's lives';
- a time when the fundamental police mission is being questioned by a programme of reform, and people need certainty in a complex world;
- a managerial environment of over-complexity and a plethora of strategies; and
- police organizations with an increasing range of skills within themselves.

In shaping their need for leadership within this context, the police are similar to a large proportion of the public services—health being an obvious analogy—and many parts of the private sector. This context requires four aspects of modern leadership to be emphasised in the police.

VISION-BASED LEADERSHIP

Depending where they are in the organizational hierarchy, leaders need either to articulate their own specific vision or to make clear their own support for the vision articulated by the organization. It has always been important to have clarity of purpose, but the shift, not so much in the police mission but in the way it is likely to be delivered in the next few years, makes it imperative that police leaders:

- make clear their vision of the organization; and
- Involve staff both in its creation and its delivery.

The component parts of such a vision, including integrity, fairness, the handling of diversity, the delineation of priorities and the values and value of public service need to be made clear.

TEAM-BASED LEADERSHIP

The cult of personality in leadership has been very dominant in the nineteenth and twentieth centuries. To the names of the generals mentioned at the beginning of this article may have been added those of leaders from other spheres, such as exploration, government and business; but the central theme has remained broadly the same. Leadership may be learned about by studying the personalities and habits of successful leaders; and those leaders have usually been of the charismatic variety.

However, this may be an increasingly inappropriate model for the development of successful leadership in policing. The growing number of different skills involved in the successful delivery of police operations means that team-based rather than individually charismatic leaders are now the requirement. The ever changing number of specialists and the complexity of the social and political landscape require skill sets beyond that of any individual. It is often said that there is no 'I' in a team: never has this been more true.

CROSS-BORDER LEADERSHIP

This is the logical extension of team-based leadership. It is no longer enough for the leader to lead solely his or her own organization or part of the organization. The key skills are now those of negotiating and influencing. The way ahead appears to be working with multi-disciplinary teams, such as Youth Offending Teams or Drugs Action Teams; forming joint bids with local authorities: the prospect of policing priority areas; and the need to be able to lead the mixture of police and civilian, volunteer and professional, headquarters and basic command unit personnel, which forms the modern task group—a mixture which is becoming more mixed as the twenty-first century goes on.

Police leaders, in common with executives in many other parts of the criminal justice system and the public sector, will increasingly have to lead teams across organizational borders, and in interaction with different communities: with all the consequent difficulties over language, information sharing, data quality, accountability and reporting lines that that task imposes, and the opportunities it carries with it.

LEADERSHIP THAT LEARNS

In his excellent report on the Metropolitan Police's diversity strategy, Lord Ouseley makes the powerful point that the Met will never move on until it genuinely learns from its own mistakes. From where I sit, this is not just a question of some part of the organization sending out instructions on how to avoid employment tribunals, but a whole change in mind-set. The Met, in common with other forces, constantly learns and adapts its operational processes, but it is not nearly as good at learning in other aspects of its work.

The leaders of tomorrow will have to engender a culture that is less risk-averse, in which mistakes can be part of genuine learning, in which the learning available in one part of the organization is available to others. It is also vital that leaders continuously question their own adaptability to changing circumstances. To return to the military analogy: the donkeys who led the lions into the carnage of the First World War had been young men of vision and courage during the Boer War and the other vestiges of imperial conflict.

This, then, is the challenge for the future. Is police leadership different or similar to leadership elsewhere? If it is genuinely different, then we need to acknowledge and to teach those differences in a specialised environment. If it is not broadly different, as I have argued, then the whole concept of a leadership centre at Bramshill must be placed in a different context. There is no reason why that leadership centre should not exist; but it could only do so in competition with leadership faculties throughout the public sector and academia.

Other than a few specialist skills, there would be no purpose in training senior police officers apart, because the skills they will need to learn will be best acquired in working with and learning alongside managers and leaders from other disciplines. After all, as they move up the ranks, police officers will find themselves working alongside senior colleagues, directly employed by the service, but who are not police officers—and some of my non-police ACPO colleagues are fine role models of the aspects of leadership described above.

This is not only my contention, of course, but also my experience. With my length of service I have been through the Special Course, the Intermediate Command Course and the Strategic Command Course. I have been through sergeants' and inspectors' courses, CID foundation training and public order training: in fact, pretty much everything except traffic. I have discussed leadership on most of those courses. I learned something from each of those discussions. Indeed, I have had the privilege to serve with some very fine police officers, some retired, some still serving, and some already 'on another shore.' I have learned enormous amounts from them. With them, I have shared the burdens of leadership in the police service, the demands on integrity and family life, the requirement to face horror, betrayal and disillusion and rise above them.

Nevertheless, the most significant learning experience of my life have been in mixing with leaders from other disciplines, understanding that the dilemmas they faced were, if not exactly the same, then parallel to the challenges in front of me. The most powerful of those experiences was a two-year learning set with colleagues from local government, health, housing, the BBC and the voluntary sector, in which we met infrequently to compare experiences, to offer support and to learn from each other. All of us were surprised by the richness of the experience and the stretching nature of the encounters, as opposed to the comfortable certainties of our own professional worlds.

So my belief and experience is that those long past senior officers were partially right. As there will be from leadership in every other field, there was something to be learned from military endeavour. But not exclusively from such a source.

Our task now is to go out and garner learning from wherever it exists and increase the richness of our leadership culture—without claiming it to be so specially and exclusively our own.

CHAPTER 13

Women Leaders: a Catalyst for Change?

Jennifer Brown

Professor Brown argues that the contribution that women could have made to the improvement of the leadership of the police—in a time of public sector reform—was either ignored or sabotaged. Indeed, women police leaders have been:

> Stressed, trapped, ignored, patronised, undervalued, misunderstood and labelled as troublemakers. (Maddock, 1999)

However, women police leaders remain a potential catalyst for change.

CHALLENGING WOMEN: GENDER CULTURE AND ORGANIZATION

Much research on gender and leadership asks whether men and women do it differently. Rosner (1990) suggested that the first few female executives adhered to many of the rules of conduct that brought success to men. She argues that the second wave of leading women adopted different styles. She also argues that changing business practices suited non-traditional (and feminine) styles of leadership in that they were more collaborative and co-operative: which maximised the chances of successful organizational change in the post-Fordian business climate of the 1980s. The results of her survey of managers showed that women were more likely to engage in interactive leadership which encouraged participation, shared power and information, enhanced other people's self-worth and got others excited about their work. Men were more likely to use rewards and punishments to enhance workers' performance and to use their power and formal authority to achieve tasks. Su Maddock (1999) also supposes that feminine qualities and practice were well-suited to effect the transformation of public sector management that occurred in Britain during Margaret Thatcher's governments.

Feminist practice emphasises connectiveness, co-operation and mutuality over separateness, competition and individual success (Silvestri, 2000). As such this challenges norms that favour masculinity and the assumptions of 'one-size fits all' solutions. Maddock (1999: 36) proposed, 'Gone are the days when women could succeed by learning to play men's games. Instead the time has come for men on the move to adopt a more feminised approach to management games.' She postulates that women, with their different model of leadership, could have delivered the changes which were sought in the public services. But they were frustrated by masculine occupational cultures in which leadership and management adapted rather than transformed. This chapter will argue a similar scenario for the police service.

We can discern several waves of government interventions throughout the 1980s, the 1990s and into the new millennium that have tried to inform and reform police management and practice, making them conform to requirements of economy, efficiency and effectiveness. Three processes can be identified that have contributed to these ends: equal opportunities, new public sector management and police reform. The key question that this chapter examines is whether there has been a paradigm shift in police leadership as a consequence of these processes, through which the police force was liberated from its masculine dominated command and control culture to one that embraced more feminine qualities within a service orientation. Furthermore, if such a transformation has occurred, what role have women officers played?

When Barbara Raffel Price (1989) asked these questions over ten years ago she presented the empirical evidence then available, which indicated a tendency for women to adopt the police role as it was and to be changed by it rather than effect any changes to it. Martin's (1990) conclusion was that for women in US police leadership roles the price for personal accomplishment is high in terms of social isolation, lack of professional support and cost in personal relationships. Silvestri (2000: 2296) draws a similar conclusion in her recent study of British women senior officers. She finds evidence of a pragmatic reading of the police world as it is. Strategies involving some form of feminist activism are at too high a cost. She concludes that for senior policewomen 'the job of policing is worth playing the game without changing the rules'. The picture in Australia is much the same. Adams (2001: v) notes:

> The sample of females in this study had already successfully negotiated through a strongly masculine organization, and therefore had either assimilated with, or adapted to, the culture. In this way, the senior women ... demonstrated their resilience and adaptability to the police culture.

In all these jurisdictions, women constitute about 16 per cent of the police establishments. There seem to be different views prevailing in the research literature about possible feminising influences being discernible on the practice and management of policing. Threshold arguments (Fielding, 1999) propose that changes will follow once women have reached some magic proportion of the workforce. On the one hand, women are said to have a transformation impact just by being there (Ledwith and Colgan, 1996); whilst on the other hand, discrimination of minorities within a workforce will 'bureaucratise' out inequalities once a gender balance is achieved (Kanter, 1977). Other commentators argue that this is unsustainably optimistic (Halford, et al., 1997). They suggest that even if more women are appointed to senior positions, male dominated organizations will not lose their essential male characteristics. Such is the potency of the male occupational culture, not only will women will be co-opted into it, but they will also be marked out by men who will undermine their power.

Influences of equal opportunities, new public management and police reform offered the potential for a paradigm shift in police leadership and management; but that project for change has been frustrated. Whilst some changes have been effected these have been on the surface rather than at a deeper structural level. The service has not transformed itself as a consequence of external requirements, but has responded with strategies that reinvented old patterns. This resonates with Chan's (1996) position that without changes within both the criminal justice system as a whole and wider society, police practices simply revert to old dispositions.

An essential characteristic of policing is its maleness. Cavender and Jurik (1998) argue that the presence of women in the police disrupts and undermines the historical links between 'good' police work and masculine prowess. The emphasis placed on the ability to confront violence and danger is a key element in the construction of a police officer's identity, which collectively creates the immovable image of street policing being a tough and dirty job requiring strength and physicality to preserve order. Hunt and Magenau (1993: 119) describe this premise as follows:

> Coercion, force and violence are inherent in police work, however, and some brutality is probably an inevitable accompaniment. Pumped up by the 'huff-and-puff' of a chase, or when the adrenaline flows as a cop's authority on the street is challenged, it happens. Violence is a part of police work—part of the culture of policing. Controlling and minimising it among all the affected parties is a constant challenge to civil society and to the police as its agent.

For management cops this translates into command and control, which achieves results through people and focuses on the achievement of the task. Thus, in the aftermath of equality legislation in the 1970s an accentuated 'cult of masculinity' was described by Smith and Gray (1985). This became the performance culture of the 1990s (Brown and Neville, 1996), and finally 'smart machismo' in the wake of police reforms in the new millennium (Silvestri, 2000). The transformation is one of externals, which assimilate some feminine qualities but with little contribution of or concession to women as contributory players.

PARADIGM SHIFTS

Radical transformations in thinking that influence scientific or political revolutions have been called 'paradigm shifts' by Kuhn (1962). Paradigms are the resources and tools that provide the framework for established modes of operating. Confidence in models or frameworks can become eroded with the accumulation of difficulties and unresolved problems resulting in failures that are laid at the door of prevailing wisdom. This can often trigger a crisis such that new ways of operating develop. A paradigm shift represents a fundamental alteration in underpinning concepts and beliefs and their substitution by new ones. This inspires new thinking and development of new techniques that are incompatible with the old ones. Concepts from equal opportunities, new public sector management and police reform have all offered the possibility of a paradigm shift for the police service that could have revolutionised its leadership. Jones and Newburn (2002) outline the Bayley and Shearing thesis that policing has fundamentally changed through the ending of the policing monopoly and the search for a new identity as a consequence. When assessing the evidence for this thesis as applied to British policing they conclude (p. 143) that there have been undeniable far-reaching changes but these have been less radical than some would have us believe. So let us turn our attention to some of these underlying beliefs that underpin the conduct of policing and which can be explored though the concept of police occupational culture.

Cop culture

Reiner (1985) indicates that the original working-class recruitment and military structure laid the foundations for this distinctive masculine style. He suggests (p. 187): 'Cop culture has developed as a patterned set of understandings which help to cope with and adjust to the pressures and tensions which confront the police.' Cop culture is surprisingly universal and provides a set of values and beliefs underpinning and guiding behaviour in an increasingly ambiguous world (Waddington 1999). He states (p. 295) that the purpose of cop culture is to give meaning to experience and that it sustains occupational self-esteem.

Another feature of the police occupational culture described by Reiner (op. cit.) is the isolation and internal solidarity experienced by officers. This not only acts as protective armour for individuals against minor infractions of the rules but also shields the organization as a whole from public scrutiny and official accountability. Interestingly, Reiner proposes that this potent mix compromises senior officers who sometimes collude with misconduct when they present a unified front in the face of external criticism. Internal solidarity is achieved through recognition of similar outlook and values of the dominant norm of white males. A formula combining the historical origins and largely working-class recruitment, the sense of mission with its ethos of seeking excitement and danger, together with collusive solidarity cultivates an occupational culture that positively reinforces masculinity.

Three consequences have been identified to result. Firstly, there is a resistance to external scrutiny and change and a strong sense that the nature of the task can only be understood and explained by those inside the organization (Bradley, *et al.*, 1986). Secondly, there is an emphasis on an exclusionary 'old fashioned machismo' which eschews otherness such as women or ethnic minority officers (Reiner, 1985). Thirdly, a tension is constructed between the enforcement and the social service tasks of policing in which the latter are demoted to 'rubbish work', incidentally often delegated to women (Walklate, 1996).

Equality legislation and the cult of masculinity

The promise of equal opportunities policies is not only that these give individuals chances to be involved in occupations or professions that have a strong gender bias, but that gender balancing will have some transforming effect on the organization itself. Sex discrimination legislation offered an official re-definition of the role of women officers and, as Jones (1986a: 6) points out, challenged 'the notion that policing should be a mainly masculine occupation.' The then Home Secretary, Roy Jenkins, told a Police Federation Conference in 1974:

> Until relatively recently policing has been regarded as a pre-eminently masculine profession necessarily depending in part for its success upon the size and physical strength of its membership...The time has come for these attitudes to alter.

Discrimination against qualified girls and women is not only insulting and unfair; it
is also wasteful of the skills and abilities of half our population.

By changing the gender balance, it was argued, there would be a
paradigmatic shift of emphasis in the priorities of policing, its management and
probity (Brown, 1997). But equal opportunities policies have not significantly
delivered on structural change or cultural transformation.

The three police staff associations mounted strong opposition against the
inclusion of policing within the provisions of the 1975 Act. Objections were made
on the grounds of:

- the unsuitability of police duties for women;
- their physical and emotional deficits;
- the risks they posed to male colleagues (these were twofold: the
  distractions caused by possible sexual entanglements, and their inability to
  provide back-up to male colleagues); and
- their economic worth (the likelihood that they would leave after marriage
  and/or child bearing).

However, the legislation was passed, and the police service in its inimitable
style complied, although with little enthusiasm or preparation, and integrated its
women officers, without having made any serious concessions to the
implications of a diverse workforce.

Sandra Jones undertook a review of progress some ten years after the
passing of the legislation (Jones 1986a, 1986b, 1987). She found the persistence of
widespread adverse male attitudes in officers recruited before and after
integration towards women colleagues, which inhibited the reality with which
women could fulfil their new, integrated roles. Jones demonstrates that whilst
numbers of women entering the police service increased after the
implementation of the legislation it was clear that this had more to do with the
need to make up for acute manpower shortages caused by comparatively poor
pay than an attempt to redress the gender balance. Once pay for police had been
increased male recruitment again dramatically outstripped that of women.

When Jones undertook her review no force had a published equal
opportunities policy or a recognisable grievance procedure. Two forces that she
researched in depth restricted women's entry into specialist roles such as CID,
dog handling, scenes of crime and traffic. Women were more frequently assigned
inside station duties, were allocated 'safer' beats and less risky or unpleasant
deployments. They were more often deployed on traditional tasks such as those
dealing with women and children. The combined effect of this was both
disheartening and demoralising in women's attempt to gain further experience,
and it also adversely affected women's promotion prospects. Jones' analysis
showed that the rank and file occupational culture sustained the grounds for
resisting the inclusion of police within the Sex Discrimination Act of 1975 by
means of a set of 'ritual arguments' which guided their daily interactions with
women officers. These arguments were about the general ability of women to
perform all police duties; the emotional unsuitability of women; women as a

discipline problem; and the physical unsuitability of women for policing. Jones (1987: 296) concluded:

> The fact also that informal deployment practices seem to be tacitly condoned by middle and senior management, usually on the pragmatic grounds of the risk of exposing women to all aspects of general patrol work, leads to their acceptance as a substitute for the formal policy embodied in the legislation. This calls into question the commitment of the police organization to genuine equality of opportunity and treatment.

The core beliefs that policing involves strength, action, danger and male fellowship were not eroded by the challenge of equal opportunities legislation. Jones comments not only on the rigidity with which these beliefs are held but the perpetuation of them to the next generation of young officers. She observes (1986b: 139):

> One cannot help but speculate whether this is not reinforced by awareness amongst young male officers of the tacit acceptance and lack of direct sanctions by middle and senior management.

Levine (1994) discusses the identity crisis experienced by men during the First World War when an extreme version of masculinity was demanded, which valorised aggression and conquest. Levine argues that in such an environment the encroachment of women into policing was resisted as this undermined models of masculinity. Thus, women were caricatured as overtly masculinised (de-feminised); or discounted on the grounds of ineffectual femininity (de-professionalised). Coyle and Morgan Sykes (1998) argue that feminism and gay politics have contributed to a de-construction of traditional masculinities resulting in a conservative backlash in which the 'Iron John' persona is valorised: i.e. more extreme versions of masculinity. Smith and Gray (1983: 372) report evidence for an accentuated 'cult of masculinity' within which women in the newly integrated Metropolitan Police found:

> The dominant values of the force are still in many ways those of an all male institution ... [with] the emphasis on remaining dominant ... on masculine solidarity ... on backing up other men ... on drinking as a test of manliness ... the importance given to physical courage and the glamour attached to violence.

This resulted in structural inhibitions such as unofficial quotas limiting the numbers of women to more prestigious departments or deployments and a debilitating working ethos that deprived women of informal social support or mentoring.

It was not until the publication of Home Office Circular 87/1989 that any significant shift at policy level was discernible. The circular set out chief constables' responsibilities towards all members of their force, recommended a code of practice and offered a model grievance procedure. When Anderson, *et al.* (1993) reported on the progress of women officers, their national survey found widescale examples of discriminatory practices and sexual harassment of women officers. The ritual arguments and differential deployment practices described by Jones (1986) remained intact.

Heidensohn (1992: 101) had argued that equal opportunities policies could help 'feminise' policing by undermining traditional attitudes and opening up opportunities for women to encroach upon previous male- only territory and transform operational practice. In assessing this proposition, Walklate (1996: 198) finds evidence of a certain cynicism or equal opportunism. In her analysis, forces frequently fell back on the statement that they were an equal opportunities employer in order to demonstrate their 'service' orientation, especially towards women. Thus, we may see the thinking behind one response to Home Office Circular 60/1990, which called for innovation in the policing of domestic violence. The creation of specialist domestic violence units absorbed women officers, who were thus diverted into an area of work historically unvalued by men and labelled as 'rubbish.' At the same time, this area of work was undervalued as appropriate for promotion. Walklate argues that this essentially re-invented the separate policewomen's department and endorsed a belief that general police work is too dangerous for women and as ' dirty work ' it should be left to men. She concludes (op. cit.: 199) that it ghettoises women's issues and leaves the rest of the police work relatively untouched in both style and service delivery.

A further example may be drawn from part-time working initiatives. They were introduced in 1990 as an equal opportunities policy to assist women officers in returning to work after maternity leave. Thus, 94 per cent of part-time officers are women. The policy was immediately made into a problem by police managers as representing a part-time mentality rather than being seen as a flexible employment option. Tuffin and Balai (2001) comment:

> The equal opportunities background to the introduction of part-time working, its use as a means of reducing hours in existing posts, and gaining more control of working hours, seems to have led managers to think of part-time working as a potential problem and administrative burden ... A manger of a specialist task force in a focus group explained how pleased he was to have been able to refuse part-time working in his area and he added equal opportunities had caused immense problems. A participant in another group stated ... that part-time officers tended to be in cushy office roles.

Given that the majority of officers working part-time are women, this reinforces stereotypes that they do not want to work nights, provide short-notice cover or work hard shifts. Tuffin and Baladi note that part-time officers were not seen to fit in with a working culture whose officers 'could be handed their jackets and told to get out there at any time.' Moreover, front line managers whom they interviewed were very defensive about utilising part-time working options, because of a culture of fear in which they were concerned about being 'bashed' by management for not being able to provide cover, or for causing staff discontent for not handling part-time working properly. Basic command unit managers prefer managing staff on a rotating 24-hour, three-shift cover. In addition, in the long hours culture of the police, used as an informal measure of commitment, going home early was viewed negatively and was a potential inhibitor of promotion. So here is a further example of the 'business as usual' mentality.

New public sector management and the performance culture

In the mid-1980s pressure was exerted for the police to be incorporated within the Thatcher reforms of the public sector, resting on the doctrine that differences between public and private management could be eliminated. This required a shift from following procedural rules towards getting results (Leishman, *et al.*, 1996). In essence the organization of business changed from a hierarchical workforce with alienated assembly line workers to one which downsized, flattened hierarchies and used computer technology to augment physical labour. For the public sector this meant the introduction of competition, customer centredness and value for money. Personnel became human resource management, creating and motivating an inter-dependent work force.

Maddock (1999: 131) argues that this was a paradigm shift. Hierarchical public sector organizations were to be swept away. There would be no more buck-passing, or operating in cultures of inertia with staff rarely coming into contact with the consequences of their work. Rather than patronising clients, acting as dictators, following rules irrespective of appropriateness, closing their eyes to the impact of red tape to keep the system running, and positively revelling in inter-departmental jealousies, civil servants would finally be accountable.

Maddock suggests that the majority of those who were insistent that collaborative ways of working were essential to responding to such requirements were women. The more challenging exponents argued that there had to be changes in management structures, rewards systems and performance measures. They were not seeking a total feminisation, but a shift from the command and control model to a perspective that recognised human processes of change. Maddock concluded from a study of women involved in the public sector at this time that this project failed because of a lack of interest in process: 'Male colleagues justified their fear of process and practical implementation by snubbing women's efforts' (*op. cit.*: 163).

She goes on to argue that the women managers whom she studied in the public sector were 'overwhelmed by the pressure to avoid reality and hide behind old practices' (*op. cit.*: 166-7): 'Stressed, trapped, ... ignored, patronised, undervalued, misunderstood ... and labelled as troublemakers.' Their innovations were unheard or ignored, or were met with huge resistance or personal hostility. Thus they became disillusioned with New Public Management and managerialism which focussed on efficiency and an actuarial method of accountability. Women found that concepts such as contracting-out intensified competition rather than facilitated collaboration and reinforced the blame culture:

> What initially appeared as a liberation from red tape resulted in forms of performance management systems which rewarded cheap activities, fast results, macho and individualist behaviour ... What women desired from the dismantling of the bureaucracies was an openness to inclusive management, but what they got were tighter management systems. (*op. cit.*: 207)

The police service was one of the last major public bodies to be subjected to new public sector management principles. The Audit Commission studies of the late 1980s had revealed a bureaucratic maze of secrecy and rigid, antiquated fiscal arrangements. Funding was based on inputs rather than outputs (McLaughlin and Murji, 1996). Three significant initiatives were taken: the 1993 White Paper on police reform, an inquiry into police roles and responsibilities and a Home Office review on core and ancillary tasks.

The police service responded in two ways: resistance and retaliation. Resistance was well orchestrated and the three staff associations (Police Federation, Police Superintendents' Association and Association of Chief Police Officers) acted in concert to challenge the reform process. This remarkable coalition resulted in an untidy, mixed implementation. There was some new managerialism but it was an amalgam of humanistic management with the old quasi-military model. McLaughlin and Murji (1996) argue that ACPO considered that the existing cadre of senior officers, topped up with MBAs, could deliver the surviving reforms. They concluded that there was no real shift in the ingrained belief that if only sufficient resources were made available the job could be done with no embracing of a culture of efficiency, i.e. of doing more for less.

A further response by the police service itself was a self-initiated examination of the occupational culture and the development of the Quality of Service (QS) approach, which Waters (1996) suggests could have been the basis of a paradigm shift. Wolff Olins undertook a review of the Metropolitan Police and the report *A Force for Change* (1988) recommended a re-engaging of the community by a shift from force to service. Together with the impetus of various government inspired inquiries, this resulted in the collaboration of the three staff associations in the Operational Policing Review (1990). Its recommendations set the scene for a return of the service ethos and a re-statement of police professionalism and the birth of the Quality of Service initiative.

A major theme of Quality of Service was changing the police culture. It also suggested the introduction of qualitative performance indicators as a counter to the quantitative performance targets set by government. A Bramshill seminar 'Getting Things Right' stressed the importance of trust and openness in the organization and the benefits of consulting and empowering staff. This model of policing owed much to the pragmatic need to upstage government-inspired change; and was an attempt by the service to redefine itself rather than having new definitions imposed upon it (Brown and Waters 1996). In commenting upon its impact, Waters (1996: 212) indicates that there was some ambivalence about Quality of Service initiatives, and a belief that the canteen culture of junior ranks and operational demands of the sharp end would undermine QOS philosophy. There is some evidence (Brown and Campbell, 1994) that middle-ranking officers inhibited the Metropolitan Police Service's 'Plus' programme of cultural change inspired by the Wolff Olins report (1988). Waters (1996: 217) concluded:

> Although police leaders driving the quality movement utilised the concepts of total quality and sought to transplant these into the sphere of policing, there was arguably no serious attempt to emulate a business model in the pursuit of quality.

The cult of masculinity and the performance culture
Brown and Neville (1996) also proposed there was no fundamental change in the old order, which positively valued danger, excitement and 'good' arrests. These were mapped directly onto the 'new' order: valuing achievement of performance targets. Fielding (1994) argues that whilst women certainly perform patrol duties,

their time may be impeded by demands on them to engage in 'emotional' labour functions such as those dealing with the more vulnerable of police clientele. So women can be marshalled into serving the quality of service functions (as described by Walklate with respect to domestic violence above), whilst crime arrests become the quantitative performance measure left to men.

So the cult of masculinity slides seamlessly into the performance culture. Whilst having a different emphasis and a different language, performance culture has the same underlying principles of competition and the condoning of rule bending and rule breaking in order to achieve targets. According to Fielding (1994), it is harder for women to achieve these, partly because they are excluded from crime fighting activity. Brown and Neville (1996: 302) concluded that:

> Arrest is a significant performance indicator that both fulfils the competitive nature of the informal culture and satisfies the Audit Commission and Home Office requirement for tangible results.

Reiner (1994) articulates a similar point as follows when commenting on the raft of Conservative Party police reforms:

> What the government's current line amounts to is essentially saying to this rank and file culture, in which feeling collars is the only 'real' police work: 'You were right all along, boys. The rest is all bullshit'.

An investigation by Beck (2001) revisited the research site of Jones' (1986) study. Beck found evidence for the persistence of beliefs by policemen that they are better at the tough stuff of policing (arrests, firearms and public order) and women are better at dealing with other women and sexual offences. Beck reports that whilst women at senior level were perceived as having the potential to manage differently, they were thwarted and the transformational project frustrated. They were treated as outsiders and felt isolated and excluded from informal information exchange. Beck reports examples of exclusionary talk, derogatory attitudes and punishing women for promotion success.

It would seem that there are few examples of Rosener's (1990) second generation of women leaders in the police. Silvestri's (2000) analysis of senior police women argues that this is due to occupational cultural constraints on women: their creativity was channelled into designing survival strategies of adaptation and conformity. Fielding (1999) puts it thus:

> We cannot look to the arrival in the police of female officers to change the way the police deliver their services ... While understandable as an adaptation ... Such officers are unlikely to challenge the established way of doing things.

New Labour: new policing?

If the police service thought that its alliance with the Labour Party in opposition would lead to any let-up in police reform when that party came to power, it was mistaken. Leishman, *et al.* (1999) argue that if anything, the political challenge to the police service presented by the present Labour government is even greater than the Conservatives' attempts at reform, for the following reasons.

- Firstly, they suggest that Labour's Best Value agenda for the public services is more radical than the Conservatives' Value for Money initiative. The essential principle of Best Value is delivering what works rather than who delivers the services. There is a statutory requirement to demonstrate the increasing efficiencies, effectiveness and quality of public services. There is a duty to set a target of 2 per cent efficiency gains year-on-year and the Home Office has powers to intervene if police authorities fail in this regard.

- Secondly, early measurement within the public sector was designed to examine resources inputs and employee performance outputs. The emphasis now is much more on outcomes.

- Thirdly, there is a greater concentration on consultation with consumers when determining the priorities and design of service provision, with emphasis located on the socially excluded and hard-to-reach groups.

- Fourthly, the human rights agenda will create challenges in morally ambiguous areas of criminality such as drugs and public order. The police will be required to develop reflective practice when considering training, supervision and management.

- Fifthly, the Labour administration requires evidence-based practice where increasingly policy and expenditure must be justified. Overall, Leishman, *et al.* (1999: 2) propose that:

  > What distinguishes the present scenario from that prevailing in the 1990s is the sheer scope of the challenges to the status quo of policing in Britain.

- A further challenge to policing is the Crime and Disorder Act 1998. This signalled a movement away from the police being the primary agency concerned with prevention and detection of crime to being one of several. The local authority has a statutory duty to form crime reduction partnerships, which involves auditing crime and disorder problems in their individual areas. There is a requirement to consult with the community and harmonise plans with the various partnership agencies such as the probation, health services and so forth. The key change this heralds is an end to the monopolistic powers of the police to police.

The Home Secretary, David Blunkett, expounded upon the modernising project of the present round of police reform in a speech to the Police Superintendents' Association in September 2001, in which he stated that the aim was to raise standards and improve performance. Deployments were to be made on the basis of analysis and intelligence. Basic Command Units, to make more flexible use of staff, were both to meet the diverse needs of the workforce and deliver efficient and effective services to the local community. The emphasis for the new generation of police leaders will be on quality and integrity. Fast tracking could see movement from constable to BCU commander in five years.

A new patriarchy: smart macho policing?
Hopton (1999) proposes that this version of managerialism is a new form of patriarchy that simply perpetuates masculine values. In a helpful analysis Maddock and Parkin (1993) define a typology of working practices that represents a response to new managerialism. These include 'smart macho' where managers are fierce, tough, forceful, quick thinking and risk taking. Maddock (1999: 92) suggested that the smart macho culture is:

> Prevalent in health care organizations and reinforces a functional approach to management. Managers are expected to be workaholics and to be ruthless in their pursuit of goals and targets at the expense of staff and social relationships.

Silvestri (2001) argues that this characterises police management in the new millennium. It is a response to demands for resourceful Best Value requirements, increasing media scrutiny and public criticism, especially in the aftermath of the MacPherson report (1999). She concludes (2001: 301):

> The new smart macho culture ... has impacted on women's decisions to move up the ranks. The reduction of management posts appears to have strengthened the predominant 'male' culture of long hours and aggressive and competitive behaviour. The inclusion of long working hours into the construction of management continues to be justified on the grounds of operational necessity. In turn, this also contributes to the process of gender demarcation and exclusion. The imagery of the policing career tends to define the career as at odds with domestic responsibilities. As a result it appeals primarily to single people, men and women who can devote themselves single-mindedly to the police ... If women in management choose to limit their working hours they do so in the knowledge that they may also be limiting their career opportunities.

Watson (1992) showed that in Australia a version of new public sector management argued that 'femocrats' offered a model of feministic working practice within managerialism. This utilised alternative conceptualisations about work and offered new ways of dealing with problems. Watson argued that the Women's Electoral Lobby developed a political agenda that coincided with a reforming government committed to opening up public services which reflected changing community needs.

The 'Gender Agenda'
Although not couched in recognisably feminist language, the Gender Agenda initiative launched in 2001 by the British police service does present a potential paradigm shift in reforming working practices within the police. By asking the women's question, the Gender Agenda raises consciousness about the long hours culture, including breakfast and twilight meetings. It challenges stereotypical thinking and offers alternative working practices. Its vision is that of a 'moral and ethical approach which ensures that all staff, regardless of their membership of any identifiable category, are neither advantaged nor disadvantaged in pursuing their duty or their career.'

The Gender Agenda sees that tackling the women's question will benefit the whole organization. It will utilise feminine as well as masculine ways of doing things, engage in an organizational style of interaction with its staff and customers that is reasonable and fair, and bring fresh and flexible approaches to working practices. It is a potential paradigm shift in reforming working practices within the police.

The full impact of this on the police service and whether this heralds a more radical way to transform the police and deliver on the new wave of police reforms awaits evaluation. Pessimistically, past evidence would suggest that the police occupational culture will absorb and neutralise this attempt at reform as it has neutralised others. There needs to be a more radical shift towards better styles of leadership and greater numbers of women at senior rank before real change will occur.

REFERENCES for *Chapter 13*

Adams, K (2001), *Women in Senior Police Management*, Payneham, South Australia: Australasian Centre for Policing Research.

Anderson, R, Brown, JM and Campbell, EA (1993), *Aspects of Sex Discrimination in Police Forces in England and Wales*, London: Home Office Police Research Group.

Beck, R (2001), *Integration or Exclusion? Perceptions and the Reality of Gender Equity in Policing*, University of Cardiff: Unpublished research.

Bradley, D, Walker, N and Wilkie, R (1986), *Managing the Police: Law, Organization and Democracy*, Brighton: Wheatsheaf.

Brown, JM (1997), 'Equal Opportunities and the Police of England and Wales: Past, Present and Future Possibilities' in Francis, P, Davies, P, and Jupp, V (eds.), *Policing Futures: The Police, Law Enforcement and the Twenty-First Century*, London: Macmillan.

Brown, JM and Neville, E (1996), 'Arrest Rate as a Measure of Policemen and Women's Productivity and Competence', *Police Journal*, LXIX 299-307.

Brown, JM and Waters, I (1996), 'Force Versus Service' in Waddington, D, and Critcher, C (eds.), *Policing Public Order*, Aldershot: Avebury.

Brown, JM and Heidensohn, F (2000), *Gender and Policing: Comparative Perspectives*, London, Macmillan.

Cavender, G, and Jurik, N C (1998), 'Jane Tennison and Feminist Police Procedural', *Violence Against Women*, 4 10-29.

Chan, J (1996), 'Changing Police Culture', *British Journal of Criminology* 36 109-134.

Fielding, N (1999), 'Policing's Dark Secret: The Career Paths of Ethnic Minority Officers', *Sociological Research Online*, 4/1 http://www.socresonline.org.uk/socresonline/4/lawrence/fielding.html.

Halford, S, Savage, M and Witz, A (1997), *Gender, Careers and Organizations*, London: Macmillan.

Heidensohn, F (1992), *Women in Control: The Role of Women in Law Enforcement*, Oxford: Clarendon.

Jenkins, R (1974), Speech to the Police Federation, *Police*, 12 August, 24.

Jones, S (1986a), *Policewomen and Equality*, London: Macmillan.

Jones, S (1986b), 'Caught in the Act', *Policing*, 2, 129-140.

Jones, S (1987), 'Making it Work: Some Reflections on the Sex Discrimination Act', *Police Journal*, 60 294-302.

Jones, T, and Newburn, T (2002), 'The Transformation of Policing? Understanding Current Trends in Policing Systems', *British Journal of Criminology*, 42, 129-146.

Home Office (1989), *Equal Opportunities in the Police Service*, Circular 87/89, London: Home Office.

Home Office (1990), *Domestic Violence*, Circular 60/90, London: Home Office.

Hopton, C (1991), 'Militarism, Masculinism and Managerialisation in the British Public Sector', *Journal of Gender Studies*, 20, 225-239.

Hunt, RG, and Magenau, JM (1993), *Power and the Police Chief: An Institutional and Organizational Analysis*, London: Sage.

Kanter, R B (1977), 'Some Effects of Proportions on Group Life: Skewed Sex Ratios and Response to Token Women', *American Journal of Sociology*, 82, 965-990.

Kuhn, T S (1962), *The Structure of Scientific Revolutions*, Chicago: University of Chicago Press.

Ledwith, S, and Colgan, F (eds.) (1996), *Women in Organizations: Challenging Gender Politics*, London: Macmillan.

Leishman, F, Cope, S and Starie, P (1996), 'Reinventing and Restructuring: Towards a New Policing Order' in Leishman, F, Loveday, B and Savage, S P, *Core Issues in Policing*, London: Longmans.

Leishman, F, Loveday, B and Savage, S (eds.) (2000), *Core Issues in Policing*, Harlow: Pearson Educational, second edition.

Levine, P (1994), 'Walking the Streets in a Way no Decent Woman Should: Women Police in World War I', *Journal of Modern History*, 66, 34-78.

Macpherson, Sir William of Cluny (1999), *The Stephen Lawrence Inquiry*, Cm. 4262, London: Stationery Office.

McLaughlin, E and Murji, K (1996), 'Times Change: New Foundations and Representations of Police Accountability' in Waddington, D, and Chritchner, C (eds.), *Public Order Policing*, Aldershot: Avebury.

Maddock, S (1999), *Challenging Women; Gender, Culture and Organization*, London: Sage.

Maddock, S and Parkin, D (1993), 'Gender Cultures: Women's Choices and Strategies at Work', *Women in Management Review*, 8, 3-10.

Martin, S (1979), *Breaking and Entering*, Berkeley: California University Press.

Martin, S (1990), *Women on the Move: A Report on the Status of Women in Policing*, Washington: Police Foundation.

Police Federation Joint Consultative Committee (1990), *Operational Policing Review*, Surbiton: Police Federation.

Price, B R (1974), 'Is Police Work Changing as a Result of Women's Contribution?' Paper presented to the International Conference on Policewomen, The Netherlands, 19-23 March.

Reiner, R (1985), *The Politics of the Police*, Brighton: Wheatsheaf.

Reiner, R (1992), 'Policing a Post-modern Society', *The Modern Law Review*, 55, 761-781.

Reiner, R (1994) Address to ACPO in Association with ACC and AMAS, 1994 Summer Conference, Bournmouth.

Rosener, J B (1990), 'Ways Women Lead', *Harvard Business Review*, Nov/Dec, 119-25.

Silvestri, M (2000), *Visions of the Future: The Role of Senior Policewomen as Agents of Change*, University of London: PhD Thesis.

Smith, D and Gray, J (1985), *Police and People of London: The PSI Report*, London: Public Service Institute.

Tuffin, R, and Baladi, Y (2001), *Flexible Working Practices in the Police Service*, Home Office Police Research Paper No. 147.

Walklate, S (1996), 'Equal Opportunities and the Future of Policing' in Leishman, F, Loveday, B, and Savage, S (eds.), *Core Issues in Policing*, London: Longmans.

Waddington, P A J (1999), 'Police (Canteen) Culture: An Appreciation', *British Journal of Criminology*, 39, 287-309.

Waters, I (1996), 'Quality of Service: Politics or Paradigm Shift?' in Leishman, F, Loveday, B, and Savage, S (*op.cit.*)

Watson, S (1992), 'Femocratic Feminisms' in Savage, M, and Witz, A (eds.), *Gender and Bureaucracy*, Oxford: Blackwells.

Wolff Olins (1988), *A Force for Change: A Report on the Corporate Identity of the Metropolitan Police*, London: private publication. Available at the National Police Library, Bramshill.

CHAPTER 14

The Mask of Police Command

John Grieve

John Grieve believes that the police have something to learn from the army, in its *organized* studies of both professional history and doctrine. Although police leaders may be described as unheroic, their task is still a highly demanding one; and successful police leadership requires the acceptance and management of risk. All this can make great demands on the psyche, and the task is full of paradox: 'One of the difficult things about policing is that you have to care about people to become a really good police officer: but you cannot care too much.' In this chapter John Grieve shows that he cares about good leadership.

In his excellent book *The Mask of Command* (1987) Sir John Keegan explores the notion of successful generalship by considering the mask that a leader dons. He describes the masks that a leader may assume as heroic, anti-heroic, unheroic or falsely heroic, and exemplifies what he means by each style, mask or model of leadership by means of a lengthy examination of a leading practitioner.

Thus, Alexander the Great (356–323 BC) was a heroic leader, who exposed himself to maximum risk because that was an integral part of his style of command, which emphasised courage, risk and theatricality, and to which the power of inspirational oratory was central.

The Duke of Wellington (1769–1852), by contrast, was anti-heroic. His image, if not necessarily the reality, was of a cold, aloof and aristocratic director of operations, who despised oratory and made no attempt to inspire the ordinary soldier—although he could show an explosive temper and withering sarcasm with those of his associates who displeased him.

General Ulysses S Grant (1822–1885) was a man of the people in a people's war, and his style of command was both effective and deliberately unheroic. Grant would expose himself to danger if he had to do so, but did not see it as the role of the leader to share the risks of his men. His philosophy of war was an extremely simple one, and his style of generalship was designed to put it into effect.

Finally, Adolf Hitler (1889–1945), as Supreme Commander of the Wehrmacht, was falsely heroic. He made great play of the fact that he had shared the risks and privations of the common soldier in the Great War—as indeed he had. However, during the Second World War he retreated to his various command posts, a long way from any fighting, and directed operations from afar: leaving Dr Goebbels, the so-called Minister for Enlightenment (and spin doctor *par excellence*) to sustain the myth of the Führer who shared the pain of his people.

In Keegan's view, all save Hitler's styles were both valid and effective in their time and place. Hitler's style of command was fundamentally flawed and led ultimately to catastrophic defeat.

In reflection on military leadership as it has been displayed since 1945, Keegan does not reject heroic leadership as an obsolete style of command: indeed, he points to its effectiveness in the Falklands War. But there is much more to leadership than the risks courted by the leader. According to Keegan there are five imperatives that any system of leadership must accommodate:

1. Kinship
The leader surrounds himself with intimates identifiable by his followers as common spirits with themselves. (Hitler, of course, surrounded himself with sycophants and toadies whose only real task was to listen to his incessant monologues, and he failed to make contact with those whom he led.)

2. Sanction
Followers are rewarded or punished according to an accepted value system. (Wellington, the aristocratic leader, made considerable use of flogging. Grant, by contrast, who led a predominantly volunteer army, was reluctant to punish, although he would do so when necessary.)

3. Example
The leader accepts for himself the risk he imposes on others. (Wellington and Grant both avoided unnecessary risk, but did what was necessary to direct combat. Alexander the Great was what would now be described as a compulsive risk- taker, and his style of command was inseparable from personal example. Consequently, he was always in the thick of the fighting, and frequently injured.)

4. Prescription
The leader explains the need for risk-taking in direct speech to his followers. (Of the four examples, Alexander was the master orator. Hitler used both rallies and propaganda as reinforcement. Wellington and Grant, by contrast, practised no oratory with their troops at all, in any formal sense. Both went on to high political office after military command.)

5. Action
This translates leadership into effect, of which victory is the desired result.

Commentary
We have turned to a military source for our first exploration of leadership, and must briefly explain both why this is potentially controversial and why we have chosen to do it.

The relationship between command of soldiers and command of police officers, more particularly of detective officers, is a source of deep paradox. As we have seen in *Chapter 1*, there is an ambiguous relationship between the police and the army that has its roots deep in the origins of the modern police service and lives on in its ongoing campaign to distance itself from its quasi-military origins. Moreover, in Villiers' opinion, police leadership presents a more complex challenge than leadership in battle, where the task is normally rather more straightforward, and the result easier to judge.

Why do the police, then, need to look to the military for lessons on leadership? For the simple but very cogent reason that military history is very much better documented than the history of policing, and there are many pragmatic lessons to be drawn. One day, perhaps, the police will carry out proper debriefs and produce its own histories. Until then, it must look elsewhere.

LEADERSHIP, COURAGE AND PHYSICAL PRESENCE

The concept of the 'Mask of Command' enables us to challenge assumptions and probe their real value. For example, we may have made the assumption that any sort of leadership, but especially in the police, requires heroism, and that the leader as hero always leads from the front. Is this necessarily so? Or is there a need sometimes, as military leaders discovered long ago, for some distance, psychological as well as physical, between the leader and those whom he leads? We may take this further and ask if the leader need always be present at all with those whom he leads. What does he fear will happen, when he is away? Has he created the right sort of team, if his presence is necessary to ensure the right behaviour?

SHARING THE RISK

There will be occasions when the presence of the leader at or near the point of conflict is appropriate. However, good police leaders need not always be present to command their officers, nor share the physical dangers that they face in order to merit their respect. The leader's physical presence is not always necessary. But what we might call his moral presence is another matter.

If he need not always be present, the police leader must share the moral risks that any police officer faces. Leadership means more than investigating what has gone wrong and apportioning blame, after the event in question. The good leader shares in the risks of the decision-making process, and thereby both sets an example to those whom he commands and emphasises his kinship with them.

Heroic leadership may be necessary in a riot. But the enduring challenge to the police leader is, perhaps, the less heroic but more difficult one of being able to make unheroic but competent decisions, under pressure, with inadequate information, time and time again: and of being able to sell those decisions not only to an angry or disbelieving public, but on occasion to one's own workforce.

Those decisions need to be balanced, consistent with the values of the organization, and defendable in a court of law. They concern what is acceptable at the margins of permissible police behaviour. In other words, they are in the area of assessing and managing risk.

The risk model currently in use in the Metropolitan Police Service comprises physical, psychological, political, legal, economic and moral dimensions. It is intended to help commanders to evaluate, assess and manage risk. The model was originally prepared for police informant handling and management, and has been extended to include undercover operations, armed interception and general leadership in areas of high tension and critical incidents. The activity of thinking about risk and whether or not to accept it is one method of reducing its negative impact. As in testing a new aeroplane, however, the police decision-maker comes to a point where simulation is not enough, and, like the test pilot, he must strap himself into the machine and fly it.

THE PEACE MODEL: THE SEVEN 'C'S

Where do we turn for a model for contemporary police leadership? The work of Bill Peace, a senior manager in the commercial sector whose work has had considerable influence within the Metropolitan Police Service, can be viewed as an overarching framework within which other schemes can be accommodated. It is conveniently described as the seven Cs.

1. Creating a vision
This means expressing a clear idea about the nature of the work and about its values and standards. It is directly related both to quality of measurable service and to moral leadership. It is about defining roles and goals and is a process that is inherently high in potential conflict.

Sir Peter Imbert, Metropolitan Police Commissioner from 1987 to 1993, created the vision for me by seeking cultural change in an organization policing a very different society to that of 1829, when Sir Robert Peel founded the Metropolitan Police. The statement of common purpose and values to which the Association of Chief Police Officers adheres is the basis for proper policing in the United Kingdom. It is the vision.

The remaining six Cs provide a means for the police to make the vision a reality.

2. Communication
This means both speaking and listening. Active listening includes listening to what is not being said, remembering it and referring to it later. Listening too much is a very rare fault.

3. Competence
The competent leader knows what the individual skills are that his team needs in order to achieve its collective task, and the pressures that they bring with them. He is able to recognise, identify and develop the skills of his team, and to provide support where necessary.

4. Caring about people
One of the difficult things about policing is that you have to care about people to become a really good police officer: but you cannot care too much. You have to be objective, to stand apart whilst at the same time to care for everyone, be they victim, alleged offender or colleague. At the same time, you cannot be experienced as patronising. There is then a considerable temptation to don a mask and to be unhelpful rather than helpful. We may need to help someone to grow by giving them information, even if it is not necessarily information which a police organization would have revealed in the past. Mrs Lawrence said at the public

inquiry into the murder of her son, to which we shall refer again later: 'We weren't given information: we were patronised'.

5. Confronting the issues

Sir John Smith, the former Deputy Metropolitan Police Commissioner (1991 to 1995), referred to this 'C' as the courage to confront the real issues. This may include declaring a view on a moral controversy of the day, such as the use of drugs or the inadequacies of the criminal justice system. Other issues will arise within the police service which equally require confrontation, such as corruption; and the good police leader may be required to examine his own organization and openly identify its weaknesses. Police chiefs are not the elected spokespersons of society. But they are moral agents with moral views; and integrity begins with honesty.

We may offer a practical example here, which will strike chords for many police officers in a number of situations, and where legal advice and the fundamentals of leadership may come into opposition.

Suppose that the police unit that you lead has been strongly and publicly criticised for its handling of a particular episode or series of episodes.

In your personal and so far private opinion, there may well be some validity in these criticisms, no matter what political motives may inspire those who express them. Perhaps the unit in question *was* rather slow in responding to the problem in question. Perhaps it *did* fail to show the level of professionalism that you would like to have seen in dealing with the issues. And perhaps you *can* understand the anger and frustration felt by the victims or their relatives and associates, who wished for an explanation of what occurred, but came up time and time against a stolid wall of apparent indifference.

The question is, what are you to do with your private thoughts and emotions? The official response, we would suggest, is that the police leader should admit nothing that could be used against the service in terms of liability. He cannot take refuge in silence if he is to face the press conference at all. But he must be extremely cautious in what he says. If he wishes to strike a note of regret that someone has been robbed, raped or murdered, he may do so. But what he must never do is apologise for what has happened, and the police role in it. For an apology may be construed as a legal admission of culpability, which can be used against the police in court. It may also imply to those under command that the officer in charge has a less than perfect confidence in their abilities.

To confront the issues is to face this dilemma, as others, and to decide that on some occasions an apology may be the proper response.

6. Consistency

Consistency is a fundamental moral virtue, and a necessary but not sufficient quality in a leader. We may, after all, be consistently wrong. But the leader who acts arbitrarily or irrationally, so that his actions and reactions cannot be predicted, is giving no moral clues to those whom he leads as to what he really believes in and supports.

7. Charisma

Charisma, in the sense of involvement, can be developed. We need to be very good at promotions or transfer celebrations, at recognition and at the challenge of not taking oneself too seriously. Humour is a much under-rated leadership and fellowship tool. People will live up to your expectations provided they believe that you are not just using them. (I was never in any doubt that the driving school empowered me as Head of Training to lead them even though I am a detective, don't drive and failed their most basic course. They never failed to mention it at every celebration). It is equally important to attend and speak at farewell functions and funerals.

CONCLUSION

Chuck Yeager, the test pilot who broke the sound barrier in the X1 aircraft, described risk management as the difference between landing safely and drilling a 40-foot hole in the runway. He also said there was no sense of being a test pilot that did not involve getting into an aircraft and flying[1]. By analogy, police leadership must be both practical and applied.

There are very real risks in policing. I wish to emphasise moral risk in the minefield of policing, as opposed to the risk of physical violence. In my mind there is no sense of any aspect of policing in the twenty-first century that does not involve some elements of moral risk. The main challenge to the leader is to ensure that he has adequately prepared both himself and those whom he commands to assess those risks properly; and that he is prepared to take the lead in confronting them.

Editorial note
The Stephen Lawrence Inquiry of 1997-1999 was a significant event in contemporary policing, and one which demonstrated a significant contrast of approach amongst police leaders, in the Metropolitan Police and elsewhere.

The Lawrence Report (Macpherson, 1999) into the unsolved murder of a black London teenager, Stephen Lawrence, stated that the Metropolitan Police were guilty of institutional racism, and that this had contributed to their inability to solve the crime. Institutional racism was defined as something like unwitting racism: in other words, a prejudice so deep-seated within the organization as unwittingly to guide it in thought and action. This is not the same as to say that a specified police officer is individually and consciously racist.

The Commissioner of the Police of the Metropolis was asked if the charge fitted, and replied that it did not. The Metropolitan Police were not institutionally racist. John Grieve, the Deputy Assistant Commissioner appointed to command the special task force set up to investigate racial and violent crime in the aftermath of the Lawrence murder, was asked the same question. He saw the need to answer this question with complete honesty, as a moral agent; and replied that in his opinion the charge fitted and the police were institutionally racist.

We need not imply less moral motives to the commissioner, nor to any other police leader who honestly reached another answer. Ethical examination does not always lead to the same results, for the essence of ethics is about making informed and justifiable choices, and sticking by them once made.

The key point here, for the purposes of our doctrine of police leadership, is that John Grieve recognised that his admission would have two consequences:

- he would be perceived by the public, or at least part of it, as admitting to a general charge of racism on the part of the police; and
- he would be perceived by the police force itself, or at least part of it, as an unheroic leader: someone who was not prepared to stand up for the men and women he commanded, but who pleaded guilty to a specious charge.

From the ethical standpoint this was a difficult choice.

A consequentialist such as Jeremy Bentham (1748—1832) might argue that John Grieve should have denied the charge, since at least in the short term its results were bound to be disadvantageous for the organization, and therefore for the general happiness. Why? Because the effectiveness of the police service would be reduced through a lessening of confidence in its abilities.

A deontologist such as Kant (1724—1804), on the other hand, would have applauded the choice as based on the best of motives, whatever its outcome.

The ethicist might also point out that the moral agent can only be held responsible for what he has decided, and not how it is perceived by others, provided that he takes reasonable steps to explain the reasons for his decision.

From the point of view of leadership theory, the leader who is looking for a short-term fix may take the apparently easy way out. The leader who is seeking to identify and uphold the long-term interests of the organization, however, is perhaps more likely to find that honesty and long-term interests coincide.

As in so many moral dilemmas, however, we suspect that the path of history is likely to prove ambivalent in indicating whether or not the right choice was made. The acceptability of an organization such as the Metropolitan Police Service does not depend upon the decisions of one person, no matter how important, but on how the bulk of its activities are perceived over time. It would be impossible to calculate the impact made by one decision as to whether to admit or deny a charge, upon the general welfare of either the police or those whom they serve.

Under such conditions, we need to ask other questions. How did the leader feel, having made the decision in question? What happened, when he had to live with it? Did he succeed in communicating what he was trying to achieve to the reasonable person? Would he do the same thing again, if faced with the same choice?

In the end, leadership, as ethics, is a matter of choice. What would we have done? John Grieve's conclusion is our own. Good leaders need to grapple with moral dilemmas and be aware of how to assess the risk of the various options open to them. They need to take the standpoint of the moral agent, and decide upon the right course of action accordingly. And they need the emotional resilience, as well as the moral courage, to be able to live with the consequences of an unpopular decision. The police service needs not heroism but stoicism, and the aphorism of Sir Robert Mark fits here as elsewhere: 'The police can only win by appearing to lose'.

The assessment of risk

We agree with John Grieve that risk cannot be avoided but must be assessed, while pointing out that there is an inescapable element of subjectivity about the assessment of risk that must be recognised. Risk and how human beings cope with it is the subject of a fascinating study by Professor John Adams (1995). Some calculations are more easily made. It is reasonable to decide not to undertake a course of action that has a high probability of leading to a disastrous outcome, if there is a choice. By the same token, it is reasonable to decide to do something which is unlikely to lead to an undesirable outcome, and where that outcome would not in any case be disastrous.

However, most options are not so easily calculated in terms of costs and benefits. Moreover, some people—and organizations—are more disposed to accept a higher level of risk than others. But to point out that we cannot calculate uncertainty with precision, for both empirical and definitional reasons, is not to recommend that we should not assess risk at all. That is the difference between reason and recklessness.

The qualities of the leader

What sort of leader is prepared, in the full sense of the word, to lead under the sort of conditions that John Grieve describes and to avoid the twin dangers of cynicism and false heroics? We return to kinship. Grant surrounded himself with the sort of men with whom he felt comfortable, not so that they would applaud his decisions but so that he remained in touch with the feelings of a volunteer army. Police leaders need to keep in touch with those whom they lead, and to share the moral risks that they face in the moral minefield of policing. And if policing by consent is to have any real significance, the kinship of police leaders must include the public whom they serve.

We agree with John Grieve's assessment. The model of the leader as omnipresent and perhaps charismatic hero may be appropriate when asserting moral leadership, or achieving cultural change in particularly challenging circumstances. But the more general task of the police leader in the twenty-first century, even in a situation of shared crisis, may be the decidedly less heroic, if more challenging, task of validating the teamwork of others by means of modesty, prudence and rationality.

REFERENCES for *Chapter 14*

Adams, J (1995), *Risk*, London: University College of London Press.
Bentham, J (1967), *A History of Philosophy*, Vol. 8, New York: Image Books. Series author: Copleston, F.
Kant, I (1965), (1967), *A History of Philosophy*, Vol. 6, New York: Image Books. Series author: Copleston, F.

---

[1] Charles Elwood Yeager was born in 1923. He was a fighter pilot in World War II and the Korean War and the first man to break the sound barrier in 1947 and to fly at twice the speed of sound in 1953: *Yeager: An Autobiography*, (1986), Yeager C and Janos L, currently available from Bantam Books, USA.

CHAPTER 15

Where Leadership Meets Strategy: Adding Value from the Top

Garry Elliott

Garry Elliott here takes a short but hard look at the role of the chief police officer, and predicts that it will have to change:

> For a police force, the question can be summed up as, how do the corporate decision-making processes add value? More directly this question asks, what value does the ACPO team add? Does it stretch the resources of the force or use them up? Does it offer a form of special understanding or discipline or does it choke progress with constraints or delays?

Superintendent Elliott then reviews four ways for the chief officer to add value, and continues:

> All of these four means of adding value are effective in the right context. The challenge for chief officers is to recognise the paradoxes and weaknesses associated with each and to be sure that the value gained does not outweigh the cost.

This is a thoughtful and realistic analysis by a reflective practitioner who is always prepared to challenge assumptions and to look for the evidence.

In the 1951 film *Captain Horatio Hornblower*, the captain saves an ordinary seaman from serious injury by shouting a warning to him. The man is deeply grateful, not just for the warning, but more because the captain knew his name. The crew would have followed Hornblower anywhere after that. Some may see this as the essence of leadership. However, what if he had been captain of an aircraft carrier with a crew of 6,000 instead of 60? How would he have displayed such obvious leadership attributes? What is expected of the leaders at the top of organizations as large as police forces? How do members of the Association of Chief Police Officers (ACPO) add value to their organizations?

The context within which the police service operates is changing. During the past ten years focus has increasingly been moving onto Basic Command Units (BCUs), partnerships and the importance of Community Safety Strategies. As this change takes place, ACPO teams need to consider how they can best influence their forces and how the current styles of leading and managing may have to be adapted. There is a great deal that can be learned from experience in other large organizations. Chief officers have much in common with the chief executives of diversified corporations. Developments in styles of corporate leadership can suggest approaches that could help the police service as it evolves in a climate of change.

THE JOB OF A LEADER

Leaders inspire. Leaders motivate. Leaders give direction. Good leaders get extraordinary performance from their people. Leaders make sure that success will carry on next year! However, leaders can sometimes stop adding some value and just start getting in the way. Examples can be seen every Saturday afternoon throughout the country. A football manager shouting from the touch-line as he sees his team fail to grasp opportunities may simply be overtaken by the emotion of the afternoon. The look of exasperation on his face as he realises his shouts are being ignored is probably not justified. He's just forgotten that his job is over for the moment and it's time to think about how well he did it. Leaders can destroy value as well as add it. They can distract, send out conflicting messages, and use resources (including their own and others' energy) wrongly. Usually, they don't realise that their efforts are taking away more than they add.

The Audit Commission recognised 'strategic management and leadership' as one of the key roles of police force headquarters[1]. The study sees the two aspects of senior policing as one. No attempt is made to define these terms tightly, but the Audit Commission suggests that they involve 'setting and co-ordinating force-wide strategy' and 'the scrutiny and monitoring of BCU performance'.[2]

The debate about the difference between leadership and management continues[3]. It is sometimes suggested that achieving the most senior position in any organization means a decreased need for managerial skills and an increased need for leadership skills. In most senior posts, is there really a difference, or should the two aspects be packaged together as the Audit Commission suggests? Yukl suggested that the huge number of different definitions of leadership and management available had little in common, but that all involved the idea of 'a process whereby intentional influence is exerted by one person over other people to guide, structure and facilitate activities and relationships in a group or organization'.[4]

At the personal level where individuals relate to individuals, how this influence is exerted is widely understood. The police service has a large number of very capable leaders at all levels who have the ability to command, inspire and influence others. The qualities and attributes of leaders are regularly appraised in assessment centres and individuals and organizations are willing to invest heavily, sometimes in surprising ways, to develop these qualities in their managers. When the leader is at the apex of the organization these personal attributes can only be part of the story. Evidence of the extra skills required comes from the findings of the inquiry into the murder of Stephen Lawrence.[5] The inquiry suggested that the Metropolitan Police was prone to 'institutional racism' which it defined as:

> The collective failure of an organization to provide an appropriate and professional service to people because of their colour, culture or ethnic origin. It can be seen or detected in the processes, attitudes and behaviour which amounts to discrimination through unwitting prejudice, ignorance, thoughtlessness and racist stereotyping which disadvantage minority ethnic people.

This statement recognises that an organization is much more than the sum of the actions of people working for it. Employees behave 'unwittingly' because they are influenced by aspects of the organization which can give rise to the 'collective failure' perceived in this case. Organizations can have their own dynamic which will affect the attitude and behaviour of individuals. That dynamic results from a broad range of issues which go beyond personal leadership. Leadership of organizations goes beyond leading people.

WHERE DOES ORGANIZATIONAL INFLUENCE COME FROM?

In the 1980s Tom Peters and Robert Waterman looked at a range of companies, searching for the sources of excellence[6]. Their findings led to the identification of seven factors which have become widely known as the McKinsey 7-S. They argued that it was the right mix of strategy, structure, systems, staff, skills, style and shared values which ensured success in an organization. Strategic leaders are not only judged on personal influence. They must consider organizational aspects such as the control of work, systems of communication, performance measurement, the level of skills in their workforce and the structure of contacts with customers. Good performance needs mixtures and interactions of both hard and soft aspects of organizations.

When the role of a leader changes from influencing individuals to influencing organizations the thrust of leadership converges with other areas of what is usually called management. The strategic leader is the strategic manager.

STRUCTURAL CHANGE

As pressure mounts for increased performance and change, the importance to police forces of effective strategic management/leadership at the start of the twenty-first century is becoming more acute. The past ten years have seen the start of the most significant structural change in the history of the police in the UK. Increasingly, the focus of the policing service is moving to Basic Command Units (BCUs). The signs of this have been growing. They are:

- the devolution of resources and accountability to BCU commanders;
- the inception of the inspections of BCUs and the publication of BCU performance figures;
- the importance of Crime and Disorder partnerships; and
- the increasing ability of local police to bid for funds direct from central government, missing out force management.

Similar changes are being experienced in other parts of the UK public sector and there can be no doubt that this will continue for the police. The Prime Minister could not have been clearer in a speech in October 2001 when he said, 'In policing, we are looking to devolve more power down to the Basic Command Units.'[7]

The job of chief constables has been slowly changing for much of the last century. This long term change from being 'commanders' to 'managers' is well documented by Robert Reiner.[8] However, although the style of the role has been changing, the view of the role by most observers has remained rooted in the tripartite arrangement where, in the words of the Audit Commission, the chief constable 'directs and controls [the] police force'.[9] It is possible that the idea of what is meant by 'directs and controls' should be fundamentally questioned. The chief officer's role is facing a more fundamental challenge as control and accountability for operational matters becomes more dispersed. As the chief officer team of a force becomes more remote from the operational strategies, what is there left for them to do? What does strategic management/leadership mean?

POLICE FORCES AS ORGANIZATIONS

The structural changes set out earlier are merely accentuating what has always been known about police work—that it encompasses a variety of different products and 'for most purposes ... is a local service'[10].

Chief constables are now chief executives of diversified organizations. Police forces could be regarded as collections of businesses which could exist independently. Divisions between business units could be made functionally or geographically. Functions like crime investigation, traffic policing, Special Branch and public order policing could easily become separate organizations. Examples of this can be seen in other European countries and the USA. Similarly it would be possible for BCUs to exist independently.

Brigading units together to achieve some economies of scale is very different from suggesting that they should be in the same organization. Partnerships already exist between forces to share expensive equipment like helicopters, and functions like recruiting and training. This does not imply that that the partners need to be one force. Similarly, the contracting out of functions has shown that it is not necessarily beneficial to own everything. Businesses are grouped together under one strategic head to realise benefits. The question which any corporation faces is summed up by Collis and Montgomery in their study of corporate strategy: 'How can executives at the corporate level create tangible advantage for their business that makes the whole more than the sum of the parts?'[11]

For a police force, the question can be summed up as, how do the corporate decision making processes add value? More directly this question asks, what value does the ACPO team add? Does it stretch the resources of the force or use them up? Does it offer a form of special understanding or discipline or does it choke progress with constraints or delays?

Goold, *et al.* recognised four ways in which a corporate parent could create value; but also recognised in each of them paradoxes which needed to be overcome[12]. The four types of influence and the way in which they apply to a police force are shown in *Figure 1* along with the consequent paradox. Looking at each of these in turn shows how force headquarters can add or destroy value.

Influence	Description	Paradox
1. Stand alone influence	The parent enhances the stand alone performance of the BCUs	That managers removed from the business and able to devote a small proportion of their time to a particular business will be able to enhance the performance of the business's own dedicated management
2. Linkage influence	Enhancing the value of linkages between BCUs	That headquarters managers are able to perceive valuable linkages which are not apparent to enlightened and energetic BCU commanders
3. Functional and services influence	Providing functional leadership and cost effective services for BCUs	That an in-house staff department can out-perform specialist providers
4. Corporate development	Altering the portfolio of the BCUs	That corporate strategies will 'beat the odds' that most corporate initiatives misfire

Figure 1

1. Stand alone influence

This view of the headquarters as a source of expertise and wisdom which can help BCU commanders better manage their own resources is one which is quite prevalent. It can be seen in:

- 'Compstat' style processes where BCUs receive the benefit of advice, scrutiny and discipline from the ACPO team; or
- force policies which direct that certain operational decisions have to be referred upwards.

The value of these activities in terms of improved performance and avoidance of problems has been widely recognised but the cost in terms of delays in decisions, distractions from tasks and imposition of inappropriate strategies is always a risk. The failure of some forces to devolve decisions was criticised by the Audit Commission. It noted:

In some cases, it appears that devolution has not been considered because of an assumption that standards can only be assured through direct supervision ... BCU commanders are quite rightly frustrated by such situations.[13]

As the work of BCU commanders increasingly focuses on local needs, partnerships and priorities the ability of a manager from headquarters to add value to local decisions must be questioned.

2. Linkage influence

It can be argued that headquarters are able to co-ordinate and identify synergistic linkages between BCUs because they have a higher, detached view. Whilst this is an attractive argument, the real result can often be systems, structures and committees which use significant resources for questionable benefit. Most managers think that time spent in meetings could be used on more valuable activities.

Setting priorities and objectives which allow all parts of the force to focus on a single purpose is another way in which strategic managers can facilitate co-operative working of the different businesses they control. In reality, this can sometimes result in vague statements which either fail to provide the desired focus or impose inappropriate measures and demands on BCUs.

The value that is added by force 'corporate' strategies is often unclear. Many strategies appear to be the sum of BCU priorities and plans or just a reflection of Home Office constraints plus some broad objectives and a statement of mission which is similar to many others.

3. Functional and services influence

The idea of headquarters as a centre of expertise, whether it is in personnel management, catering or crime investigation, is found in all police forces. The value of concentrating particular specialisms is generally accepted but is open to question on two counts:

- In the past 30 years most forces have devolved a range of specialisms which were once thought to be best under central control. Forces have had to balance the need for operational managers to have control of the resources they use against the benefit of concentrating the expertise to gain economies of scale, more knowledgeable management and greater flexibility. If BCU commanders are to be held accountable for the performance of their units, they are likely to push for greater local control over resources. This has been recognised by the Audit Commission which concluded, 'most BCUs have insufficient delegated powers to be sure of carrying out their role efficiently and effectively.'[14]

- Most forces have contracted out functions which would once have been considered an integral part of headquarters. Recognition that external specialist providers can offer an acceptable service has been the catalyst for challenging the provision of all services in-house under the Best Value legislation.

4. Corporate development

Most force headquarters see themselves as the builders of the organization, setting long term plans for change and development and preparing the force for difficult times ahead. Goold, *et al.* found that in practice these high level plans were fraught with difficulty and would often not be implemented. Studies of the police service reveal similar problems. The Police Foundation looked at a number of policing strategies and found that few were successfully implemented, noting that:

they are predominantly exhortatory, abstract and the level of detail about the exact means of implementation under operational conditions is universally vague ... The question of 'exactly how' is rarely addressed.[15]

Each of these four means of adding value is effective in the right context. The challenge for chief officers is to recognise the paradoxes and weaknesses associated with each and to be sure that the value gained does not outweigh the cost.

SEIZING THE OPPORTUNITY

The reality is that many corporate parents do not create value in their businesses.[16] The problems outlined above often result in the parent destroying more value than it creates. Goold *et al* identified three conditions which needed to be present for a corporate strategy to be valuable:

1. there must be opportunities for the parent to improve performance which are seized in the corporate strategy;
2. the characteristics of the parent must match the opportunities; and
3. characteristics of the parent which do not match opportunities must not lead to value destruction which outweighs the value created. [17]

As the structure of forces change, there certainly are opportunities for chief officer teams to add value and improve performance, but they are probably not the same opportunities that were there ten years ago. At that time the prospects to improve performance were more plentiful and all of the styles of influencing set out above could be found in forces:

- ACPO teams significantly influenced local strategic planning and would even set out operational priorities and objectives to be followed locally.;
- force headquarters departments were specialist units that were the source of assistance and corporate policy; and
- both the role and the style of working of local units were directed from the centre.

A police force was then seen as the unit of policing and middle managers were expected to identify with the overall performance of the force rather than their local unit. Because the headquarters involved itself in setting operational objectives, the responsibility and accountability were shared between the local commander and the chief officer. Strong focus on short term performance indicators was not appropriate. Getting everyone focused on the problems of the force was the main agenda.

However, the situation today is significantly different. Local accountability means that the work of BCUs is becoming more diverse as the focus turns to local issues. Setting of priorities centrally risks causing harmful distraction rather than beneficial focus. At the same time the policing of a local area has become more specialist. Knowledge and skills need to fit the local context. Operational influence from a distant headquarters where the issues are inevitably less well understood is no longer helpful.

The past decade has seen the start of changes outlined earlier in this chapter. Local units are now held responsible for short term performance. This emphasis has sometimes been taken to extremes in 'Compstat' processes. The relationship between BCU commander and chief constable has changed, but perversely some forces are still trying to exert influence in the style that they used in 1990.

Value in forces is no longer added by the imposition of central operational priorities and policies. Corporate strategies must now concentrate more on how the effectiveness of BCUs is supported and encouraged. Corporate strategy should no longer try specifying what the BCU should do. A comparison with the vociferous football managers mentioned earlier illustrates the point. They need to learn that they have:

- selected the best players, built the team, given them the skills and appointed the captain;
- ensured that new talent is being developed and there is money to pay the wages; and
- provided facilities for the team and the fans.

They have worked round the McKinsey 7-S factors. They must now leave the players to kick the ball and score the goals.

ENDNOTES and REFERENCES for *Chapter 15*

[1] Audit Commission (2001), *Best Foot Forward: Headquarters' Support for BCUs*, London: Audit Commission, p. 5.

[2] *Ibid*, p. 11.

[3] Exemplified by MacDonald, I (2001), 'Lessons in Leading: Leadership in the Police Service', *Police Review*, Jane's Information Group, London (8 August 2001), p. 22.

[4] Yukl, G (1998), *Leadership in Organizations*, New Jersey: Prentice-Hall, p. 3.

[5] Macpherson, Sir William of Cluny (1999), *The Stephen Lawrence Inquiry*, Cm. 4262, London: Stationery Office.

[6] Peters, T J and Waterman, R H (1982), *In Search of Excellence: Lessons from America's Best Run Companies*, New York/London: Harper and Row, p. 10

[7] Blair, A (2001), 'Public Service Reform', Speech given at British Library, London, October 16.

[8] Reiner, R (1991), *Chief Constables: Bobbies, Bosses or Bureaucrats?*, London: Oxford University Press.

[9] Audit Commission (2001), *Best Foot Forward: Headquarters' Support for BCUs*, London: Audit Commission, p. 9.

[10] *Ibid*, p. 6.

[11] Collis, D. J. and Montgomery, C. (1999), 'Creating Corporate Advantage', *Harvard Business Review on Corporate Strategy*, p. 1.

[12] Goold, M, Campbell, A and Alexander, M (1994), *Corporate-Level Strategy: Creating Value in the Multi-Business Company*, Chichester: John Wiley and Sons, p. 79

[13] Audit Commission (2001), *Best Foot Forward: Headquarters' Support for BCUs*, London: Audit Commission, p. 19

[14] *Ibid*, p. 39.

[15] Irving, B L (2001), *An Independent Review of Police Management Training and Education: The Customer's Views*, London: Police Foundation.

[16] Goold, M, Campbell, A and Alexander, M (1994), *Corporate-Level Strategy: Creating Value in the Multi- Business Company*, Chichester: John Wiley and Sons, p. 82

[17] *Ibid*.

CHAPTER 16

This Complex Thing, Leadership

Robert Adlam

The terms 'leadership' and 'leader' continue to be widely invoked in discussions concerning human affairs in general. Evaluations both of the quality of leadership and the ability of the leader or leaders are usually inseparable features of those discussions. Police are no exception. Analyses, reviews and critiques of policing reveal a consistent interest in—and concern with—the standards and practices of police leadership as well as the conduct of police leaders. Whilst the new theorising of 'power law' suggests that, in fact, only a very few individuals can ever be widely esteemed and revered as 'exemplary' leaders (Buchanan, 2000) there are good grounds for thinking that the quality of police leadership—throughout the service as a whole and its separate organizations in particular—can be improved. At the very least police officers, wherever they may be positioned in the organization, can adopt a more disciplined approach to their professional practice—an approach that is informed by both the theoretical and practical knowledge that has accumulated in the field of leadership studies.

Even now, though, it is not uncommon to hear senior and experienced members of organizations generally—and police organizations specifically—express the view that leaders are 'born and not made'; leaders have, it appears, some preternatural faculty. Moreover, it is not uncommon for people in more subordinate organizational positions to express similar views. Consistent with this view is a scepticism about that which it is possible to attain through 'training' and 'development' programmes. It may even be the case that only a relatively small number of independent and emancipated thinkers—along with an equally small proportion of social inquirers—take the view that leadership is a very complex cultural phenomenon and that it is simply too facile to assert that some few people are, somehow, innately 'wired-up' or 'programmed' to lead. The overly simplistic assertions about leadership suggest widespread ignorance of the research findings. Police ignorance may be even more pronounced; it is by no means certain that senior and junior officers alike are familiar with the serious study of policing itself.

Police leadership—as a specific area of inquiry—has attracted a certain degree of scholarly attention. Reiner (1991), for example, advances a typology of chief constables, Adlam (1998a) prescribes the types of knowledge that properly might be expected of police leaders, whilst Vick (2000), implicitly acknowledging the nature of post-modern times, argues that senior police need to develop a key competency—consisting of the ability to produce 'credible' scripts.

Following the creation of a police college in 1948 a great deal of attention has been devoted to the study of senior police leadership and the provision of learning structures designed to promote and develop effective leaders. Whilst much of this has gone unrecorded—and the majority has remained informal in nature—the written material that has been stored and catalogued in the National Police Library suggests that police leadership can be viewed as an occupation-specific practice. So, for example, whilst the notion of 'command' can be usefully deployed in describing certain facets of police leadership it is not the same type of command that pervades practices within the armed services. This is because the individual constable enjoys considerable discretionary authority.

Police leadership is also tied to the occupational culture. Indeed, police leaders and their styles are constructed within and spring from a distinct cultural milieu. Police culture impresses as unique, multiform and complex. Police leadership reflects this complexity; so, for example, it embraces the simultaneous welfare and punitive aspects of that culture. Police culture also inculcates a generalised attitude of suspicion and scepticism on the part of its membership. This makes the task of leadership especially difficult because police leaders are subjected to the testing and often baleful scrutiny of their subordinates. New policies, strategies and initiatives are greeted with reserve or, worse, scorn—even when their thoroughly justified underlying rationale has been made transparently clear. An atmosphere of distrust endemic to the police organization (Adlam, 1998b) makes it difficult for police leaders to make the kinds of change that professionalism demands.

Nonetheless, despite all the attention that has been devoted to 'police leadership' it is doubtful that the discussions have been based on a thorough appreciation of the knowledge and lessons emerging from research. In fact, it is by no means clear that police leadership—at all levels—is based on the guidelines for effective leadership practice that have been wrought from applied and practical inquiries into 'leadership'.

This chapter pursues the intimation that police in general do not have proper foundations for their leadership practices. This assumption is plausible for three reasons. First, simply too many officers bemoan the quality of police leadership. Second, there exists a widespread (if relatively tacit) criticism of police leadership that is felt from outside the service (Adlam, 2001). Third, an emphasis on 'management' and the rise of the 'new managerialism' has resulted in the impoverished examination of leadership on the police professional development curriculum.

The chapter begins by considering 'leadership' as an enduring field of study and locates it within that branch of knowledge that is 'practical'. It then moves on to review relevant research findings within two branches of social and practical inquiry, namely, 'social psychology' and 'applied behavioural science', This review suggests that a great deal is, in fact, known about leadership—including the recipe knowledge concerning how to be an effective leader. The discussion turns to consider police leadership as a distinct form of social and professional practice. An analysis of the nature of police work supports this contention. Finally, against the backdrop of research and conceptual analysis a modest number of recommendations are made concerning how to improve and enhance the quality of police leadership.

LEADERSHIP AS A FIELD OF STUDY

Whilst the study of leadership has been subject to the vicissitudes of cultural fashion (Hollander and Julian, 1969, Handy, 1985) it has managed to sustain its position within social science. It finds itself mentioned as a critical variable for analysis in the comprehensive introductions to social psychology that have continued to appear over the last 50 years. Already by the early 1960s the first-time student of psychology would encounter elaborate models enumerating the variables that contributed both to 'productivity' and 'satisfaction' in human enterprises (e.g. Krech, *et al.*, 1962). Central to these outcomes were the nature of leadership style and the particulars of social influence processes. Social scientific knowledge concerning the whole field of human social interaction has been impressively summarised by Argyle (1969), and, significantly, throughout his work, 'leadership' features as both a major descriptive and explanatory concept. Succeeding works (e.g. Middlebrook, 1974, Tajfel and Fraser 1978, Hewstone *et al.*, 1988, Coats and Feldman, 1997, Wren, 1999) presenting overviews of the dynamics at play in social interaction continue to identify the significant part played by leadership in determining the course of that interaction and the fate of human projects.

Leadership also remains an area of serious study within the field of management and organizational development. In addition to works providing theoretical overviews (e.g. Northouse, 2000) the scholarly literature reveals both the richness and diversity that characterises the appreciation of the phenomenon of leadership. Thus, Sims and Lorenzi (1992) articulate a 'new leadership paradigm', Conger and Kanungo (1998) present a comprehensive model of 'charismatic leadership', Arolio (1999) details the nature of 'full leadership development', whilst Plas and Lewis (2001) focus upon 'person-centred leadership in non-profit organizations'. Leadership studies have also been influenced by the upsurge of interest in 'ethics'. So, for example, Crosby (1999) in her work on 'leadership for global citizenship' includes a chapter devoted to 'ethical leadership'.

It appears that leadership has been studied as an object of both theoretical and practical inquiry. Aristotle drew a distinction between theoretical knowledge (*theoretike*) and practical knowledge (*pratike*). The former resulted from observation plus contemplation; it was thought to be fully scientific and characterised domains of study such as biology and astronomy. To the practical branch of knowledge, in contrast, belonged subjects such as ethics, politics and poetics. Whilst these subjects were based on collecting and analysing data, these data were fundamentally different in kind to those of the full sciences. They—the data—arose out of human endeavour and were less stable in nature. Moreover, in the course of studying subjects such as ethics and politics it was (at least in the time of Aristotle) not sufficient merely to discover the facts; students were expected to find out what could be done about them.

When the study of human behaviour and experience was located within a strictly 'scientific' framework (i.e. dominated by positivism) social psychologists appear to have treated 'leadership' as if it were a branch of *theoretike* or theoretical knowledge. In some ways this resulted in the gathering of important insights. Thus, for example, two aspects of leadership were recognised (i.e. achieving the task and meeting the socio-emotional needs of the group) and some crude generalisations about the personality of 'leaders' were uncovered. New approaches to human inquiry (e.g. Reason and Rowan, 1981, Patton, 1990 and Denzin and Lincoln, 1994) have provided a powerful critique of the positivist assumptions undergirding social science—and suggest that leadership might be more properly placed within the branch of *pratike* or practical knowledge. Thus, leadership may be seen as part and parcel of human endeavour. Indeed, social psychologists such as Argyle (1969) have recognised the fluidity of the phenomena of leadership. Whilst he recognised that 'the emergence of a leadership hierarchy is characteristic of human groups', he goes on to state: 'It is found that a clear leadership structure is more likely to appear under some conditions than others' (Argyle, 1969: 229).

In other words, 'leadership' is contingent on the circumstances facing human individuals and groups. It has an 'emergent' quality. What are those conditions that bring about its emergence—or, as Argyle puts it, the emergence of a 'clear leadership structure'? When there is some urgency about achieving the task, when the group is large, and when the task facing the group is complex. So, the 'facts' of leadership (its form and appearance) are tied to the nature of human endeavours, projects and arrangements. These are themselves set in the context of time and place. They are enormously susceptible to the 'press' of cultural patternings. Handy (1985) has recognised this and commented on how the value of 'democracy' has undermined traditional styles of leadership, styles that reflected a relatively authoritative and prescriptive command and control ethos. Indeed, the pulls of democracy coupled with the allure of 'empowerment' have, perhaps, accelerated demands for new styles of leadership.

The Aristotelian distinction between different types of knowledge suggests that it might be more appropriate to place the study of leadership in that branch of knowledge that is 'practical'. It follows that something can be done with this knowledge. The student of leadership always has the possibility of 'putting the discoveries to work'. In short, he or she can choose to make leadership more effective.

What, then, is known about this practical human endeavour—'leadership'? It seems helpful to begin to abstract the knowledge that has been gleaned about leadership by first referring to research within social psychology before turning to outline the way the subject is dealt with and discussed in the more obviously practical discipline of applied behavioural science.

Leadership and conventional social psychology

The admixture of theoretical and practical knowledge that has accumulated in relation to leadership has been served by advances in ethnology and the study of animal behaviour, by the study of small groups and their dynamics, and by the study of larger aggregates of persons, i.e. organizations.

It is not uncommon to search for clues in understanding the nature of human conduct by noting parallels or similarities between humans and non-human primates—as well as other animals, especially mammals. Ethicists—such as Midgley (1997)—have pointed out how patterns of care, co-operation and reciprocity are not only plainly apparent but in many ways typify the behaviour of birds and mammals. They have recognised the link between co-operative patterns of behaviour and moral conduct—such as 'benevolence' and 'compassion'—conduct that is considered so commendable in humans actions. Similarly students of social interaction have noted other recurring patterns of social behaviour amongst many species of animal that reflect 'leadership' behaviours. The phenomenon of the 'pecking-order' or 'dominance hierarchy' demonstrates something that can be conceptualised as a form of 'leadership'. Moreover, patterns of dominance can be considered to be advantageous to the animal group; the existence of such a structure prevents aggression within the social aggregate. Put differently, 'leadership' may function to promote order, predictability and stability amongst the close relatives of humanity.

Clearly, these conditions enable the problems of living to be better addressed—and therefore serve to promote the survival prospects of the group. Indeed Argyle's (1969) study of human social interaction pays close attention to the forms of 'leadership' that are present amongst non-human primates; whilst they vary from species to species he points out that 'the most common arrangement is for a number of dominant males to share degrees of social influence'. This contention reflects the orthodoxies of the time—and can be challenged by the advances made in the field of cultural studies. However, for the discussion here, the key point is that a behavioural pattern to which can be attached the concept of leadership is widespread amongst birds and mammals including the non-human primates. Leadership has, it appears, some sort of pre-programmed biological basis.

The association of 'leadership' with the concept of a 'dominance hierarchy'—that itself is associated with powerful males, survival and 'biology'—lends support to the thesis that leaders are born and not made. Argyle, in common with most other social psychologists, avoids the trap of such a socio-biological simplification. This becomes clearer as he turns to examine the study of leadership in group settings.

The study of relatively small human groups—such as problem- solving groups—represented, for example, in the classic studies of Bales (1950, 1953) and Tuckman (1965) point to patterns of influence that regularly appear. These lead Argyle to conclude that: 'The emergence of a leadership hierarchy seems to be a universal feature of human groups' (Argyle, 1969: 230) .

He does, however, remain cautious when he turns to make theoretical sense of this phenomenon. Whilst he acknowledges the 'pre-programming' of human behaviour through neural structures he recognises the role of learning and the impact of cultural traditions on the expression of 'leadership' and its related social processes such as dominance, power, influence and control. He underlines the fact that whilst some human groups (e.g. small boys and/or gangs) can base leadership on physical power—leadership in human groups is decided more on the basis of conversation and contribution to the group's problems. Moreover he notes that, in broad terms, human problem-solving groups have to accomplish two 'things' if they are to be effective; on the one hand they have to achieve the task; on the other, they have to find ways to resolve the interpersonal tensions and to meet the socio-emotional needs of their members. The study of small groups (and therefore, to some extent, of the 'teams' of modern organizations) led Argyle to conclude that the social system developed in such groups 'provides a way of dealing with the external and internal needs of the group'.

LEADERSHIP AND ORGANIZATIONS

When the small group grows in size, when small groups are brought together, or when far larger numbers of people are assembled together an organization develops. Just as a general feature of small groups is the appearance of some form of leadership structure so a general feature of organizations is the presence of an hierarchical set of interpersonal relations. Until fairly recently, the study of leadership in organizations tended to exclude those at the most subordinate level i.e. the 'front-line' service deliverer. The more contemporary discussions of leadership (e.g. Egan, 1988, Heron, 1989) as well as theorists working within the framework of 'transformational leadership' articulated by Burns (1978) have, more thoroughly, democratised the concept. Instead of remaining solely within the province of supervisors, middle and senior managers, each and every person within an organization is considered to have the opportunity to demonstrate leadership behaviours.

The study of leadership in organizations has been closely tied to the analysis of an organization's efficiency and effectiveness. Both Argyle (1969) and Handy (1985) underline how elusive this is. Argyle remarks that: 'There is no simple solution to an organization's problems; each one is unique, and a unique and imaginative solution is required' (Argyle, 1969: 299).

The uniqueness to which Argyle refers is intrinsic to Handy's observation that: 'Organizational phenomena ... should be explained by the kind of contextual interpretation used by an historian' (Handy, 1985: 14).

Yet, despite Handy's identification of more than 60 variables that impact powerfully upon organizational effectiveness, 'leadership' is still abstracted as one of the most useful explanatory concepts that can be used to make sense of organizational behaviour. Argyle, too, underlines the salience of the 'leadership' dimension in organizations by isolating 'leadership' as a principle factor in relation to the organization's overall performance. He moves on to present a social scientific overview of the research into leadership effectiveness. In this context, he cites Halpin and Winer (1952) who uncovered two main dimensions along which individual military leaders varied in relation to their leadership behaviours. Subsequent studies of leaders—including those in industrial settings—revealed the same two dimensions. Standardly they are described as 'initiating structure' and 'consideration'. Argyle characterises 'initiating structure' as follows: 'The extent to which the leader maintains standards of performance, follows routines, makes sure his [sic] position and functions are understood, and distributes tasks' (Argyle, 1969: 300).

He moves on to define 'consideration' as: 'The degree to which the leader shows warmth in personal relationships, trust, readiness to explain action, and listens to subordinates' (Argyle, 1969: 300).

The two dimensions coincide with the two aspects of leadership behaviour that emerge in small groups—i.e. those pertaining to the task and the socio-emotional needs of individual group members. Other students of management—such as Blake and Mouton (1964)—analyse the behaviours of managers in terms of 'concern for production' and 'concern for people'. These dimensions correspond to those of 'initiating structure' and 'consideration'. The practice of 'democratic leadership—brought about through an admixture of persuasion, explanation and group discussion (i.e. the use of special social skills and techniques)—reflects a combination both of 'initiating structure' and 'consideration' for people. Other styles of leadership—e.g. 'autocratic'—do not reflect the same levels of 'initiating structure' and 'consideration'. For example, the 'autocrat' is disposed to issue orders without explanation and to employ coercive and punitive methods of discipline. Argyle summarises a number of studies that have examined the effects of these two types of leadership and concludes: 'The main finding is that democratic leaders, those fairly high both on initiating structure and on consideration, are more effective' (Argyle, 1969: 301) .

Indeed, it is tempting to advance the idea that the few existing case studies of individual police leaders provide support for this claim. Thus, for example, in a brief biography, the former commissioner of the metropolis, Peter Imbert is described by Fido and Skinner (2000) as renowned for his 'geniality and informality'; he secured the affection of the work force because he understood and appreciated the different tasks of policing. This understanding was allied to a genuine concern for the well-being of his fellow officers.

Whilst there are circumstances under which democratic leadership is not the most effective Argyle observes that it is better to regard these cases as 'exceptions to the general rule'. So for example, when decisions have to be taken very quickly and in times of crisis—typifying, for example, situations of combat, battle and riot—more 'authoritarian' leadership is needed.

It is worthwhile providing some explanation as to why democratic leadership 'works'. First, a social style that moves between persuasion and consultation combines both the task and socio-emotional requirements of leadership. Second, participation in decision-making means that the members of the group are more likely to become committed to the action that is decided upon. Third, group discussion enhances communication and this leads to cohesiveness and co-operation within the group. This set of reasons constitutes a powerful rationale for attempting, in general, to practice 'democratic leadership'. Additional research studies help to refine the picture concerning the detail of effective leadership. Thus, for example, Fiedler (1958) found that leaders were more successful if they discriminated between the most preferred and least preferred co-workers. In addition, Hersey (1983) has emphasised how at higher levels in the organization the character of leadership changes. So, for example, at the most senior level in the management hierarchy—i.e. executives and strategists—a visionary perspective is needed—as well as the skills to guide the organization in such a manner that makes the vision a reality. This visionary (or strategic) perspective implies that high levels of conceptual skill are needed by the top-team leaders.

After reviewing the knowledge about effective leadership that had emerged from social scientific research Argyle concluded by endorsing the efficacy of the 'democratic-persuasive' style of leadership—even though, at the time of writing he thought that this would constitute a major change in the nature of organization. In effect what Argyle highlights is the intensive nature of 'people work' that is such a vital ingredient of effective leadership. This has been endorsed very recently in Alimo-Metcalfe and Alban-Metcalfe's (2000) work that underlines the importance in contemporary leadership of showing 'respect for the individual'.

LEADERSHIP AND APPLIED BEHAVIOURAL SCIENCE

The social scientific study of leadership in psychology—and social psychology in particular—led to the development of an increasing theoretical sophistication in understanding its nature. This knowledge began to find itself 'put to work' in the newly emerging discipline of 'applied behavioural science'. The inception of this branch of study can be traced to the work of Kurt Lewin—work that culminated in the creation of the National Training Laboratories and the 'T' group design. Graham remarks:

> Lewin … whilst at the Massachusetts Institute of Technology during the 1940s, recognised that training in human relationship skills was greatly neglected He advocated the establishment of groups for training such skills, the first of which met in Maine in 1947 … Social scientists saw such events as potential microcosmic laboratories in which to study aspects of group behaviour, particularly leadership functions, identity formation and decision making processes. (Graham, 1986: 50)

He goes on to say that shortly after the National Training Laboratories were created employers began to send students to these groups (the 'T' group) in order to develop their managerial skills and their interpersonal sensitivity. Schaffer (1978) stresses the fact that the training group was not established to provide 'therapy' but was designed to help managers and executives within relatively large organizations 'become sensitive to the interpersonal and group dynamic aspects of their work settings'. He notes:

> To provide an appropriate atmosphere for this kind of learning, the T-group leader (or 'trainer' as he [sic] came to be called) strove to create within the group a sense of openness, trust and emotional intensity. Hence, an administrator with strong authoritarian tendencies might find out through feedback from the other group members, just how controlling he was. The group dynamics principle that he would hopefully learn in the process is that undemocratic styles of leadership are resented by subordinates (and thereby inefficient in the long run). (Schaffer, 1978: 126)

Thus, both the practice of effective 'leadership' and effective 'management' were amongst the central goals of the T' group process—and its subsequent but related educational designs. These laboratories of learning—focused as they were on enhancing 'practice'—encouraged the development of theories and models within the discipline of applied behavioural science. By the early 1990s it was possible to identify several models, proto-models, frameworks and/or guidelines that, as result of research inquiry—spelt out the details of effective leadership practices (Pfeiffer, 1991, Biech, 2000, Anderson, 2000). Following the development of the early 'T' group 'technologies' for training leaders that advocated 'democratic leadership' as well as enhanced interpersonal sensitivity, the analysis of leader effectiveness has seen three key developments.

Leadership as analysis of the presenting situation

Tannenbaum and Schmidt's (1958) classic model not only identified a 'leadership continuum' but also served as a framework for subsequent attempts to provide a synthesis of leadership effectiveness (e.g. Handy, 1985). Tannenbaum and Schmidt were able to identify the classes of intervention choices available to leaders. They distinguished 'boss-centred' (authoritarian) from 'subordinate-centred' (participatory) leadership styles. 'Authoritarian' forms of intervention occur when the manager/leader identifies problems, decides on solutions, and informs subordinates of the actions that they will take. The most completely 'participatory' form of leadership occurs with full-blown team decision-making and where the manager/leader is part of the group. Tannenbaum and Schmidt perceived the need for leaders and managers to vary their intervention style according to the demands of the situation. They also succeeded in reducing the complexity of leadership by identifying three sets of forces that needed to be considered prior to adopting any intervention style. They are:

- forces in the leader (him or herself);
- forces in the subordinates; and
- forces in the situation.

Schein (1988) provides a succinct summary giving some examples of the constituent aspects of these three 'forces' as follows:

> Examples of forces in the leader are his [*sic*] value system, his confidence in the group, his own natural inclinations or style, and the security he feels in the situation. Examples of forces in the group are their prior experience in making decisions, their actual competence, their tolerance for ambiguity, their ability to become involved in the problem, and their expectations and need for growth. Examples of forces in the situation are the amount of time pressure, the type of problem to be solved, and the type of organization in which the process is occurring. (Schein 1988: 91)

Tannenbaum and Schmidt's model came to be widely used in training environments and encouraged the practice of leadership to be based on an analysis of the multiplicity of factors at play in any given situation. It also encouraged leaders to consider making diagnoses of the situations they confronted. In addition, their identification of three sets of forces in many ways anticipates the framework constructed by Adair (1983). Their work drew attention to the social encounter between leader and follower(s). This paved the way for a sustained analysis of the dynamics involved in this relationship.

Leadership: the dynamic relationship between leaders and followers
Livingston (1969) asserts that leaders' expectations of their followers stand as a critical factor determining the levels of performance and achievements of those followers. His basic contention is that leaders who have genuine confidence in their own ability to develop and stimulate followers to high standards of performance will expect much of those followers and will treat them in a manner that is commensurate with this confidence. In other words, they combine a mixture of psychological disposition and a form of interpersonal conduct— conduct that impacts positively on followers. The subsequent work of Bennis and Nanus (1985) can be linked directly to Livingston's thesis. Bennis and Nanus underline how 'self-esteem' is a crucial factor in the follower's ability to be successful. Put most simply, if a person has a high regard for him or herself then he or she is more likely to expect to achieve higher standards. Leaders who build the self-esteem of their followers create basic psychological conditions for 'success'. This focus on the 'psychology' and interpersonal behaviour of the leader occasioned Pfeiffer (1991) to provide a summary of the characteristics that most researchers believe successful leaders have in common. Those characteristics are:

- a belief in their ability to develop the potential of their followers and the provision of the appropriate amounts of direction and support that the followers need in order to be successful;
- an ability to establish and communicate goals that are challenging, realistic and attainable;
- positive assumptions about the potential of others—an ability to see them as 'winners';
- a commitment to excellence and a genuine, intense enthusiasm for what they and others do; and
- a focus on the human aspects of the task in addition to a focus on procedures, conceptual frameworks and technology.

It is significant that Pfeiffer concludes his listing of the characteristics that make leaders effective by stating: 'The human aspect is the one that leads to improvement' (Pfeiffer, 1991: 145).

Pfeiffer's summary reflects the increasingly sophisticated understanding of what outstanding or exemplary leaders actually do as they interact with those around them. It resonates with the conclusions provided by both Kouzes and Posner (1987) and Kinlaw (1989). Kouzes and Posner contend that highly effective leaders are distinguished by the fact that they share five 'behavioural practices' (each of which is marked by additional leader 'commitments'). Thus, exemplary leaders:

- inspire a shared vision;
- enable others to act through 'spirit-nurturing' relationships;
- model the way through setting an example;
- challenge the process through a willingness to question and confront the status quo; and
- encourage the 'heart' through, for example, recognising accomplishments.

What Kouzes and Posner succeed in highlighting is the capacity of the leader to engage the energies of followers, to be 'in-touch' with followers, and, to convey optimism, purpose and hope. They are, in a sense, 'pioneers'—who innovate and experiment and who treat mistakes as opportunities for learning. Importantly, Kouzes and Posner underline the fact that exemplary leaders are 'expressive'. They let others know that their efforts are appreciated and they are proud of their achievements. Kinlaw (1989) presents a similar set of conclusions following his studies that, *inter alia*, revealed the practices of 'superior leaders'. He believes that superior leaders share six sets of common practices. These are:

- establishing a vision;
- stimulating people to gain new competencies;
- helping people to overcome obstacles;
- helping people to overcome failure;
- leading by example; and
- including others in their success.

Kinlaw's summary indicates the very high degree of overlap that exists in relation to the conclusions that applied behavioural scientists have drawn in relation to identifying the constituent elements of effective leader behaviour.

An elaboration of the 'relational' or 'interactive' or 'expressive' character of effective leadership has been captured through the elaboration of the concept of the 'transformational' leader. Burns (1978) is most typically credited with formulating the idea of 'transformational leadership'. Bass (1981) provides an appreciation of its nature by noting that transformational leaders are often described as 'visionaries', 'leaders of reform', 'innovators', 'movers and shakers' and/or 'heroes'.

Transformational leadership acknowledges the fact that leaders can 'tap into' or create the goals, motives and values of followers in order to influence them—their followers—to act in desired ways. It recognises that as followers respond a mutually beneficial relationship develops—a relationship that brings leaders and followers together.

To appreciate better the character of transformational leadership Burns (1978) contrasts it with the less effective—but more common—transactional leadership. In the transactional mode the practice of leadership takes the form of an exchange—an exchange that reduces the employee or subordinate to an instrumental functionary. Transactional leadership makes little or no appeal to higher order motives (after Maslow, 1970). Bass (1981) characterises transactional leaders as 'bargainers', or bureaucrats'; in broad terms, transactional leaders reflect leadership that has a 'favour-for-favour' character (Anderson, 2000).

Transformational leadership is differentiated from transactional leadership because it is based on the principle of mutual stimulation and elevation. Transformational leaders inspire their followers to find ways to satisfy higher-order needs such as self-actualisation and self-esteem. In addition, transformational leaders have the power to metamorphose their followers such that followers become leaders and leaders become moral agents. Moral agents are committed to effecting positive social change especially with regard to securing those conditions that promote human flourishing. In this sense, transformational leadership has claims to being not only inspirational but also emancipatory. Plainly, the idea of transformational leadership meshes well with the strategic emphases to 'reinvent' policing through the creation of a genuine 'quality of service' culture that simultaneously champions human rights (Woodcock, 1991).

Leadership: responsibility and autonomy—leadership by each individual 'self'

The practice of leadership, as noted earlier, reflects the nature of human endeavours and projects as they are situated in time and place. Effective leadership reflects therefore the subtle shifts in cultural values and more general cultural trends. Manz and Sims (1989) capture the increasing democratisation of leadership as they argue that the traditional models—i.e. those resting on role or position power—are no longer effective. This is because they fail to promote 'self-leadership' practices by—in principle—all the organization's personnel. Manz and Sims believe that 'superleadership'—the leading of others so that they come to lead themselves—is likely to be both more appropriate and more effective.

This approach to leadership approximates to the 'reflective practitioner' ethos that has been articulated by Schon (1983); it also has much in common with Heron's (1974) earlier characterisation of the 'educated person—a person who is self-directing, self-monitoring and self-adjusting, and who takes responsibility for setting goals and objectives'. Indeed Heron's highly emancipated approach to personal and professional development was, in essence, adopted as the foundation for developing the future leaders of the police service by the 'new-style' Special course in the mid-1980s. It is certainly not something alien to the police. Nonetheless, it is important to stress that Manz and Sims underline how 'self-leadership is applicable to everyone who works in an organization'. It consists of a form of conduct where employees accept responsibility for their performance and productivity. Whilst Manz and Sims outline a number of specific behavioural and cognitive strategies that reflect the disciplines of self-determination, self-direction and personal mastery this emphasis is tantamount to grounding leadership in the personal development psychologies and their associated practices that have been elaborated over the last 50 years.

POLICE LEADERSHIP AS A DISTINCT FORM OF SOCIAL AND PROFESSIONAL PRACTICE

Adair's (1983, 1989, 1990) model of effective leadership—with its emphasis on the important part played by 'inspiration', its recognition that the dynamic exchange between leader and followers is crucial, its delineation of the necessary social and analytical skills and its emphasis on the 'team ethos'—reflects, in many ways, a synthesis of the many lessons that can be abstracted from the research. Adair perceived that working groups share areas of common need. In turn, they need:

1. to accomplish a common task;
2. to maintain (or be maintained) as a cohesive social unit; and
3. to meet the diverse psycho-social needs of the individual group members.

Again, his work makes salient the need/emotion complex that has to be engaged with in the course of effective leadership practice.

One consistent theme identified throughout the relatively long history of research into leadership has concerned the way the 'shape' of effective leadership alters in relation to the exigencies of the task. Adair's practical training in leadership, for example, reprises Tannenbaum and Schmidt's (1958) classic work which underlined the significance of taking into account the 'forces within the situation'. In the context of police leadership, this focus on the 'task' raises a very basic question for police leadership, police management and designs for police professional development; thus, is there something about police work—the 'tasks' of policing—that necessitates an original, un-derived and singular approach to leadership?

Since police work—along with its component tasks—is inextricably linked to the more general social construction of the police role, an analysis of this role should go some way towards clarifying whether or not police leadership is a markedly distinct form of practice.

An appreciation of the nature of police work has continued to develop since the establishment of the 'new' police in London in 1829. The apparently straightforward priorities articulated by Rowan and Mayne in their celebrated 'instructions to police officers' (Metropolitan Police, 1829) privileged the 'prevention of crime' over the detection (and subsequent punishment) of the offender. Scarman (1981) effected something of a revision in the fundamentals of policing philosophy by emphasising the primary need to ensure that order—the 'Queen's Peace'—was maintained. Kleinig (1996) argues persuasively that the most appropriate way to construe the role of police is in terms of 'social peacekeepers'. All police activities should be derived from and contribute to this fundamental purpose. Alderson (1998) finds a basis for policing in a theory of 'protectionism'. These discussions have all served to elucidate the nature of the police role. Laugharne and Newman (1985) set out to clarify the fundamental duties of police by adopting an historico-constitutional and jurisprudential perspective. Their work suggests that the concrete practices (i.e. the tasks) of policing reflect an esoteric background—composed of principles, conceptual knowledge and understanding—as well as liberal democratic values. They note that:

> The primary aims and duties of the Metropolitan Police are to uphold the Rule of Law, to protect and assist the citizen and to work for the prevention and detection of crime and the maintenance of a peaceful society, free of the fear of crime and disorder. They will carry out these aims and duties in consultation and co-operation with others in the community. (Laugharne and Newman, 1985: 9)

By identifying the primacy of upholding the Rule of Law they invite a consideration of the principles which must be adhered to for it—the Rule of Law—to be sustained. They find that:

> A respect for citizens' individual rights and freedoms and the avoidance of arbitrary or unlawful action are fundamental to the constitutional meaning of the Rule of Law and thus to the whole meaning and purpose of police duty. (Laugharne and Newman, 1985: 10)

They proceed to underline how police action must be consistent with the 'fundamental values of British society'—values which, for them, 'emphasise a just balance between order and freedom'. These values are underpinned by 'procedure', 'legal rules' and 'assumptions'. Amongst these they identify:

- the right to free speech;
- the right to free association;
- restrictions on powers of arrest and detention;
- the right of access to legal advice;
- the prohibition of discriminatory behaviour towards individuals, classes of persons and minority groups;
- the observance of suspects' rights;
- integrity in the collection and presentation of evidence; and

- the need to use only such force as is necessary to accomplish a legitimate purpose.

Whilst this articulation of the rights to which citizens are entitled (and which it is a duty of police to protect) has been, to some extent, superseded by the enactment of the Human Rights Act 1998, it should be emphasised that Laugharne and Newman succeeded in constructing a comprehensive ethical framework in which to ground the police role. Vividly, they show how persons who take on the role of 'police officer' claim (and enjoy) a particular social status commensurate with which is the requirement to fulfil a range of duties, obligations and professional commitments. To be a police officer is to enter into a specific and special sort of relationship with a wide and diverse range of citizens—citizens who, in a liberal democracy, tolerate such officers only if they adhere to the kinds of principles explicated by Laugharne and Newman. This analysis of the role of the police begins to provide strong grounds for believing that police work has a certain uniqueness. Support for such a contention stems from the 'Quality of Service' committee's publication, *Getting Things Right* (ACPO, 1993). In a lengthy appendix the 'features that make policing unique' are described. Its authors assert that 'police staff must competently undertake a remarkably broad sweep of activities'. The 'wide menu' of police responsibilities includes:

- enforcement of the criminal law;
- maintaining public order;
- helping and befriending; and
- reassuring the community.

The analysis continues by highlighting the significance of the 'large degree of discretion' that exists in relation to police decision-making. It notes that this discretion 'cannot be delegated to others either upwards or downwards'. Seven other features of police work are subsequently identified (e.g. the need for 'instant decisions', the 'reliance upon individual skill, judgement and initiative' as well as the 'emotional demands of policing') which, and particularly when taken together, justify the notion that police work is, as its authors claim, unique.

Effective police leadership has to find ways of resisting the tendencies to reduce the practice of policing to a simple hierarchical ordering. It has to find ways of communicating the over-arching values that suffuse and legitimate the very office of constable itself. It has to find a style that interweaves both direction and prescription as well as support and autonomy. It also has to be wedded to the ongoing requirement of effecting change.

Improving the quality of police leadership: an emphasis on practice

The following set of recommendations has been kept deliberately short and reflects the knowledge that has accumulated in relation to the study of effective leadership as well as the more specific social study of police and policing. Emerging from the wealth of detail that has been amassed as a result of decades of work studying leadership it seems important to make a brief theoretical observation. Effective leadership appears to be closely tied to the nature and structure of human needs and their related emotions. Leaders arouse emotions and influence the degree to which a whole range of human needs are made salient and are met. The inspirational and liberating leader enables people to find purpose and meaning in their endeavours.

APPLYING THE LESSONS FROM RESEARCH

At the most general level police leadership should align itself far more closely and systematically with the lessons that have emerged from the research. In the most straightforward and practical of terms police leaders should adhere to the guidelines and practices recommended by the models outlining effective leadership practices. More specifically police leaders—throughout the service—should rest their practice on three desiderata; they are given below.

1. Embracing the professional responsibilities attaching to the police role

Ker Muir (1977) observed that police deal with the 'big questions' of human existence. The philosophical analysis of policing (e.g. Laugharne and Newman, 1985, Kleinig, 1996, Alderson, 1998) reveals the profound and demanding nature of the foundations upon which policing rests. Put most simply, police help to secure those social conditions within which human flourishing can take place and worthwhile projects can be pursued. Laugharne and Newman derive an extensive set of police ethical principles from an analysis of the constitutional foundations of policing and the police role. They note for example the intimate connections between policing and the social advances made possible through commitments to upholding fundamental human rights. Their work begins to illustrate how the practices of policing demand forms of leadership that are unique precisely because of the unique role and responsibilities of police in a liberal democracy. Police leaders through their use of language give meaning to police work. The crude and ineffective leader allocates tasks that amount, metaphorically, to little more than 'breaking stones' whilst the effective leader transmutes those same tasks into 'building cathedrals'.

A part of the 'reform' of police leadership will include making changes to some aspects of the occupational culture that serve to restrict responsible role filling. In particular the infantilisation that police officers experience as a result of the routines, rituals, norms and patterns of interaction at the core of their culture comes to act as a major barrier to mature ways of 'going on'. In fact, far from acting as autonomous professionals, police often behave in dysfunctional, dependent and childish ways. Processes of induction and subsequent training go some way towards creating these outcomes. However, leadership and management styles oscillate between those of the antiquated disciplinarian and the cloying carer. The quasi-welfare culture of police does little to empower the individual officer.

2. Embarking on the disciplines of the reflective practitioner

Kleinig (1996) examines the shared features of the 'professions' and recognises that professionals are expected to demonstrate responsible autonomy. To be professional is to be committed to improving the quality of one's professional knowledge, understanding and practice. And this means engaging in the intense admixture of personal and occupational scrutiny that constitutes a part of being a 'reflective practitioner'. At the heart of the reflective practitioner lies the 'inquiring I'. The individual embarks on a process of 'living-and-working-as-learning'. The reflective practitioner seeks to abstract lessons from experience, to plan how to intervene more effectively in situations of practice, to risk new forms of intervention and to evaluate the extent to which those interventions led to improvements in situations of practice. The reflective practitioner works as a self-managing learner. To the extent that 'leadership' in the complex situations of policing requires acts of creativity, imagination and the achievement of change it cannot be reduced to formulaic procedure. Its subtleties and refinements are generated through those educational processes made possible through critical reflections on practice.

3. Doing 'self' work

As Heron (1989) remarked: 'a person is a signature in action'. A person 'signs' him or herself idiosyncratically across the conduct of their leadership. Persons are also susceptible to the frailties of their psychological constitution. In consequence—and partly as a reflection of Foucault's (1991) 'science of discipline'—a remarkably extensive array of 'self-development' techniques and methods have emerged to facilitate the development of personal and interpersonal effectiveness. They have often been included within the practical arm of humanistic psychology—but are more generally dispersed throughout the body of literature devoted to 'training'. Heron (1989) for example, provides a thorough and detailed analysis of the types of 'intervention' that are central to 'personal development' work. He notes that 'their purpose is to facilitate self-directed living' and goes to add that 'this means learning how to live', 'how to handle feelings' and 'how to think and act differently in different sorts of situation'. The most basic form of 'self' work entails using the experiential learning cycle. For Heron, this consists of four stages; 'living', 'uncovering', 'reflecting' and 'preparing'. 'Living' produces different sorts of experience. This experience constitutes the ground from which learning (and change) might spring. He goes on to say:

> Uncovering ... means recalling some experience in full, exploring one's feelings about it and one's understanding of what was going on. Reflecting means pondering on the uncovered experience, getting insight into it, learning about oneself, others and the world through it. Preparing means getting ready to take this learning back into living. (Heron, 1989: 91)

This is the basic model to use for extending the height, breadth and depth of leadership practice. Leaders also need to ask themselves some confronting questions—questions designed to uncover 'blind spots' and to test perceptions of reality. In the context of police leadership, I suggest the following:

- 'What value—seriously—have I added to achieving the central (the core) goals of the organization today?'
- 'Can I show, concretely, that I am making a real difference towards achieving social peace and/or the protection of the public?'

- 'What positive change or improvements am I really making to the provision of policing services?'

Finally, here, I should like to recommend an additional practice that can improve aspects of leadership. Cultures, in general, employ totems—or power objects—which when touched or contemplated evoke a design for living—a style of conduct. They can energise, motivate and discipline the person. I do not think it too fanciful to suggest that police leaders secure their own 'totem' of good leadership practice. By way of example, a 'wise' piece of text may suffice. Sun Tzu remarked that:

> Leadership is a matter of intelligence, trustworthiness, humaneness, courage and sternness. (Sun Tzu, 1991: 4)

He goes on to note that the 'way of the ancient kings was to consider humaneness foremost'. Since it appears to be the case that police officers are left disappointed with the degree of consideration extended towards them by their super-ordinates and unable to trust the integrity of their 'leaders', Sun Tzu's words impress through the excellence of their counsel.

CONCLUDING REMARKS

If it is the case that a reasonably robust body of knowledge has been amassed that both identifies the general principles underpinning effective leadership and indicates the general forms of conduct by which it is constituted then it becomes possible to specify some general leadership standards—the leadership practices and disciplines—that might, justifiably, be expected of leaders. What might these include? They would, for example, emphasise the importance of doing whatever it takes to meet a wide range of needs experienced by organizational members. Minimally these would include a sense of belonging, of esteem and of personal fulfilment through work. In addition leaders must be able to show how they contribute tangibly towards enhancing the work performance of their subordinates. They should be able to illustrate how their practice adheres to some model (or models) of good leadership practice. Encounters with leaders should result in that kind of *frisson* that energises and inspires.

It is probably unnecessary to generate a large range of micro-behavioural practices against which to classify and 'measure' the conduct of leaders. Instead, it is much more important for leaders to embrace and internalise a few sound maxims of good practice. Paramount amongst these is the need to sustain the dream that a better state of affairs will be achieved—and that the people upon who the leader impacts feel supported, included, appreciated, acknowledged, respected and valued. Whilst this appears simple enough it does, in fact, take real discipline. This discipline is insufficiently developed in police organizations. This must change.

REFERENCES for *Chapter 16*

ACPO (1993), *Getting Things Right*, London: Association of Chief Police Officers.

Adair, J (1983), *Effective Leadership*, Aldershot: Gower.

Adair, J (1989), *Great Leaders*, Guildford: Talbot Adair Press.

Adair, J (1990), *Understanding Motivation*, Guildford: Talbot Adair Press.

Adlam, R (1998a), 'Uncovering the "Ethical Profile" of Police Managers and the "Moral Ethos" of Police Organizations: A Preliminary Study', *International Journal of Police Science and Management*, September, Vol. 1, No. 2, pp. 162-183.

Adlam, R (1998b), 'What Should We Expect From Police Leaders?', *Police Research and Management*, Spring, pp. 17-30.

Adlam, R (2001), 'Police Leadership and the Provision of Police Leadership Development Opportunities, Bramshill: Problem, Solution and a Critical Engagement', *International Journal of Police Science & Management*, Vol. 3, No. 3, London: Henry Stewart Publications, Spring.

Alderson, J (1998), *Principled Policing: Protecting the Public with Integrity*, Winchester: Waterside Press.

Alimo-Metcalfe B and Alban-Metcalfe, R J (2000), 'Heaven Can Wait', *The Health Service Journal*, Hospital and Social Services Publications, London.

Anderson, T (2000), *Every Officer is a Leader: Transforming Leadership in Police, Justice and Public Safety*, New York: St. Lucie Press.

Argyle, M (1969), *Social Interaction*, London: Tavistock Publications.

Avolio, B (1999), *Full Leadership Development*, London: Sage Publications.

Bales, R (1950), *Interaction Process Analysis*, Cambridge, Mass.: Addison Wesley Publishing Co.

Bales, R (1953), 'The Equilibrium Problem in Small Groups' in Parsons, T, Bales, R and Shils, E (eds.), *Working Papers in the Theory of Action*, Glencoe Ill.: Free Press.

Bass, B (1981), *Stodgill's Handbook of Leadership*, New York: The Free Press.

Bennis, W and Nanus, B (1985), *Leaders: The Strategies For Taking Charge*, New York: Harper and Row.

Biech, E (ed.) (2000), *The 2000 Annual*, Vol. 1. 'Training', Vol. 2. 'Consulting', San Francisco: Jossey Bass/Pfeiffer.

Blake, R and Mouton, J (1964), *The Managerial Grid*, Houston: Gulf Publishing Co.

Buchanan, M (2000), *Ubiquity: The Science of History or Why the World is Simpler than we Think*, London: Weidenfeld and Nicolson.

Burns, J (1978), *Leadership*, New York: Harper Row.

Coats, E and Feldman, R (eds.) (1997), *Classic and Contemporary Readings in Social Psychology*, London: Sage Publications.

Conger, J and Kanungo, R (1998), *Charismatic Leadership in Organizations*, London: Sage Publications.

Crosby, B (1999), *Leadership for Global Citizenship: Building Transnational Community*, London: Sage Publications.

Denzin, N and Lincoln, Y (eds.) (1994), *Handbook of Qualitative Research*, Thousand Oaks, California: Sage Publications.

Egan, G (1988), *Change Agent Skills: Managing Innovation and Change*, San Diego, California: University Associates Inc.

Fido, M and Skinner, K (2000), *The Official Encyclopaedia of Scotland Yard: Behind the Scenes at Scotland Yard*, London: Virgin Publishing.

Fiedler, F (1958), *Leader Attitudes and Group Effectiveness*, Urbana: University of Illinois Press.

Foucault, M (1991), *Discipline and Punish: The Birth of the Prison*, Harmondsworth: Middlesex: Penguin Books.

Graham, H (1986), *The Human Face of Psychology: Humanistic Psychology in its Historical, Social and Cultural Contexts*, Milton Keynes: Open University Press.

Halpin, A and Winer, R (1952),*The Leadership Behaviour of the Airplane Commander*, Columbus: Ohio State University.

Handy, C (1985), *Understanding Organizations* (third edition), Harmondsworth, Middlesex: Penguin Books.

Heron, J (1974), *The Concept of a Peer Learning Community*, Guildford, Surrey: Human Potential Research Project, Department of Educational Studies, University of Surrey, Guildford, Surrey.

Heron, J (1989), *Six Category Intervention Analyses*, Guildford, Surrey: Human Potential Research Project, Department of Educational Studies, University of Surrey, Guildford, Surrey.

Hersey, P (1983), *An Intensive Experience in the Process of Change: Situational Leadership*, Escondido, California: Leadership Productions Inc.

Hewstone, M, Stroebe, W, Codol, J-P and Stephenson, G (eds.) (1988), *Introduction to Social Psychology*, Oxford: Basil Blackwell Ltd.

Hollander, E and Julian, J (1969), 'Contemporary Trends in the Analysis of Leadership Processes', *Psychological Bulletin*, 71, 387-397.

Ker Muir, W (1977), *Police: Street-Corner Politicians*, Chicago: University of Chicago Press.

Kinlaw, D (1989), *Coaching for Commitment: Managerial Strategies for Obtaining Superior Performance*, San Diego, California: University Associates.

Kleinig, J (1996), *The Ethics of Policing*, Cambridge: Cambridge University Press.

Kouzes, J and Posner, B (1987), *The Leadership Challenge: How to Get Extraordinary Things Done in Organizations*, San Francisco: Jossey-Bass.

Krech, D, Crutchfield, R and Ballachey, E (1962), *The Individual in Society*, New York: McGraw-Hill.

Laugharne, A and Newman, K (1985), *The Principles of Policing and Guidance for Professional Behaviour*, London: Metropolitan Police, New Scotland Yard.

Livingston, J (1969), 'Pygmalion in Management', *Harvard Business Review*, July-August, pp. 81-89.

Manz, C and Sims, H (1989), *Superleadership*, New York: Berkeley Books.

Maslow, A (1970), *Motivation and Personality* (second edition), New York: Harper and Row.

Metropolitan Police (1829), *Instructions to Police Officers*, London: Metropolitan Police.

Middlebrook, P (1974), *Social Psychology and Modern Life*, New York: Alfred A Knopf Inc.

Midgley, M (1997), 'The Origins of Ethics' in Singer, P (ed.) (1997), *A Companion to Ethics*, Oxford: Blackwell Publishers.

Northouse, P (1999), *Leadership: Theory and Practice* (second edition), London: Sage Publications.

Patton, M (1990), *Qualitative Evaluation and Research Methods* (second edition), London: Sage Publications.

Pfeiffer, J (ed.) (1991), *Theories and Models in Applied Behavioural Science*, Vol. 3: 'Management and Leadership', San Diego: Pfeiffer and Co.

Plas, J and Lewis, S (2001), *Person-centred Leadership for Non-Profit Organizations: Management that Works in High Pressure Organizations*, London: Sage Publications.

Reason, P and Rowan, J (eds.) (1981), *Human Inquiry: A Source Book of New Paradigm Research*, Chichester: John Wiley and Sons.

Reiner, R (1991), *Chief Constables*, Oxford: Oxford University Press.

Scarman, Lord (1981), *The Brixton Disorders 10-12 April 1981*, London, HMSO: Cmnd. 8427.

Schaffer, J (1978), *Humanistic Psychology*, Englewood Cliffs, New Jersey: Prentice Hall Inc.

Schein, E (1988), *Process Consultation*, Vol. 1: 'Its Role in Organizational Development' (second edition), New York: Addison Wesley Publishing Co.

Schon, D (1983), *The Reflective Practitioner*, New York: Basic Books.

Sims, H and Lorenzi, P (1992), *The New Leadership Paradigm: Social Learning and Cognition in Organizations*, London: Sage Publications.

Sun Tzu (1991), *The Art of War* (trans. Thomas Cleary), London: Shambala Pocket Classics.

Tajfel, H and Fraser, C (eds.) (1978), *Introducing Social Psychology: An Analysis of Individual Reaction and Response*, Harmondsworth, Middlesex: Penguin Books.

Tannenbaum, R and Schmidt, W (1958), 'How to Choose a Leadership Pattern', *Harvard Business Review*, March-April, 36, 2, pp. 95-101.

Tuckman, R (1965), 'Developmental Sequence in Small Groups', *Psychological Bulletin*, 63, pp. 384-399.

Vick, C (2000), 'Aspects of Police Leadership', *Police Research and Management*, Summer, pp. 3-14.

Woodcock, J (1991), 'Overturning Police Culture', *Policing*, Vol. 7, No. 3, Autumn pp. 172-182.

Wren, K (1999), *Social Influences*, London: Sage Publications.

CHAPTER 17

Leadership by Consent

Peter Villiers

Policing by consent is the central idea of British policing. However, although often referred to, this interesting aspect of doctrine has never been authoritatively defined, and even its parameters remain largely unexplored.

As we near the end of this book, it is time to lay our cards on the table and set down a philosophy of policing by consent. From this, we intend to lay out a doctrine of leadership by consent: but let us deal with first things first! We should start in the best academic manner, by defining both policing and consent.

The police are the department of government that is concerned with the maintenance of public order and safety and the enforcement of the law (*Shorter Oxford English Dictionary*: 1730 definition).

The dictionary states that to consent means voluntarily to accede to or acquiesce in a proposal or request. In the broadest sense, consent therefore means agreement, as in consent to marriage. It does not necessarily mean that the parties to the agreement are equal, or that they made their agreement on the basis of equal information. However, we may say that whether the marriage be based upon the beguiling myth of romantic love or the possibly more solid foundations of a mutual family interest, some acquisition of information would appear essential if the union is to be a long-term success.

We now have a preliminary notion of the meaning of policing by consent, but no proof that it exists in practice. It is easy enough to assert that one polices by consent; but where is the proof? And perhaps more importantly, where is the disproof? What would count as reasonably convincing evidence that a constabulary were *not* policing by consent? These questions are easier to ask than to answer. In our usual way, let us try to work methodically towards their resolution.

It is a preferred police method in investigating a serious crime such as murder to proceed by the identification and elimination of possible suspects, until only the more serious candidates are left 'in the frame'. Whilst policing by consent is not a crime, we should like to borrow from this methodology in its investigation.

1. THE ABSENCE OF FORCE PROVES CONSENT

Consent is sometimes taken as the opposite of coercion or force, and the assumption made that because police officers do not need to exercise force to ensure compliance on every occasion, so they must be policing by consent.

That is, of course, a false assumption. Conditioning, habit and inertia may help a police force to go unchallenged in at least some of its day-to-day activities: but that does not give legitimacy to the presumption that the absence of the need to use force on all occasions means consent.

2. RATIOS PROVE CONSENT

It is sometimes argued that because the police service is vastly outnumbered by the public at large, so it must in some way be operating with the consent of the public; but this assertion must clearly be false:

1. *All* police forces, even those which are most heavily armed and belligerent, and operate within oppressive dictatorships, are vastly outnumbered by the populations whom they police.

2. What counts is the tactical situation, and not the overall ratio in a country as a whole as to the number of police officers and those whom they police. A force may be strategically outnumbered by the population as a whole, but tactically superior in numbers to the mob whom it faces. Moreover, if we compare the police in operation with a crowd or mob, the police generally have the advantages of training, equipment, discipline and ethos, which make a simplistic comparison of ratios invalid. It is a principle of war that an army should outnumber the opposing army at the point where battle is joined, by at least three to one; but that is an aspiration and not a necessity for victory. In the police context, a large assembly may be controlled by a smaller but purposive and disciplined force.

3. USE OF FORCE SHOWS AN ABSENCE OF CONSENT

There is a double paradox here which we need to spell out. The absence of continuous opposition does not prove consent: but nor does the use of force prove that consent has been withdrawn. After all, no-one expects every citizen to agree with every action of the police on every occasion, and there must be occasions when the police act without the consent of those whom they are policing, at least in the immediate context. What the police are looking for is a sort of generalised consent, which we might paraphrase as the consent of the reasonable person. That person may not be the rioter who is being clubbed, gassed or restrained, but the person watching the riot on television, who decides that the actions of the police were proportionate in the circumstances, and therefore worthy of support.

The astute police commander does not simply consider the opposition that he or she is facing on the ground, but the attitude of those not present, upon whose support the commander will wish to rely when tactics are reviewed after the event. The police leader will be seeking to impress the silent majority, the reasonable person, or 'the man on the Clapham Omnibus', or however else he or she chooses to refer to the voice of public opinion. Hence the wisdom of Sir Robert Mark's oft-quoted aphorism that the police can only win by appearing to lose.

POLICING BY CONSENT AS A MYTH

1 A Marxist view

If we cannot rely upon the conventional proofs for the existence of policing by consent, let us for the moment assume a wholly opposite position, and dismiss it as a myth. This is an argument that has been put forward in syndicate discussion at Bramshill by some very hard-headed police officers, and can easily find intellectual support for itself: particularly if we take an historicist view of the development of the modern police.

A Marxist-inclined historian might be inclined to dismiss the whole notion of policing by consent as a fiction whereby the iron fist of capitalism imposes its grip ever more strongly on the down-trodden workers, by the imposition of a police service wearing the velvet glove of consent. We cannot devote a major proportion of this text to an analysis of the defects of the Marxist approach to history, but shall echo Hamlet that there is more in heaven and earth than is dreamt of in its philosophy. In our view policing by consent is neither a convenient fiction nor a cunning exercise in mass deception. Its pragmatic virtues for the working police officer—it is easier, after all, to police with public co-operation than without it—do not render it invalid as a philosophy. Nor is the fact that some police officers are not convinced that they police by consent, a conclusive argument that it does not exist. That view may rather point towards an ideological naivety, and another reason to clarify and establish doctrine.

There is in reality a world of difference between policing by consent and its opposites, such as policing by fear, for example, or simply policing by authority. Neither the United Kingdom nor France is a police state, for example; but they have very different traditions of policing.

2 The power of central government

There is a notion, again propounded by some hard-headed police officers, that policing by consent is a myth in that it rests on a set of constitutional presumptions, which are not in fact true. The police are not independent of political control, and do not in practice retain operational independence either from local or central government. Indeed, it is naïve to suppose that the police are not an arm of the state. All states have police forces. Whether those forces are described as national or local, they must ultimately work to support the institutions of the state and the policies of the government in power at the time. This was shown, for example, during the Miners' Strike of 1984, when the British police were accused of acting as Prime Minister Margaret Thatcher's 'boot boys'.

In brief, we would say whilst that there is a refreshing breath of *realpolitik* about this argument, it is overstated. No doubt, in some ways central government would like a far greater control over policing, as over local government itself. However, politics is the art of the possible, and there are forces working against the urge to centralise as well as forces working for it. The tripartite relationship remains in being, the Home Office does not control a national police service, and chief constables retain sufficient autonomy to practise policing by consent should they choose to do so.

The supposed necessity for local accountability

The police are a creation of local government. They are accountable to local government, and there must be a distance between them and central government. This is a distance which we see, or appear to see, in Great Britain, but which is not evident in France, where the official ideology is one of policing by authority and the centralisation of control has been perceived, at least until recently, as a virtue and not a vice.

However, this account is not historically true, and therefore cannot be used to bolster the general ideology of policing by consent. Modern British policing began with the creation of the New Police by Sir Robert Peel in 1829, and the New Police— now the Metropolitan Police Service—were thus the direct creation of the Home Secretary, whom he placed under the day-to-day direction of two commissioners chosen by himself. That force went on to develop a style of policing which emphasised a style of policing by persuasion and co-operation rather than by force, certainly: but here the word style is crucial.

The style of policing that is now associated with policing by consent was developed by an entirely new police service that was the direct creation of the Home Secretary. It had no accountability to the citizens of London, and was at first profoundly unpopular with them. The Metropolitan Police had to work very hard and for a very long time to build up a relationship with those whom they policed, which was not based the simple equation of obedience through fear. It was only at the end of the twentieth century that realistic mechanisms for accountability began to be discussed in the metropolis, although the tripartite relationship between police, central and local government had been developed elsewhere.

The New Police in fact co-existed for some time with locally accountable police forces in London, such as borough watchmen, who might have put forward a better claim to represent indigenous traditions of policing. The county and borough police forces that could claim local accountability were created after the Metropolitan Police, and saw the latter force as their exemplar.

We must also reflect that not everyone saw the local ties and accountability of a local force as an advantage. Metropolitan Police officers were regarded by some very important decision-makers as more professionally competent than their country cousins, and less likely to be influenced by local factors to the dereliction of their duty. For example, in 1910 there was a coal strike in South Wales in which the then Home Secretary, Winston Churchill, perceived the possibility of a serious threat to public order and even the possibility of the beginnings of a Marxist-inspired revolution.[1] Churchill appointed a soldier with considerable imperial policing experience, General Sir Nevil Macready, to take charge of the situation. General Macready moved MPS police officers to the area, as he had much greater confidence in their professional skills and impartiality than in the local force, and he was able to resolve the situation by negotiation and good use of intelligence, with little conflict (Macready, 1924).

KEY FACTORS TENDING TO INDICATE THE PRESENCE OR WITHDRAWAL OF CONSENT

We have, perhaps, circled around our subject for long enough, and even the most long-suffering reader will be wondering when we are going to show our hand. What we shall argue is for key factors, a combination of which tends to suggest the presence of policing by consent, and an absence of a significant number of which may indicate or precipitate its withdrawal. Those factors are not necessarily constant over time, and nor are they finite in number. However, there is what we might call a critical combination of successful factors, which good police leaders need to keep in mind if they are to be able to continue to police without force, or with only such force as is tactically necessary. Those factors include:

- upholding the rule of law, which means, most importantly, the police not seeing themselves as above the law;
- not acting as a political police, but preferring to deal with 'crime ordinary';
- maintaining a visible presence in the community;
- remaining an unarmed and civil police, and not a paramilitary organization;
- preferring to use persuasion rather than coercion where possible;
- tending to use the official power of the law as a last resort;
- attempting to balance the rival interests at stake in any conflict, and find a common sense solution in which no-one is an absolute loser ;
- emphasising the original authority and discretion of the constable as an officer of the law—which means considerable variation in how problems are dealt with;
- playing a specific and constrained role in the criminal justice system;
- defining its other duties inclusively rather than exclusively;
- not being directly accountable to central government, but recognising and applying the principle of accountability in everything that it does;
- attempting to be and remain locally recruited, responsive and accountable; and
- showing that the idea of the police as a friend in need is not entirely mythical.

Policing by consent is a *renewable* doctrine. It implies that the police service engages with a *dialogue* with the public both as to its duties and *modus operandi*. That dialogue will, of course, include the propensity of the public to complain about the police. Complaints are a good thing, in that they indicate that the complainant believes that it to be both safe and worthwhile to make a complaint. The same logic applies to the police complaining about the public, for example in not volunteering information that would help to solve crimes.

Policing by consent is an *organic* doctrine. Its tenets cannot always be neatly separated into philosophy, doctrine or style; and it is not necessarily the case that top police leaders deal with policy, intermediate commanders with strategy, and more junior officers with tactics—although police training manuals would like to have us believe that this is so. In reality, policing by consent is an organic doctrine that cannot easily be separated into its constituent parts, nor applied by one section of a police service in isolation from its other parts.

Policing by consent is a *realistic* doctrine One of the problems of the performance management culture, in its various manifestations, is the sometimes fantastic disparity between what the organization is supposed to be doing, according to its official policies, priorities and procedures, and what is actually going on. Our comments here are certainly not restricted to policing, but apply to other public sector organizations. We would suggest that what happens at street level is both the reality of policing, by definition, and more likely to correspond to the practice of policing by consent. Police officers are street-corner politicians, and their essential role is to negotiate between conflicting parties and find a way forward (Ker Muir, 1977).

The reality of policing by consent includes negative as well as positive factors. Policing by consent is not necessarily the best solution to any problem. It may not appear the most efficient way to make use of the resources available to the police; and it is bound to give rise to disparities between the apparent productivity of one force and another. We would argue, however, that improvements in efficiency do not necessarily lead to corresponding improvements in effectiveness; and that policing by consent is the most effective form of policing for the United Kingdom.

IMPLICATIONS FOR LEADERSHIP

This doctrine, philosophy or style makes very considerable demands upon its officers and their leaders.

To interpret the situation, weigh up public opinion, and decide upon the course of action which best suits the public interest whilst at the same time satisfying the other requirements placed upon a law enforcement official is on occasion very difficult. Following set national procedures or political directives is in theory easier—and lends itself to the supposedly desirable but in fact wholly inappropriate military style of command, in which senior officers give orders to juniors and hold them accountable for the results. Moreover, the local nature of policing by consent, which exists despite our dismissal of the veracity of its supposed historical origins, makes agreement and co-operation between police forces an endless exercise in negotiation and compromise.

INTELLIGENCE-LED POLICING

In essence, intelligence-led policing sees the police as an independent and autonomous group that must direct their energies and skills towards where they will do most good. This means concentrating on major crime and major criminals by combining specialist detective work with a multi-agency approach to addressing the most significant perpetrators of crime. (Al Capone was famously convicted for income tax evasion, because he could not be convicted of gangsterism; and the method remains valid.)

Intelligence-led policing is active, rather than re-active. It does not wait for the public to ask for its help, but sets out to find the major perpetrators of crime and remove them from circulation, on the assumption that if they are removed then the total volume of crime will fall, the police will have fulfilled their essential function, and society will be better off as a result.

Consider, for example, the drugs problem. If the major importers of illegal drugs can be identified, arrested, charged and convicted then there will be a much smaller amount of drugs for the street traders to sell. The activities of petty criminals will dry up with the dwindling of supplies, and crime as a whole will decline.

It is an attractive theory, and in many cases a thoroughly sensible basis for police work. What it is not, however, is an example of mainstream policing by consent. There is no dialogue with the public at large as what should be the priorities for police action, since in reality the police must decide those alone. There can be no wholesale sharing of information, since intelligence-led policing must by its very nature rest upon the acquisition of high quality information which will need to be rigorously protected. There is no obvious way in which ordinary members of the public can assist the police in their work; and no priority path by which their needs, wishes and desires can find a way onto the system. And finally, there is no need for the police service to be organized in such a way as to be able to respond to every public demand for its services, whether or not it prioritises its response.

Intelligence-led policing does *not* mean a visible police presence in the community. Indeed, it could be carried out by plain-clothes officers alone; and areas where crime is confined to local nuisance could be left untouched by formal policing altogether. In fact, the more we describe the system, the more we realise that we are describing the model for a specialised detective agency; and the reference to Al Capone becomes more and more appropriate. Intelligence-led policing may be the right model for the FBI, or in the United Kingdom for the National Criminal Intelligence Service, the National Crime Squad, or a number of other national institutions. It is not the obvious model for a county police force to adopt.

Intelligence-led policing represents a different philosophy of policing, and requires a different type of leadership. It may, indeed, require *more* leadership, in the sense of an active and thrusting style of command, than the infinite negotiations and compromises of its alternative. But we must recognise that it is different, and a specialised approach rather than a true basis for a widespread philosophy of policing.

POLICE LEADERSHIP AND HUMAN RIGHTS

The connection with policing by consent and human rights is indirect. Historically, policing by consent is linked to the notion of an unwritten constitution and the traditions of the common law—neither of which deal with rights, in any formal sense.

Until the passage of the Human Rights Act in 1998 and the rather steep learning curve to which British police officers then addressed themselves, human rights were not seen as a mainstream issue in British affairs. Indeed, there was a huge ignorance on the whole subject of rights and their evolution, not only in the police but also in the population at large whom they represented.

To the ordinary Briton, the Council of Europe in Strasbourg was a very remote organization. The judgements of its Court were generally ignored, save by the most specialised of specialists. If they came to wider attention, as in the Gibraltar shooting case (*McCann v. UK*, 1995) in which the United Kingdom was found to have breached the right to life in its planning of the operation to neutralise the activities of an IRA murder squad, then the reaction of the Deputy Prime Minister of the day was for Mr Heseltine to say that there would be no reaction.

Given this as the official view, it is hardly surprising that human rights did not figure strongly on the policed training curriculum at Bramshill or elsewhere—although we must in fairness point out that the British Police Code of Ethics as launched at Bramshill in 1992 went to the trouble of correlating ethics and rights, with specific reference to both the Universal Declaration of Human Rights of 1948 and its slightly later European edition, signed in Rome in 1950 (Villiers, 1997). However, the content of the European Convention On Human Rights did not become widely known in the United Kingdom until the passage of the Human Rights Act of 1998.

Jeremy Bentham and utilitarianism
Human rights doctrine is not part of the tradition of policing by consent, which rests upon a far more informal and intuitive idea of rights, and offers much greater scope for negotiation. Moreover, the British philosopher Jeremy Bentham, who has had an enormous influence upon British thought, was opposed to human rights, not because he believed that the state should wrong its citizens but because he thought it fatuous to declare a right without a remedy. Furthermore, his philosophy of utilitarianism can be interpreted to justify the suppression or even extinction of one or more of the rights of an individual, or the members of a minority group, in favour of the rights of the majority, according to its formula that the purpose of any social policy is to work to achieve the greatest happiness of the greatest number.

This formula has been of appeal to the police, who face constant and difficult challenges in terms of how they should allocate their resources when demand will usually outstrip supply. Under such conditions, the police commander is likely to decide to deploy resources where they are likely to have most effect. This may mean comparative or absolute inattention to other demands, or *in extremis* a sacrifice of the interests of the few for the interests of the many.

Traditionally, then, the police officer has tended towards a utilitarian ethic rather than an absolutist one, and tends to consider the general good rather than the individual's rights. We believe that police officers will continue to consider the concept of the greater good, as they define it, in deciding what to do when they face competing priorities of equal, or equally defensible value.

However, it is not impossible to adjust the traditional doctrine of policing by consent in order to accommodate human rights, at least as far as the rights enshrined in the Human Rights Act of 1998 are concerned; and it is a help that the Act is written in clear language, is designed to be applied, and allows for the analysis of police or other public authority decision-making in terms that any reasonably informed person can understand.

Proportionality may have been a comparatively new word to the police in 1998; but the concept, which the word expressed, was far from new. If the fundamental implication of the Human Rights Act is that public authorities should exercise their legitimate powers in accordance with the principle of proportionality, then that is an excellent underlying principle for policing by consent. Theory and practice come together; and the wise police officer is unlikely to police in such a way as to offend gratuitously the public whose support is needed—for example, by using official powers disproportionately.

We do not see a fundamental dichotomy between policing by consent, and policing in order to sustain and uphold human rights. Policing by consent does *not* mean finding out what the majority wants, and then giving it to them. Such a policy could lead to mob rule and the domination of the vigilante. It is right and proper for the police to protect even the most hated of criminals from the blind instincts of the mob. The consent to which the police appeal, here as elsewhere, is the consent of the reasonable person, rather than of the inflamed bystander who is being prevented from wreaking vengeance; and the police must retain the fundamental right to control their own activities, rather than handing over the right to dictate their affairs either to central government or the local citizenry.

We must acknowledge that human rights doctrine will not suit all occasions or master all problems. There will remain times when astute police officers will solve the problems they face to general acclaim, but without reference to any formal procedure or recognised doctrine at all. This, we believe, is what is meant by pragmatism; and pragmatism is a very British approach.

The public wants its police officers to be fair. This allows for the vigorous enforcement of the law on occasion; but it must be enforced fairly. Arbitrary, prejudiced or unnecessary law enforcement is not fair, and offends against the unwritten rules of policing by consent. In addition, it is likely to be in breach of human rights: so we reach the same destination from two starting places.

POLICE LEADERSHIP IN THE LIGHT OF THE LAWRENCE MURDER AND INQUIRY

Three of the contributors to this volume, John Alderson, Sir Robert Bunyard and John Grieve, have referred independently to the Lawrence Inquiry (Macpherson, 1999) as a central event in shaping their thoughts on police leadership.

John Alderson referred to its exposure of manifest faults in police procedure, and dedicated his article to the search for the principles upon which proper policing should be founded.

Sir Robert Bunyard saw it as a failure of supervision in two stages, and highlighted the fact that the initial police inquiry into what went wrong was a whitewash that found no fault in what had occurred.

John Grieve confronted the accusation of institutional racism, and saw his need to answer the charge as a moral agent, despite the negative short term consequences could be expected to follow an admission to such a charge.

The murder of Stephen Lawrence raises profound issues for police leadership, and we must emphasise the need for active police leadership and the indispensability of personal inquiry. We shall also take the opportunity to examine the Lawrence investigation in the light of human rights. Whose rights did the police fail to uphold, and why? How could human rights doctrine help us to examine their behaviour, and how it might be improved?

The right to life (European Convention On Human Rights, Article 2)

Like anyone else, Stephen Lawrence had a right to life. The police have a general obligation to uphold the right to life. In practice, *pace* Osman (*Osman v UK*, 1999) this means that the police must take a known threat to life seriously and take reasonable measures to protect that life. However, this does not impose an unconditional obligation upon the police to protect any possible victim against any possible threat to life.

In this case, there was no known threat to a particular life. Stephen Lawrence was not killed as a result of a premeditated attack in which he had been chosen as the victim, and which the police might have been expected to know about beforehand, but as the result of a casual encounter with white racists who stabbed him at a bus-stop—an attack which arose out of nothing and lasted only a few seconds.

No one, so far as we are aware, has argued that the police should have been in a position to anticipate and prevent any such attack. To expect the police to be able to prevent any crime is an unrealistic assumption. Moreover, to attempt to make it a reality would require, we would suggest, granting to the police such powers to investigate the activities of ordinary citizens and to regulate their behaviour, that the United Kingdom would in effect become a police state.

Given, then, that the police did not know of any specific threat to the life and well-being of Stephen Lawrence—because such a threat did not exist—we would appear to be on strong ground in arguing that they cannot be blamed for having failed to prevent his murder.

On the other hand, the police were aware that there were gangs of racist thugs in London who were capable of carrying out such an attack on any suitable victim, especially in the area where Stephen Lawrence was killed. There had been previous such attacks, and there were offenders known to the police. A major duty of the police is to carry out a generally protective role on behalf of society, and especially its more vulnerable members. In other words, the police are required to keep the Queen's Peace, of which murder is a spectacular breach.

Were they culpable in failing to provide that service? Could a more vigorous or a better intelligenced pattern of preventative patrolling have prevented the murder? Might the potential killers in question have thought: *We'd better not do this? It's not worth it? We're bound to be caught?* And were the police influenced, at some level in their assessment of what it was necessary or not necessary to do in south London, by institutional racism? Did they, perhaps, not take the general threat seriously enough, because of the race of the potential victim? And did they respond so inadequately, because there was an assumption that it was 'only' a black who had been killed—and a young black male who might have been selling drugs anyway?

There is an arguable case here, and it is certainly an enduring element of the thinking behind the authors of the Lawrence Report, who present a mass of data to support their view. It is not a logic that would necessarily lead to a conviction of the police service, we would suggest, for a breach of Article 2 on the basis of dereliction of duty. The causal relationship between institutional or unwitting racism and professional negligence may be easy to assert, but is difficult to prove.

The assertion is, however, something that police leadership needs to take into account; and is part of the assessment of risk and its consequences that John Grieve emphasised as necessary for proper police leadership.

- Who are the most vulnerable members of our society?
- What are we doing to protect them?
- What more can we do?

These are questions to which that the good police leader needs to return—again and again.

Article 2 further applies in regard to the investigation of a murder. The potential victim of any crime, but perhaps especially murder, has the right to expect that the state will make the best use of its resources not only to prevent that crime from occurring in the first place, but in properly investigating it should it still occur. Moreover, the idea of a proper investigation includes the need for the police to be able to describe and account for their actions. In this case, the police were severely criticised both for their lack of professionalism on the night of the crime and in the conduct of their investigations after the event, including their in-house review of the case. The organization as well as the individuals were at fault, and that is a major failure of leadership.

Indeed, the Lawrence Report is a withering indictment of police incompetence in every way, shape and form, throughout the initial reaction to and investigation of this murder; and an Assistant Commissioner of the Metropolitan Police apologised unreservedly to the inquiry for what had occurred.

Such an apology was merited. The authors of the report constantly, and in our view fairly, criticised the men who led the initial inquiry, uniform and CID alike, for their complete absence of any display of leadership as conventionally understood.

As the inquiry indicates, the senior police officers did not shirk their duties altogether. They did not ignore the murder, or fail to visit the scene of the crime, or fail to discuss both with the detectives involved and with each other, how the investigation was going. *However, it is clear that overall their presence and inquiries failed to add any value to what was going on.* They sought, consciously or subconsciously, to be reassured, rather than to bring a critical acumen and a wealth of professional experience to bear upon the process and reshape it as necessary. And they were far too happy to remain at the level of the surface, rather than drilling down, in John Grieve's words.

The report said in regard to the activities of the most senior police officer directly involved in the investigation, DAC Osland, that:

He now accepts that some of the problems of the family liaison were attributable to the police themselves ... This is another example of a senior officer seeing a problem but failing to address it ...

The difficulty which faces us is that Mr Osland was at pains to say that he was involved in almost daily visits to the Incident Room and conversations with the [Senior Investigating Officer] in particular, yet he distanced himself from any decision made on the ground by the SIO, indicating that any tactical decision in connection with arrest and other steps to be taken in the investigation were not for him to make.

This is to abjure leadership, and to fail to come to terms with the implications of the Human Rights Act for the police service, which posits a need for active and investigative leadership.

To uphold rights and fundamental freedoms, whether human or common law, must be an essential tenet of police doctrine; and its implications are inescapable. The police leader must on occasion be not counter-majoritarian but anti-majoritarian. During the miners' strike, one of the arguments put forward in order to provide a moral justification for police activity, was that non-striking miners had a right to work. (Interestingly, this was presumably a common law right, since it is not recognised in the European Convention On Human Rights.)

It did not matter if only one man wanted to go to work, when several hundred wanted to stop him (in which case it would have been much cheaper, considering the police bill for protection involved, if he had simply been paid *not* to work.) The principle applied. No matter what the arithmetic, that one strike-breaker had a right to work; and the police had a duty to uphold that right. The fundamental task of the police cannot be calculated economically, and if the government of the day really wants the police to do something, they will provide the money by means of which it can be done—as was the case in the miners' strike.

If the police leader needs on occasion to consider the needs of the individual rather than the demands of the majority, then the performance management culture is again shown to be dysfunctional. That culture rests on setting easily measurable and comparable targets, such as how long it takes the police to reach the scene of a crime. *But there was no problem with the time that it took the police to reach Stephen Lawrence, who was still alive on their arrival. The problem lay in what they did, or rather failed to do, when they arrived.*

The police service sets out to provide an infinitely adjustable service in which quality is the significant factor, and one failure may count for more than a thousand successes. Some of the critics of the Lawrence Inquiry stated that it placed a disproportionate emphasis on the failure to investigate properly the murder of one person, and gave no credit to the police for their successes elsewhere. That, however, is to miss the point. Statistically, one death is insignificant. In terms of the reputation of the Metropolitan Police Service and its relationship with the very mixed community which it is required to police, a single death was of enormous importance.

THE ROLE OF THE POLICE IN THE CONSTITUTION

It is interesting to note that police studies is a relatively new phenomenon, and that the police are given very little space in any classic account of the British Constitution. It is also the case that the standard biographies of Sir Robert Peel, the founder of the New Police, give very little attention to that aspect of his career: which is, we would suggest, of rather greater long-term importance than his attitude to the corn laws. Indeed, some biographies do not mention his police activities at all.

We find this sad but not surprising. The police are the Cinderella of the British constitution, and their Prince Charming has yet to arrive. At best, they are accepted as necessary. But, like Victorian children, there is a perception that they should be seen but not heard. The police were created to keep the dangerous classes under control in Victorian society, and Peel deliberately chose that they should not be officered by gentlemen, except at the very top. This was decided partly in order that they should know their place, and not challenge the fundamental assumptions of the society in which they operated (Villiers, 1998).

How might they have challenged those assumptions, if they had *not* known their place? For example, as John Alderson analysed in his lucid exposition of principled policing, by asking why society should have concentrated so much on retributive justice, and ignored what John Rawls was later to call distributive justice. In other words, much of the crime and disorder of Victorian England, which the police were there to control, was not in fact the result of the genetic and incorrigible criminality of the dangerous classes at all, but may simply have arisen because of the social conditions of the time. We have a modern parallel to this in Professor Scruton's contribution (*Chapter 4*), when he suggested that police leaders should challenge political decisions that they consider unprincipled; and we are sure that his thoughts will have prompted many further ones amongst our readers from their own experience.

We wish to argue a contrary view to the traditional constitutional assumption of the relative unimportance of the police. There is a positive and reciprocal relationship between policing by consent, and creating and sustaining the requisite values of a liberal democracy—as two of the writers in this volume, the former chief constables John Alderson and Sir Robert Bunyard, showed by personal reflection on their conduct as chiefs, and as other contributors have also indicated.

It is in fact the police, together with but ahead of the other public services, who contribute decisively by their actions to the success of a liberal democracy. For the police, to the ordinary citizen, are the reality of state power. If the police wish to uphold and sustain the virtues of a liberal democracy, then their actions can contribute considerably towards its success. If they wish to destroy it, or simply fail to act to uphold its virtues—and there are more than enough studies of the role of the police in Nazi Germany, to demonstrate that parts of the police were capable of taking both positions—then they may do so.

Police leaders, as Deputy Metropolitan Police Commissioner Ian Blair emphasised in his article, must demonstrate integrity in everything that they do. Integrity is a difficult taskmaster, which does not tolerate the easy option or the expedient solution. Police leaders need to be aware of the significance of their constitutional contribution. Policing by consent rests upon the discretion and individual judgement of the constable, and the principled leadership of his or her commander; and the primary role of the commander is not simply to satisfy the demands of either local or central government, no matter how pressing they may be. Senior police officers are accountable not only to those who pay their wages but also to the ideals of the service; and here the judgement of their peers may be as or more important than the thoughts of the police committee.

Who shall guard the guards themselves?

It has been argued that the police should police themselves, for only by self-regulation can they attain the full status of a profession. We do not agree. Firstly, in an era of verifiable professionalism, the concept of an entirely self-regulating profession has become obsolete. Secondly, the unique constitutional powers of the police, including the use of lethal force, entail that the public must have the optimum means of reassurance that those powers are used properly. Finally, the police are the investigative branch of the criminal justice system. Under the right to a fair trial, any complainants within that system should have access to an independent and impartial tribunal if they believe that their rights have been breached.

New sources of police leadership?

The conclusion of Milan Pagon, our contributor from Slovenia, may require that the police change its leadership altogether. He challenged the assumption that it must be necessary to have worked one's way up through the ranks in order to be aware of the challenges that the constable faces, and believes that in the new era of policing the police may need to look to outside sources for its leadership.

Some of the older questions of police leadership have been debated to the point of exhaustion, and attitudes have become so entrenched that, as in some of the battles of the Great War, the gaining of a few watery, shell-destroyed yards is hailed as a victory, even though they will be lost in the following week. But we cannot avoid the conflict altogether. For the record, then, let it be said that we support the Pagonian view, and would like to see police leadership open to the talents. Good leadership is about asking the right questions; and good leaders use and build on others' experience. The police service should neither recruit and develop its leaders exclusively from within its own ranks, nor rely entirely on outsiders, but instead find a way of combining the best of both worlds. And now, please, in the twenty-first century, could we finally move on from this sterile debate?

LEADERSHIP BY CONSENT

Policing by consent means leadership by consent. It requires a certain type of leadership, which we shall label ruthless integrity, and a style that we shall call, in acknowledgement of its emphasis in Professor Miller's contribution, verifiable professionalism.

There is no one style of leadership that suits every occasion; and police leaders will need on occasion to be democratic and on occasion autocratic. Even when behaving autocratically, however, their behaviour should be that which the reasonable person would approve after the event. (Hence the need for verifiable professionalism, for otherwise approval must rest on trust rather than rational analysis of the facts.)

Frank Panzarella has quite properly pointed out that the same person may not be equally psychologically suited to leading either democratically or autocratically, and that most leaders will have a preferred style. We would suggest that, *pace* Ian Blair, one of the special if not unique requirements of the police leader is the ability to be versatile, able to switch styles as the situation demands. If that versatility needs to be improved, then a means must be found for doing so. This is not beyond the capability of dedicated training and development, and is part of the need of the reflective practitioner.

TRUST, SUPERVISION AND DISCRETION

Trust is important, but does not mean that leaders should accord their subordinates absolute discretion. Nor does it mean that they should never challenge, investigate or correct their subordinates' behaviour, nor punish those who have chosen to act wrongly. As Sir Robert Bunyard has argued, the police service has a history of failing to investigate systematic misbehaviour by its own officers, and this is a norm that must change, as some leaders have realised: Deputy Assistant Commissioner John Grieves saw the willingness to find out what is really going on as one of the cardinal virtues of a police leader; and he refers to it as drilling down. Nor is the habit of ineffective supervision confined to the United Kingdom. Frank Panzarella castigated the New York Police Department, and other North American forces, for failing to investigate the behaviours of their own operatives on the ground, but instead taking refuge in improving procedures, so that in the world of the perfect bureaucracy, nothing can go wrong.

The dilemma of misplaced loyalty

Trust does not mean that the leaders should deny any criticism of their officers by others. Indeed, on occasion they may have to take part in that criticism themselves—as John Grieve reflected. But what if the interests of the force and the interests of the public appear to be in opposition? That is a far from hypothetical dilemma. For example, a force may be accused of serious misconduct, such as brutality or the use of excessive or unnecessary force, when the facts may be capable of more than one interpretation. Should chief constables seek to defend and protect their officers, whatever the accusation, in order to demonstrate solidarity with those whom they command?

Although such a course of action may require both commitment and courage, we think that it is not necessarily the right option. Leadership is not as easy as that. The good leader has a responsibility to find out what really happened, and act accordingly. As our current Prime Minister Tony Blair has pointed out more than once, it is a mistake to confuse popularity with leadership.

We believe that in any real situation it is comparatively easy to recognise the force that is policing with some measure of public assistance and co-operation, and the force which, no matter how well organized, disciplined, or apparently productive, is struggling to do so.

If policing by consent is a style, it is a very important one; and it requires a certain type of leadership. Good police leaders must have a clear understanding of the principles on which their profession is based. They need to show ruthless integrity and to practice verifiable professionalism. Their role is not simply to satisfy government directives in a 'performance management culture'. Such a practice tends to confuse management, as a systems-based activity, with leadership, which must involve challenging goals as well as examining means.

The police are not simply an arm of the state, and are not there to uphold the party in power but to serve the long-term interests of the community as articulated through a pluralistic democratic process in which they themselves participate in two ways:

- by holding the ring, as it were, so that others may debate controversial issues without conflict and oppression; and
- By expressing an opinion themselves, as rational and responsible citizens. Bentham's formula for deciding how to achieve the greatest happiness of the greatest number included the rule that each should count for one and none for more than one; and that rule may be applied to police participation in public debate. To participate in a debate, however, does not imply subservience to its outcome, although it may on occasion necessitate obedience. Senior officers must pay attention both to public opinion and current political priorities, but cannot allow either to dictate their conduct. Police leaders need to be impartial, fair and just. They need not, however, be silent.

REFERENCES for *Chapter 17*

Ker Muir, W (1977), *Police: Street Corner Politicians,* Chicago: University of Chicago Press.

Macpherson, Sir William of Cluny (1999), *The Stephen Lawrence Inquiry,* Cm. 4262, London: Stationery Office.

Macready, Sir Nevil (General the Rt. Hon., Bart., GCMG, KCB) (1924), *Annals of an Active Life,* London: Hutchinson and Co.

McCann v United Kingdom (A/324) (1996), 21 EHRR 97 (1995).

Osman v. United Kingdom (1999), 1 FLR 193.

Villiers, P J (1997), *Better Police Ethics,* London: Kogan Page.

---

[1] General Macready, a very politically aware officer, did not share Churchill's alarmist view of the coal strike, and found the mine-owners harder to do business with than the strikers themselves. He was later rewarded for his sagacity by being appointed Commissioner of the Metropolitan Police on 31 August 1918, when a police strike was imminent; and his memoirs contain some fascinating reflections on the state of the Metropolitan Police at the time. General Macready's final public appointment was as Commander-in-Chief of the British Army in Ireland during the War of Independence (1919-1921) that resulted in the creation of the Irish Free State. General Macready resisted this appointment also, believing (rightly) that he faced an impossible task: 'Whatever we do, we shall be bound to be wrong.' He was successful in resisting joint command of the army and of the Royal Irish Constabulary, as he believed that he could not do justice to both appointments. He thereby lost the opportunity to co-ordinate both intelligence and operations by the 'security forces'. Charles Townshend (*The British Campaign in Ireland,* 1919-1921, Oxford University Press, Oxford, 1975) is the acknowledged expert on this period and has much to say on military and police command which is still of relevance.

CHAPTER 18

Golden Rules: Effective and Enduring Principles of Police Leadership

Robert Adlam and Peter Villiers

The quality of police leadership has been the subject of intense interest, heated debate and critical scrutiny over the past few years. As a result considerable time, energy, effort and analysis have gone into exploring the character of effective police leadership. The picture outlined here draws upon more than 150 published reflections on and evaluations of practice as well as other sources, and is intended to convey a portrait of the good police leader which is both effective and enduring.

Although it should be emphasised that effective police leadership calls for particular dispositions, knowledge, skills and competencies at the different ranks in the police hierarchy, it is possible to articulate a more general model that characterises best practice, irrespective of rank.

1. THE PRINCIPLE OF SERVICE

Whatever their level in the police organization, effective leaders are committed to providing the best possible service to the people policed. The task in hand may be 'macro' (e.g. how best to achieve crime reduction across the territory served by the constabulary) or 'micro' (e.g. how best to help this specific victim of crime or solve this particular crime). Notwithstanding this variation, effective leaders strive continually to meet the needs of the customers of policing.

2. THE PRINCIPLE OF UNSELFISHNESS

Leaders demonstrate a genuine concern for and interest in both staff and colleagues. Fundamental and significant to the process of effectively leading people is the need to be visible and to put the interests of the staff, the organization and the public before the personal interests of the leader.

3. THE PRINCIPLE OF STRATEGIC AWARENESS

Effective police leaders ground their practices upon a range of personal powers and qualities that make a real difference to their followers. This includes a range of intellectual virtues that, in combination with professional knowledge and experience, generate credibility and confidence. Effective police leaders are sensitive to the wider social, cultural, political and business environment within which the police service operates. They are able to communicate with a diverse public and with all levels of the service itself.

4. THE PRINCIPLE OF SUPPORT

Effective police leaders possess a wide range of 'people' skills amongst which 'listening', 'supportive confrontation', 'conflict management', 'negotiating' and 'collaborative problem solving' are fundamental. They deploy these and other skills in ways that 'enable' and 'empower' the staff both as individuals and in relation to building and maintaining effective teams. In short, good leaders support, value and encourage their staff, who find themselves enjoying a working milieu in which they can flourish. Central to the process of 'getting the best' from staff is the ability to provide a clear vision and sense of direction. The ability to offer a vision—a clarity about purposes and goals—is, according to one group of researchers, like 'gold dust'.

5. THE PRINCIPLE OF PROFESSIONAL EXCELLENCE

Good police leaders are exemplary practitioners who set and maintain high personal and professional standards in the workplace. Put differently, they are rigorous professionals striving for excellence, who demonstrate both intellectual and moral virtues. Effective police leaders are trustworthy, open, honest, fair and compassionate. They are willing to confront poor performance as well as dysfunctional and inappropriate behaviour. Effective police leaders have a vibrant 'can do' approach to the challenges facing their part of the police organization. They are recognisable as individuals, and impress because of their integrity, genuineness and warmth.

6. THE PRINCIPLE OF ENDURANCE WITH INTEGRITY

Good police leadership requires the qualities of stoicism and endurance. As John Grieve put it *(Chapter 14)*, heroic leadership may be necessary in a riot. But the enduring challenge to the police leader is, perhaps, the less heroic but more difficult one of being able to make unheroic but competent decisions, under pressure and with inadequate information, time and time again: and to be able to sell those decisions not only to an angry or disbelieving public, but on occasion to one's own workforce.

Roger Scruton *(Chapter 4)* discussed the pressure on senior police officers to endorse and enforce laws which their professional knowledge and judgement may suggest to be in error; and argued that they face a categorical imperative, in Kantian terms, to make their own views clear on the issue in question. This does not mean that the police should actively defy or refuse to apply laws that they believe to be ill-founded. In a pluralist democracy that believes in policing by consent, however, the police have a right to be heard. Police leaders need to be both impartial and neutral: but they need not be silent.

COMMENTARY

A number of things need to be said about this conceptualisation of effective police leadership.

- First, this model reflects an ideal. No one, in reality, could be expected to meet all its stipulations on each and every day. Nor would it this be desirable: a good leader is human, and is, therefore, full of idiosyncrasies and occasional shortcomings.
- Second, it suggests that the service has 'moved on' from an earlier 'top-down' command and control style of leadership prevalent in the mid-1980s.
- Third, it highlights the fact that a 'quality of police service' emphasis is a central component of effective leadership.
- Fourth, in common with the wider research findings, effective leadership focuses upon achieving tasks through supporting and empowering people.
- Fifth, the sketch provides a foundation for best practice; it recognises that, in addition, different aspects of leadership will need to be emphasised and demonstrated at different ranks.
- Sixth, it is worth emphasising that effective police leadership requires certain levels of specialised knowledge and experience.

THE FOURFOLD CHALLENGE

Falklands veteran and now leadership consultant Christopher Keeble, a valued contributor to the development of leadership doctrine at Bramshill, has referred to the fourfold challenge of leadership as being physical, intellectual, moral and spiritual. Deputy Commissioner Ian Blair wrote in *Chapter 12* of: 'the burdens of leadership in the police service, the demands on integrity and family life, [and] the requirement to face horror, betrayal and disillusion and rise above them.'

Horror, betrayal and disillusion are dangerous adversaries, and require a robust and enduring capacity to withstand their onslaught. In order to be able to cope with this challenge, leaders need physical, intellectual, moral and spiritual resources. Physical health and stamina can be developed, but this is not a one-off project; physical fitness is a life-long endeavour. In the same way, intellectual, moral and spiritual resources need to be developed and protected.

Leaders will not find all these resources within themselves, nor even within family and friends, who may be overburdened by their demands, whether made consciously or not. If they are lucky, and work at it, they will find most of the resources that they need within their followers. Leaders do not need to be the best at everything. Indeed, as John Grieve pointed out (*Chapter 14*), they may not even have some of the basic skills that subordinates tend to take for granted: he was head of the Metropolitan Police Driving School without possessing a driving licence. But they do need to know themselves; and they do need to be outstanding in recognising and developing the talents of others.

A LIFE-LONG LEARNING PROCESS

How we should live our lives is a question that has preoccupied Western philosophers since the emergence of the Athenian Republic. This is not the place to present a potted précis of moral philosophy, and we shall simply point out that police leaders must address this task for themselves. Frankena (1973) described the good person as leading life according to these virtues:

- benevolence and justice;
- a disposition to think clearly;
- conscientiousness and integrity;
- moral courage and respect for the moral law;
- the ability to realise vividly, in imagination and feeling, the inner lives of others.

We believe that these virtues are necessary for police commanders; and we support Richard Rorty (1997) in underlining the importance of a sentimental education in acquiring them. Such a list of virtues is demanding, to say the least; and to live one's life consistently at such a level may prove impossible. To aspire to do so, however, is not an ignoble project. Leadership can be a dangerous and painful task. It is always likely to be a lonely one. In order to be able to function effectively, leaders need to acquire and cultivate resources at every level; to keep a sense of proportion; and to exercise a sense of humour.

REFERENCES for *Chapter 18*

Frankena, W (1973), *Ethics*, Englewood Cliffs, NJ: Prentice Hall Inc.
Rorty, R (1997), 'Human Rights, Rationality and Sentimentality' in Ishmay, M (ed.) (1997), *The Human Rights Reader*, London: Routledge.

Index